GW00645139

Epica Book 26
Creative
Communications

EDITOR

Andrew Rawlins

ART DIRECTOR

Patrick Taschler

SYNOPSES

Mark Tungate

EDITORIAL ASSISTANT

Lucia Ongay

COVER IMAGE

Sebastian Hudert
(Volkswagen Golf GTI 35,
courtesy of Tribal DDB, Berlin)

PUBLISHER

Fairchild Books, an imprint of
Bloomsbury Publishing Plc

Printed in China

EPICA
65 rue J.J. Rousseau,
92150 Suresnes, France
Tel: 33 (0) 1 42 04 04 32
www.epica-awards.com
info@epica-awards.com

Epica has made every effort to publish full and
correct credits for each work included in this
volume based on the information provided on
the Epica entry forms. Epica and Bloomsbury
Publishing Plc regret any omissions that may
have occurred, but hereby disclaim liability.

Contents

Photo: Laurie Catelli

How great work inspires us to do better

Advertising passes; it is temporary and is created to be replaced by more advertising.

You could say that advertising is meant to be forgotten. But somehow, some advertising manages not to be: great advertising.

Great advertising makes us remember what it was for, what it said and how it said it. It becomes part of our conversations – and in some cases part of our culture. The problem is that great ideas are usually replaced with "greater" ideas. In some notable cases, this happens within the same brand over and over again.

So the value of publications like this book is enormous. Because it helps us remember what was great and why it was great. I think that learning from the great work of the past is the best way to become better at what we do. We must be able to admire other people's work in order to achieve greatness.

I know our business is changing, but I feel the fundamentals will remain. Strong, simple and powerful ideas will continue to shine in any environment. They will continue to change minds and help us make choices. I believe the power of good ideas will change the balance between client and creative.

Today it is no big deal to make wine for example. Wine can come from anywhere and can be pretty good. There is an installed capacity to make wine that by far exceeds demand. So brands really make a difference. I think very soon winemakers will compete for the privilege to work with the best talent.

And this is true of almost everything that surrounds us: cars, furniture or luxury timepieces.

Brands with the most famous advertising/communications will be more famous, and brands with forgettable ideas will be forgotten. And we all know where the smart brands want to be.

Soon, I hope, the people who produced the ideas in this book will get calls to do more work like that, from people whose products did not have ideas good enough to be included.

Great ideas change things, big and small. The really great ones may even change our business.

Jose Miguel Sokoloff,

President of the Lowe Global Creative Council, Co-Chairman and Chief Creative Officer of Lowe/SSP3, Bogotá

Epica d'Or (Film)

Epica d'Or (Press)

Epica d'Or (Outdoor)

Epica d'Or (Interactive)

GRAND PRIX

EPICA D'OR (FILM)	M2FILM, AARHUS	MIDTTRAFIK, "THE BUS"
EPICA D'OR (PRINT)	DDB, HELSINKI	McDONALD'S, "LARGE COFFEE" CAMPAIGN
EPICA D'OR (OUTDOOR)	DLKW LOWE, LONDON	THE MICROLOAN FOUNDATION, "PENNIES FOR LIFE"
EPICA D'OR (INTERACTIVE)	LEO BURNETT, DETROIT	TROY PUBLIC LIBRARY, "BOOK BURNING PARTY"

FILM WINNERS

FOOD	BETC, LONDON	COW & GATE, "SUPERGROUP"
CONFECTIONERY & SNACKS	McCANN, MANCHESTER	ALDI, "CHOCOLATE BUNNIES"
DRINKS	WUNDERMAN, BUENOS AIRES	COCA-COLA, "SECURITY CAMERAS"
COMMUNICATION SERVICES	THE NEWTONS LABORATORY, ATHENS	WIND HELLAS, "BANK ROBBERY"
TRANSPORT & TOURISM	M2FILM, AARHUS	MIDTTRAFIK, "THE BUS"
RETAIL SERVICES	CREATIVE ARTISTS AGENCY, LOS ANGELES	CHIPOTLE, "BACK TO THE START"
FINANCIAL SERVICES	TRY ADVERTISING AGENCY, OSLO	DNB BANK, "THE TREASURE"
HOMES, FURNISHINGS & APPLIANCES	ADAM&EVEDDB, LONDON	JOHN LEWIS, "THE LONG WAIT"
HOUSEHOLD MAINTENANCE	DLKW LOWE, LONDON	OMO, "SET FREE"
PUBLIC INTEREST	WANDER, LOS ANGELES	RAINFOREST ALLIANCE, "FOLLOW THE FROG"
HEALTH & BEAUTY	HAVAS WORLDWIDE, LONDON	VO5, "PAGEANT"
CLOTHING, FOOTWEAR & PERSONAL ACCESSORIES	OGILVY & MATHER, FRANKFURT	JAKO-O, "THE SCHEDULE"
AUTOMOBILES	WEAPON7, LONDON	SMART FORTWO, "SKATE FORTWO"
AUTOMOTIVE & ACCESSORIES	FORSMAN & BODENFORS, GOTHENBURG	THE NEW VOLVO FH TRUCK, "THE BALLERINA STUNT"
MEDIA	TRY ADVERTISING AGENCY, OSLO	CANAL DIGITAL NORGE, "THE MAN WHO LIVED IN A FILM"
RECREATION & LEISURE	TBWA\PARIS	UGC, "EMOTIONS"
PROFESSIONAL PRODUCTS & SERVICES	HAVAS WORLDWIDE, PARIS	EURO RSCG C&O, "BEST WISHES 2012"
CORPORATE IMAGE	QUAD PRODUCTIONS, PARIS	CARTIER, "CARTIER ODYSSEY"
ANIMATION	UNIT IMAGE, PARIS	UBISOFT ZOMBIU, "ZOMBIU GAME TRAILER"
DIRECTION & CINEMATOGRAPHY	BETC, PARIS	CANAL+, "THE BEAR"
EDITING & SPECIAL EFFECTS	RAINEY KELLY CAMPBELL ROALFE/Y&R, LONDON	BBC ONE, "WONDERFUL WORLD"

PRINT WINNERS

FOOD	LEO BURNETT, LONDON	McDONALD'S OLYMPICS, "WE ALL MAKE THE GAMES"
CONFECTIONERY & SNACKS	BBDO UKRAINE, KIEV	WRIGLEY ORBIT, "STRAWBERRYNANA"
DRINKS	DDB, HELSINKI	McDONALD'S, "LARGE COFFEE" CAMPAIGN
COMMUNICATION SERVICES	SPILLMANN/FELSER/LEO BURNETT, ZURICH	SWISS POST, "COFFEESTAMP"
TRANSPORT & TOURISM	NEW MOMENT NEW IDEAS CO. Y&R, BELGRADE	KIELO TRAVEL AGENCY, "POOL"
RETAIL SERVICES	DDB SOUTH AFRICA, JOHANNESBURG	McDONALD'S, "MONSTERS" CAMPAIGN
FINANCIAL SERVICES	ZAPPING/M&C SAATCHI, MADRID	MAPFRE, "LIFE PASSES BY" CAMPAIGN
HOMES, FURNISHINGS & APPLIANCES	DDB TRIBAL GROUP, BERLIN	BOSCH NOFROST TECHNOLOGY, "ICEBERGS" CAMPAIGN
HOUSEHOLD MAINTENANCE	HEREZIE, PARIS	VAPONA INSECTICIDE, "STOP TRYING" CAMPAIGN
PUBLIC INTEREST	BBDO GERMANY, DÜSSELDORF	ISHR, "HANGMAN" CAMPAIGN
HEALTH & BEAUTY	PUBLICIS COMUNICACIÓN ESPAÑA, MADRID	VISIONLAB, "PRESCRIPTION GLASSES" CAMPAIGN
CLOTHING, FOOTWEAR & PERSONAL ACCESSORIES	OGILVY & MATHER, FRANKFURT	SCHOEFFEL, "CAMPAIGN WITH A VIEW"
AUTOMOBILES	DDB GROUP, SYDNEY	VOLKSWAGEN, "PARK ASSIST TECHNOLOGY" CAMPAIGN
AUTOMOTIVE & ACCESSORIES	SCHOLZ & FRIENDS, BERLIN	MERCEDES-BENZ, "DANGER DOESN'T ANNOUNCE ITSELF" CAMPAIGN
MEDIA	RAFINERI, ISTANBUL	CNBC-E TURKEY, "NEWS & SERIES" CAMPAIGN
RECREATION & LEISURE	LOWE/SSP3, BOGOTÁ	COLSUBSIDIO LIBRARIES, "BOOK EXCHANGE" CAMPAIGN
PROFESSIONAL PRODUCTS & SERVICES	OGILVY & MATHER, FRANKFURT	DPA PICTURE-ALLIANCE, "ALL YOU NEED TO TELL THE STORY" CAMPAIGN
PRESCRIPTION PRODUCTS & SERVICES	LANGLAND, WINDSOR	KENTERA, "UNWANTED SIDE-EFFECTS" CAMPAIGN
CORPORATE IMAGE	TRY ADVERTISING AGENCY, OSLO	VOLKSWAGEN, "SAFETY INNOVATION" CAMPAIGN

RADIO

RADIO ADVERTISING	PUBLICIS BRASIL, SÃO PAULO	PURINA, "ONLY A DOG" CAMPAIGN

DIRECT MARKETING

CONSUMER DIRECT	LEO BURNETT, DETROIT	TROY PUBLIC LIBRARY, "BOOK BURNING PARTY"
BUSINESS TO BUSINESS DIRECT	WIEN NORD, VIENNA	OPEL AMPERA, "THE MOST CREDIBLE TESTIMONIAL IN THE WORLD"

MEDIA USAGE

MEDIA INNOVATION - TRADITIONAL MEDIA	JUNG VON MATT, HAMBURG	STOLPERSTEINE, "ONLINE HOLOCAUST MEMORIAL"
MEDIA INNOVATION - ALTERNATIVE MEDIA	JUNG VON MATT, HAMBURG	MERCEDES-BENZ B-CLASS F-CELL, "THE INVISIBLE DRIVE"

BRANDED CONTENT

SOCIAL NETWORKS	PUBLICIS, AMSTELVEEN	BLOEMEN.NL FLOWERS, "IS THIS SPAM?"
MOBILE COMMUNICATIONS	DLKW LOWE, LONDON	THE MICROLOAN FOUNDATION, "PENNIES FOR LIFE"
BRANDED ENTERTAINMENT	LEO BURNETT COMPANY, MILAN	MONTBLANC CHRONOGRAPH, "THE BEAUTY OF A SECOND"

PR & PROMOTIONS

PUBLIC RELATIONS	STUDIO TOTAL, MALMÖ	BELARUS HUMAN RIGHTS, "BEARS OVER BELARUS"
PROMOTIONS & INCENTIVES	DMITRY & OLEG, MOSCOW	DMITRY & OLEG, "THE BEST RECOMMENDATION EVER"

CRAFT & IMAGERY

PRINT CRAFT	WIRZ BBDO, ZURICH	CARAN D'ACHE, "LET IT OUT" CAMPAIGN
ADVERTISING PHOTOGRAPHY (2 WINNERS)	MARCEL, PARIS	RAY-BAN, "RAY-BAN 75 YEARS OF LEGENDS" CAMPAIGN
	FRED & FARID, PARIS & SHANGHAI	WEIGHT WATCHERS, "TREAT YOURSELF BETTER" CAMPAIGN
ILLUSTRATION	ADAM&EVEDDB, LONDON	MARMITE LIMITED EDITION JUBILEE JAR, "CORGIS"

DESIGN

GRAPHIC DESIGN	OGILVY & MATHER ADVERTISING, SHANGHAI	COCA-COLA, "COKEHANDS"
PUBLICATION DESIGN	LEO BURNETT, LONDON	PANTONE, "PANTONE QUEEN"
PACKAGING DESIGN	FAMILY BUSINESS, STOCKHOLM	ABSOLUT VODKA, "ABSOLUT UNIQUE"

INTERACTIVE

FOOD & DRINK INTERACTIVE	ROBERT/BOISEN & LIKE-MINDED, COPENHAGEN	ANTHON BERG, "THE GENEROUS STORE"
CONSUMER SERVICES & HOUSEHOLD INTERACTIVE	ÅKESTAM HOLST, STOCKHOLM	PAUSE HOME ENTERTAINMENT, "THE HEIST"
PUBLIC INTEREST INTERACTIVE	DDB DM9JAYMESYFU, MANILA	GABRIELA, "BURY THE PAST PROJECT"
HEALTH, BEAUTY & FASHION INTERACTIVE	OGILVY & MATHER, LONDON	DOVE, "THE DOVE AD MAKEOVER"
AUTOMOTIVE INTERACTIVE	FORSMAN & BODENFORS, GOTHENBURG	THE NEW VOLVO FH TRUCK, "LAUNCH SITE ON EBAY"
MEDIA & ENTERTAINMENT INTERACTIVE	HEIMAT, BERLIN	CNN INTERNATIONAL, "THE CNN ECOSPHERE"
BUSINESS TO BUSINESS & CORPORATE INTERACTIVE	LBI DENMARK, COPENHAGEN	A.P MØLLER MAERSK SHIPPING, "WE ARE MAERSK.COM"
ONLINE ADS	SMFB, OSLO	IKEA IPAD CATALOGUE, "IKEA BERÖRA"
ONLINE FILMS	DUVAL GUILLAUME MODEM, ANTWERP	TNT, "PUSH TO ADD DRAMA"

INTEGRATED

INTEGRATED CAMPAIGNS	DDB, STOCKHOLM	SWEDISH ARMED FORCES, "WHO CARES?"

The jury

The Epica jury is made up of journalists from leading advertising magazines and websites worldwide. A total of 41 publications from 34 countries were represented on the jury in 2012.

AUSTRALIA	Campaign Brief
AUSTRIA	Extradienst
	Lürzer's International Archive
BELGIUM	Pub
BULGARIA	Sign Café
CANADA	Strategy
CHINA	Modern Advertising
CZECH REPUBLIC	Strategie
DENMARK	Markedsføring
ESTONIA	Best-Marketing
FINLAND	Markkinointi & Mainonta
FRANCE	Stratégies
GERMANY	Werben & Verkaufen
GREECE	+Design
	Marketing Week
HUNGARY	Kreativ
INDIA	exchange4media
IRELAND	IMJ
ITALY	NC Nuova Communicazione
	Brand News
	Pubblicita'Italia
LEBANON	ArabAd
NETHERLANDS	Marketing Tribune
NORWAY	Kampanje
PHILIPPINES	Adobo Magazine
POLAND	Press
PORTUGAL	Briefing
RUSSIA	Sostav.ru
SERBIA	New Moment
SINGAPORE	AdAsia
SLOVAKIA	Stratégie
SLOVENIA	Marketing Magazin
SOUTH AFRICA	Migrate
SPAIN	El Publicista
SWEDEN	Resumé
SWITZERLAND	Persönlich
	Werbewoche
TURKEY	Marketing Türkiye
UNITED KINGDOM	Creative Review
	Marketing Week
	The Drum

9

Epica Awards
2012

Annual report

The 2012 Epica Awards Ceremony and International Creative Conference took place in Ljubljana. It was held at the Cankarjev Dom Culture & Congress Centre on Friday, January 25th, 2013. The event was hosted by Slovenia's MM magazine.

Epica went global in 2012 and received 3,900 entries from 649 companies in 62 countries. As a result, a record number of countries are represented amongst the winners.

The 4 grand prix were won by M2Film, Aahus (film), DDB, Helsinki (press), DLKW Lowe, London (outdoor) and Leo Burnett, Detroit (interactive).

DDB was the most successful agency network with 8 gold and a grand prix from 7 different countries.

Germany topped the country rankings, followed by the UK, France and Sweden.

Jung von Matt Hamburg was the most successful agency with 16 awards, ahead of Forsman & Bodenfors Gothenburg with 10.

All the gold, silver and bronze winners feature in this 26th edition of the Epica book, together with a selection of other high-scoring entries.

	Entrants	Entries	Gold	Silver	Bronze
ALBANIA	2	2	-	-	-
ALGERIA	1	8	-	-	-
ARGENTINA	2	11	1	-	1
AUSTRALIA	6	55	1	1	1
AUSTRIA	10	44	1	2	2
BELGIUM	10	47	1	2	2
BRAZIL	5	25	1	3	2
BULGARIA	4	15	-	-	-
CAMBODIA	1	1	-	-	-
CANADA	11	111	-	2	2
CHINA	7	20	1	4	5
COLUMBIA	1	14	1	2	-
CROATIA	3	4	-	-	-
CYPRUS	1	1	-	-	-
CZECH REPUBLIC	14	55	-	-	1
DENMARK	15	29	3	2	-
EGYPT	1	3	-	-	-
FINLAND	21	66	1	3	1
FRANCE	39	451	8	23	17
GERMANY	78	721	9	32	25
GREECE	8	41	1	-	1
HONG KONG	3	21	-	1	1
HUNGARY	7	17	-	-	-
ICELAND	3	8	-	-	-
INDIA	5	26	-	2	3
IRELAND	5	8	-	-	-
ISRAEL	4	18	-	3	1
ITALY	20	87	1	3	6
JAPAN	5	15	-	1	1
KAZAKHSTAN	2	6	-	1	-
KUWAIT	2	11	-	-	-
LEBANON	5	18	-	1	2
LITHUANIA	3	8	-	-	-
MACEDONIA	1	3	-	-	-
MALAYSIA	2	3	-	-	-
MEXICO	1	5	-	-	-
NAMIBIA	1	4	-	-	-
NETHERLANDS	25	100	1	6	10
NEW ZEALAND	1	7	-	-	1
NIGERIA	1	1	-	1	-
NORWAY	16	93	4	5	1
PHILIPPINES	2	13	1	1	1
POLAND	6	12	-	1	2
PORTUGAL	6	33	-	-	3
PUERTO RICO	1	1	-	-	1
ROMANIA	10	41	-	-	-
RUSSIAN FEDERATION	48	226	1	5	5
SERBIA	4	18	1	-	-
SINGAPORE	2	18	-	-	1
SLOVAKIA	10	39	-	3	-
SLOVENIA	2	2	-	-	-
SOUTH AFRICA	8	16	1	1	1
SPAIN	16	85	2	-	1
SRI LANKA	1	2	-	-	-
SWEDEN	55	298	6	15	18
SWITZERLAND	12	155	2	7	5
TUNISIA	2	9	-	3	4
TURKEY	16	84	1	-	1
UKRAINE	20	65	1	1	-
UNITED ARAB EMIRATES	8	48	-	3	2
UNITED KINGDOM	46	358	13	22	20
UNITED STATES	22	194	3	8	8
TOTAL	649	3900	67	170	159

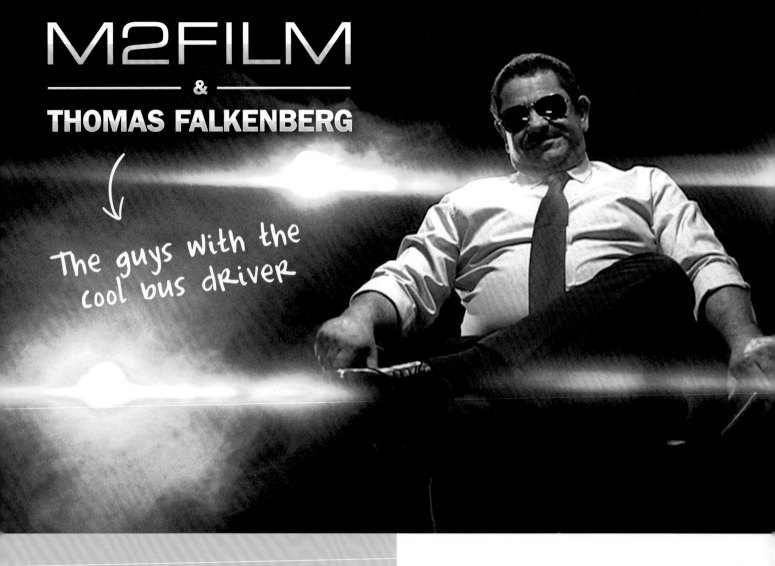

M2FILM
& THOMAS FALKENBERG

The guys with the cool bus driver

Back on the bus
by Mark Tungate

When small Danish bus company Midttrafik did some consumer research, it came up with a not entirely surprising fact: young people were not big fans of the bus. In fact, as Ronni Madsen – one half of the Epica award-winning team – puts it: "Many young Danes would rather drop dead than be seen on the bus."

This situation could not go on. If a whole generation had fallen out of love with the bus, Midttrafik was facing a long-term problem. So it turned to Ronni – vice-president of production company M2Film – and his regular freelance copywriter Thomas Falkenberg for help.

"The advertising community here is small, so Midttrafik were aware of the work Thomas and ourselves had done," says Ronni. "That's why they approached us directly, rather than going through an agency. It was based on personal relationships."

He adds that Midttrafik had rarely done any advertising. "Their approach was very rational: they needed a specific type of content and they went straight to the people who could create it. We emphasised that we were a film company, not an advertising agency, but they told us that was exactly what they were looking for."

The search was on for an idea that would get people back on the bus.

"The client very kindly dropped by with a product sample," Thomas recalls, "in the form of two tons of blue-painted steel. So we looked at this vehicle and asked ourselves how we could make it appealing to the iPhone generation."

The bus had doors, windows, comfortable seats and, of course, a driver. "That's when the solution came to us," says Thomas. "We had to sell the bus as if it really was the next iPhone. So we looked at it again as if we had never seen one before."

The resulting film is, quite simply, epic: a trailer for an imaginary blockbuster in which the bus is the star. As the vehicle glides across the screen in super slow-motion, the husky-voiced narrator praises its panoramic views, enviable length, free handles and "designer bells with cool functions". And unlike most vehicles, it comes with its own lane.

Even the driver is cool. In fact the driver – an actor whose real name is Peer Bruun – has since become something of an icon.

Media planning and buying was handled by Carat. "We only had a small budget, so it was a pretty short conversation," says Ronni. "We decided that for our target audience we needed to focus on the internet, supported by cinema advertising."

Eventually, however, the film was also screened on TV. "As this is a regional campaign, it couldn't even be shown on national television. But that gave us an advantage because the standard of advertising on local TV is generally fairly low. When our ad came along, with its big production values, the effect was like: BOOM!"

The bus ad worked – more spectacularly than anyone had envisaged. Thanks to YouTube and social media, it became a global phenomenon. "The Huffington Post and Time magazine wrote about it," says Ronni. "And because it was popular abroad, suddenly the Danish media started talking about it too."

It turned out that not everyone had fallen out of love with the bus, after all. Thomas observes: "We all have a relationship with the bus. It's a bit like an old friend – if not a super cool old friend. It's something of an underdog in the transportation world. But it turns out that all it needed was a bit of a boost."

The film succeeds because it plays on the vehicle's underdog status in an ironic and affectionate way. As you're watching it, you become convinced that you've liked the bus all along. Perhaps you even remember the time you wanted to be a bus driver when you grew up.

The film became the core of Midttrafik's image-building efforts. "In most cases you'd create a concept and then express it across various media," says Ronni. "But here you have a single piece of content driving the whole strategy. We were able to give our mood boards to the company's internal graphics people so they could work on print material that would reflect the film."

At the time of writing, Ronni and Thomas were planning the next instalment of the Midttrafik saga. A sequel? An entirely new film? Or something completely different? The boys aren't saying. But one thing's for sure, says Ronni: "People are listening to us now. The film got their attention. Now we can tell them a lot more."

So keep a look out for the next bus to come along. It will be loaded with even more cool new features.

Large Coffee. 1,50 €. i'm lovin' it

Great coffee
by Lewis Blackwell

This year's Epica d'Or for press goes to an ad from DDB Helsinki – the first Epica Grand Prix honour to go to an agency from Finland.

Overdue perhaps, as Finnish advertising has often entertained with cultured and amusing executions. The breakthrough work is at once globally accessible and yet highly local – a perfectly executed visual pun that sells McDonald's coffee.

Now how is that at all local? Let creative director and copywriter Vesa Tujunen explain: "Finns drink more coffee per head than any nation in the world – for example, we drink four times as much as somebody in the UK! We have a lot of places selling coffee, of course, a lot of competition and a lot of opportunity.

"People here did not really see McDonald's as a place for coffee, more as a place for burgers and fries, and so on. So that was our challenge, to change that. McDonald's has good coffee at a great price. We had to shift perception, really raise the awareness of it being a great place to pick up a coffee. The coffee is no different there than in many a coffee bar."

Working with art director Jukka Mannio, Tujunen started exploring what approach to take to penetrate the Finnish coffee drinkers consciousness. "We thought about angles such as talking about it being freshly ground, or great for waking you up, but really what stood out was a simple proposition: McDonald's has a really fair price for a big cup of coffee.

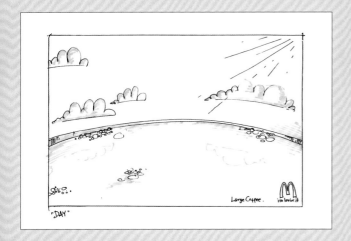

"Next thing, Jukka drew up some ideas of what 'big' could mean. We went through some different expressions, but we really wanted to get away from all the familiar things that are typical of coffee advertising. We hit on the idea of just showing a really big cup, and then we worked on that."

The old modernist mantra of 'less is more' seems to have applied at that point. Mannio adds: "We thought about having a skyline with a city in it, but it just worked better to be simpler. Illustration could also have been a route, but we thought it needed to be as 100 per cent real as it could be for the illusion to work. We also shot it for real, putting a studio image of the coffee together with photographs of sky that we had sourced. Our post-production advice had initially suggested trying to build it in 3D illustration but we said no and that proved to be right."

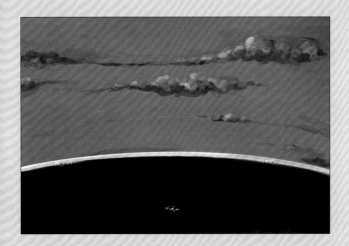

All of this called for great trust from the client as such a simple idea, sold with a minimal sketch, required belief that the art director could deliver the illusion promised. "When we pitched it I said 'Don't worry, it's going to be great!' even though I had a little worry at the time at how we were going to make that happen," says Mannio.

"It actually took quite a while – in fact, weeks – to build the sky from various elements. As for the coffee, we had a lot of shots to work with, shooting across a huge cup... it was a bit like a salad bowl full of coffee!"

The resulting two executions of the idea ran as half-page newspaper ads. The idea was particularly to engage and amuse the Finnish coffee drinker early in the day (which is perhaps a near tautology, as most Finns are clearly stoked up on coffee most of the time). Planting that seed of entertainment and positive brand and price awareness before they venture out for coffee was smart positioning. "Typically people will be picking up a takeaway coffee on the way to work, so we aimed to get ahead of that decision," says Tujunen.

The ads do that by getting into the consciousness at a highly emotional level – a combination of visual humour, with the tricking of the eye to recognise the cup in the landscape – and also just giving a visual pleasure, placing an uplifting picture in the morning paper. The takeaway message is that coffee is fantastically good value at McDonald's. This is an idea that is never explicitly claimed, but can be felt by the reader. The beautiful image of what seems like a swimming pool of coffee is combined with the simple price promise. The viewer then subconsciously marries the two pieces of information to believe in the idea of value and quality at McDonald's. It's a clever appeal to our emotions.

Once again, we see the secret of a great ad being as much in what is not said as in what is said. The art direction strength is clear, but there is also a little genius in the understatement of the copy.

15

The result is that Finland can not only punch above its weight in coffee drinking, but also with coffee advertising. They'll be selling reindeer meat to us all soon if we don't watch out.

Lewis Blackwell is an internationally published writer and editor on creative issues. A former editor of Creative Review and global creative head of Getty Images, he is now Chief Creative Officer of Evolve Images. www.evolveimages.com

Small change
by Lewis Blackwell

There is a saying that necessity is the mother of invention. While that applies to every great creative ad that we get to see, it doesn't usually apply quite so fundamentally as happened with this year's winner of the Epica d'Or for Outdoor.

The winning work from DLKW Lowe of London was on a pro-bono account, for the MicroLoan Foundation. In that it involves a sophisticated digital billboard, and a large team of digitally-savvy creatives and media folk, it would be easy to jump to the conclusion that this one-off piece of resource-intensive creativity cost a small fortune to produce and sits at odds with its charitable mission for cash-strapped people in Africa.

But, no. "We had more or less no money to work with on this," says creative director Greg Delaney. "That's not so uncommon when you are working with a charity but it certainly presents a challenge for doing something outstanding." Zero media-spend is a sobering start to a project. It was only by DLKW Lowe spotting that Ocean Outdoor were running a competition to give free space on their new state-of-the-art giant digital billboard at Westfield shopping centre, west London, and then putting together a compelling pitch to win the competition, that the campaign had any media. It went from famine to feast – suddenly having the latest display technology to celebrate its message on.

"We won with the strength of the concept," adds Delaney, "but it has to be said we were not entirely sure how we would deliver it. I guess that often applies to cutting-edge ideas, or ideas that work with cutting-edge technology. You have to think of something that hasn't been done, and so far perhaps can't be done...but will be done if you can just work through the problems. Obviously we had clever people working on it who thought we could do it, but there was a lot to sort out once we won the competition."

The concept involved enabling viewers of the screen at Westfield to text in a donation that was then added to the image on the screen. They were then personally thanked on-screen and back on the website. They were invited to share the experience with others, spreading the brand awareness and recruiting more donations. As the gifts were texted in, the image on the display

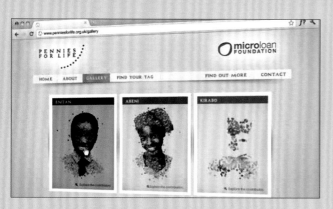

changed, pennies being added to build up a picture of a potential recipient of the micro-loan grant: typically a woman looking to start a business in Africa with a loan of about 70 euros. As donors texted in gifts via their phone account pennies would animate across the screen landing on the image and building a face, and a future for the life behind it.

It was a highly participative proposal and a great way of demonstrating the flexibility of the new digital billboards. More pertinently for the MicroLoan Foundation, it was a way to break through public indifference, provoking Westfield shoppers to become curious about the ad and get them engaged in seeing how their small change could lead to big change for the African women. And it was a way of not only raising funds for the MicroLoan Foundation but also raising awareness of the little-known charity.

A whole lot of digital ingenuity was required though to make this concept go from presentation film to real experience for thousands of participants. The audience feedback has to be near real-time. The movement on screen has to be both engaging for participants, as their coins get added, but also understandable by newcomers, who are just trying to work out what the ad is for.

So effective was the build though, that donations in just one weekend enabled 21 women to start their businesses.

"It was great that it could make that difference to people's lives, but by doing something high-profile we achieved a lot more," adds Delaney. "The charity were delighted with the recognition they gained, helping them go from being fairly obscure to a much wider credibility. It generated a lot of media coverage – the name of the charity has now travelled around the world."

From initial coverage of the technical innovation, to coverage of the award-winning quality of the work, the 'Pennies for Life' ad has broken new ground in combining outdoor and mobile. It's a piece of work that sits as a milestone along the route towards much more participative media.

Delaney expects to go further down this route. "Issues of participation certainly preoccupy us at the agency and it's also at the core of the challenges faced by charities. Every charity faces some degree of indifference and have to break people out of that and get them to engage. Using mobile is a great way of linking people up – you can see them respond and then you can broadcast back to them and celebrate their involvement.

"Of course, not every media permits two-way communication so you can't just take this thinking and apply it every time. But undoubtedly, as an agency, you have to be open to where the technology is going and embrace it fully.

"The odd thing about pushing ideas with technology is that you need to know what you can do before you have the idea. And yet you need to have the idea in order to push what you can do..." It's the digital version of chickens and eggs (which came first?).

Increasingly, Delaney sees agencies sitting at the hub of teams of 'clever people' who feed in thinking, help develop ideas, and respond through complex execution. "The copywriter and art director were of course fundamentally important (Richard J Warren and Paul Hancock) on this project, but there's a long list of other smart folk who did vital work in so many areas.

"There's an obvious irony in all this apparently expensive state-of-the-art technology helping people who have next-to-nothing. But we really did manage to do it for very little and raise money to make real projects happen," explains Delaney. "And then it's a nice irony, a celebration of the circular process of how investment works, and how helping each other works."

VOTE TO CLOSE TROY LIBRARY AUG. 2nd

BOOK BURNING PARTY AUG. 5th

facebook.com/BookBurningParty

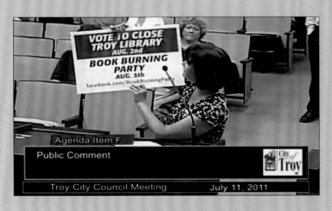

Burn after reading
by Mark Tungate

Something dark was going on in the charming Detroit suburb of Troy, Michigan – ranked number 25 out of 100 in a CNN Money survey of the nicest small cities in America. Troy's award-winning library was threatened with closure unless it could secure additional funding. A public vote on a small tax increase was scheduled for August 2nd. The trouble was, a very powerful group seemed determined to shut the library down.

That group was the anti-tax Tea Party, a misleadingly quaint name for an influential conservative movement which is committed to reducing government spending. It has a strong presence in Troy and began campaigning heavily against the tax increase, putting up posters and urging people to vote "no" on August 2nd.

Which is when Leo Burnett Detroit got involved. The agency's office is actually in Troy. Creative director Glen Hilzinger lives there and his family uses the library regularly. "As far as many people in Troy were concerned, this was a desperate, tragic situation," he says.

A group of concerned citizens formed a pro-library support group. Glen's wife, who knew the group, tentatively asked him: "Is there anything at all the agency could do?"

Glen approached executive creative director Peter McHugh, who was immediately enthusiastic. "Turns out his mother was a librarian. And of course we're all creatives, so we're liberal in our thinking about the value of the arts. Pretty soon, this became a personal issue for everyone at the agency."

A radical idea surfaced "surprisingly quickly", according to art director Bob Veasey. "In fact we presented the group with two ideas: a safe one that we said probably wouldn't work; and a vile one that we thought had a good chance of working."

The "vile" idea – on the surface at least – was simple. The agency posted signs around town saying: "Vote to close Troy Library August 2nd. Book burning party August 5th." The signs led to a Facebook page that made the party look very real indeed. The result? Anger and confusion on all sides.

"Nobody knew who was doing this," says Glen. "The library certainly didn't – some of its employees were almost as irritated as the Tea Partiers were."

The campaign required considerable planning and resources. "We did a traffic survey to identify the street corners where our signs would be most visible to drivers," says Bob. "And as they were constantly being taken down, we had to keep going out to put up new ones."

Outraged comments flooded the Facebook page and spilled over into a fierce debate on Twitter. The world may have gone digital, but people hated the idea of burning books.

The agency fed the flames by posting videos on Facebook of burning books, offering souvenirs – T-shirts and an "ironic" book bag – placing small ads in the local newspaper, putting up flyers and creating a Foursquare check-in for the party. On the Facebook page, the news that a band had been booked for the event elicited even more furious comments.

Glen says: "It was a genuine social experiment because we had to react on the fly 24/7 to the different twists and turns that the campaign provoked."

National and even international media picked up the story, with some quoting the agency's sinister name for the group that had "paid" for the signs: Safeguarding American Families (SAFE). Slowly, however, the rumour surfaced that an advertising agency in Troy was responsible.

"That's when it started getting a little scary," says Glen. "At one point we saw cars circling our parking lot at night, trying to see if there were any lights on. Meanwhile, we'd be up here on the fifth floor handing out replacement signs to agency volunteers. It got so some of them were anxious about going out there alone."

Just as emotions over the issue had reached their peak, the agency revealed its true message on the Facebook page: "A vote against the library is like a vote to burn books."

The comments, reports and social media sharing began all over again. Now the discourse was no longer about taxes – it was about the merits of libraries and books. On August 2nd, voters turned out en masse to save the library. In fact, there were 342% more "yes" voters than projected. Troy Public Library survived.

A worthwhile repercussion of the campaign was the way it generated debate about the role of libraries. Glen says: "When I was a kid, the library was a place where you could walk in and discover whole worlds. Today a library is more of a community resource. For instance, Troy library provides computer education for the elderly, homework help, assistance with job searches. It's about far more than books."

But sometimes it's about books. Shortly after the campaign had ended, Glen's son was looking for a book for a school assignment. He told his dad: "It's called Fahrenheit Four something."

The book was Ray Bradbury's Fahrenheit 451, set in a dystopian future where books have been banned by the government; any that are found are burned by squads of "firemen".

19

"We looked in a couple of bookstores," says Glen, "but you won't be surprised to hear that we finally found Fahrenheit 451 in Troy Public Library."

Mark Tungate is the author of several books about branding and communications, among them Adland: A Global History of Advertising, Luxury World: The Past, Present and Future of Luxury Brands and Branded Beauty: How Marketing Changed the Way We Look.

20 Food

Agency	BETC, London	Inquisitive toddlers sneak into a recording
Creative Director	Neil Dawson	studio where various instruments are lying
Copywriter	Clive Pickering	around. One of them even establishes
Art Director	Paul Copeland	himself behind the mixing desk. At first
Production	RSA, London	they don't know what to make of the in-
Director	Jim Field Smith	struments, but they quickly begin to work
Producers	Debbie Garvey	out how to produce sounds. Then a miracle
	Nikki Cramphorn	takes place: the sounds coalesce into a
Advertiser	Cow & Gate,	rousing version of 'Come on Eileen' by
	"Supergroup"	Dexy's Midnight Runners. These little char-
		acters are clearly being raised on Cow &
		Gate, as it "feeds their personalities."

THE FLAG-WAVING PIGGY-BACKER
WE ALL MAKE THE GAMES

THE NERVY PEEKER
WE ALL MAKE THE GAMES

THE SULKY PANTS
WE ALL MAKE THE GAMES

THE PROUDEST MUM IN THE WHOLE WIDE WORLD
WE ALL MAKE THE GAMES

THE BLUBBERING WRECK
WE ALL MAKE THE GAMES

Food **21**

Agency	Leo Burnett, London
Executive CD	Justin Tindall
Creative Director	Adam Tucker
Copywriters	Mark Franklin Rob Tenconi
Art Directors	Mark Franklin Rob Tenconi
Advertiser	McDonald's, "We All Make the Games"

Agency	CheethamBell JWT, Manchester
Creative Director	Andy Cheetham
Copywriter	Andy Huntingdon
Art Director	Martin Smith
Production	Uber Content
Director	Luis Gerard
Producer	Bridget Pelicias
Advertiser	John West Canned Fish, "Combover", "Lucky Pete" & "Blackout"

John West chooses its fish with such care that it knows the story behind every can. For example, a John West fisherman relates the time one crew-member cut off another's flapping comb-over when it struck him in the face during a gale.

A second spot tells the tale of crewman "Lucky" Pete, whose winning lottery ticket was plucked from his fingers by a crashing wave, thus instantly shortening his name to "Pete".

Finally, we hear the story of crew member Herbie Webb, who found himself in a tight spot when he began accidentally slurping the end of his mate's spaghetti during a short power cut. John West: there's a story behind every can.

Agency	Leo Burnett, Moscow
Creative Director	Mikhail Kudashkin
Copywriter	Alexander Ovsyankin
Art Director	Mikhail Yarovikov
Advertiser	Happy Milkman Dairy, "Cows"

Agency	Leo Burnett, London
Creative Director	Justin Tindall
Copywriters	Ed Morris
	Andy Drugan
Art Directors	Ed Morris
	Andy Drugan
Production	MJZ, London
Director	Rocky Morton
Producers	Chris McBride
	Bruce Macrae
Advertiser	Kellogg's Crunchy Nut Cereal, "Snake"

A TV documentary crew films an Australian snake catcher as he enters a suburban home to trap "a female red rattler". They tread stealthily into the kitchen. "Don't make a sound," the snake catcher warns, preparing his noose. Suddenly, there's an almighty "crunch". The snake shoots out from under the kitchen sink and straight up his shorts. He falls to the ground, writhing in agony. "Sorry mate," says one of the film crew, who was unable to resist munching on Kellogg's Crunchy Nut Cereal. "They're nutty."

24 Food

Agency	Publicis Conseil, Paris
CCO	Olivier Altmann
Creative Director	Steve O'Leary
Copywriter	Antonin Jacquot
Art Director	Philippe d'Orgeville
Production	La Pac, Paris
Director	David Shane
Producers	Pierre Marcus
	Armelle Sudron
	Florent Villiers
Photographer	Achim Lippoth
Advertiser	Guigoz, "Let's Speak Baby"

Grown-ups and babies often have communication issues. In this spot, subtitles translate babies' sarcastic comments about the adults around them. The adults, meanwhile, respond with fake baby noises that are pure gibberish. Except when twins trick a babysitter into repeating baby language for "I'm an airhead". Fortunately, Guigoz baby food "speaks baby".

Agency	Forsman & Bodenfors, Gothenburg
Copywriter	Anders Hegerfors
Art Director	Lars Elfman
Designer	Magnus Almberg
Planner	My Troedsson
Production	Acne, Stockholm
Director	Marcus Svanberg
Producers	Åsa Hammar
	Fredrik Skoglund
Account Team	Erica Berghagen
	Ann Spennare Bengtsson
Advertiser	Kalles Kaviar, "Tokyo"

A lone Swedish guy has set up a stall in the middle of Tokyo offering free tastings of Kalles Kaviar – a mixture of cod roe and potato flakes that's hugely popular back home. Apparently the citizens of Tokyo just think it's weird, or even disgusting, judging by their grimaces. But they're far too polite to voice their distaste. When the guy asks: "Do you like it?" one lady nods enthusiastically, even though she clearly wants to spit the stuff out. Kalles: a very Swedish taste.

Agency	New Moment New Ideas	Agency	BBDO, Moscow
	Company Y&R, Skopje	Creative Directors	Luis Tauffer
Creative Director	Dusan Drakalski		Andres Vergara
Copywriters	Nikola Vojnov	Copywriter	Evgeny Tsiklauri
	Ana Pop Stefanija	Art Directors	Roman Lych
Art Director	Nikola Vojnov		Luis Tauffer
Illustrators	Jana Miseva	Photographer	Ale Burset
	Hari Dudeski	Art Buying	Giuliana Giora
Advertiser	Pekabesko Pâté	Retouching	Diego Speroni
		Advertiser	Bering Canned Fish, "Fisherman's Tales"

Agency	Black River FC, Johannesburg
Executive CD	Ahmed Tilly
Creative Director	Suhana Gordhan
Copywriters	Avish Gordhan
	Lufuno Mavhhungu
	Nhlanhla Ngcobo
Art Directors	Mandie Van Der Merwe
	Monde Siphamla
Production	Bouffant, Johannesburg
Director	Dean Blumberg
Producers	Chanelle Critchfield
	Melinda McDonald
	Iolanthe Grobler
Account Manager	Charlotte Pettifer
Strategic Planner	Gia Callinicos
Advertiser	Nando's, "The Last Dictator Standing"

This darkly amusing spot reflects a period in which dictators all over the world are being opposed and deposed. To a rendition of the iconic 1968 track, "Those were the Days" by Mary Hopkin, a Robert Mugabe lookalike is laying places for Christmas dinner. His mind drifts back to "the good old days", when fellow tyrants Muammar Gaddafi, Saddam Hussein, PW Botha and Idi Amin would frolic at his mansion, shooting one another with water pistols and making "sand angels". Now he's alone. "This time of year, no-one should have to eat alone," deadpans the narrator. "So get a Nando's six pack meal."

26   Food

Agency	McCann, Manchester
Creative Directors	Dave Price
	Neil Lancaster
Copywriter	Neil Lancaster
Art Director	Dave Price
Advertiser	Aldi Supermarkets, "Fish Fingers"

Supermarket Aldi sells own-label products that are just like big brands – only cheaper. Here we see a fisherman taste testing some Birds Eye fish fingers (£2.48). "Oh, I like those," he says to camera. "That's nice. Pollock, am I right?" Then he tastes Aldi's version (£1.49). "Oh, I like these – same fish. There you go then – a fine pair of pollocks." Aldi: like brands – only cheaper.

Agency	DDB Group, Auckland
Creative Directors	Andy Fackrell
	Jordan Sky
Copywriters	Pete Gosselin
	Jay Hunt
Art Directors	Pete Gosselin
	Jay Hunt
Production	Revolver, Sydney
Director	Steve Rogers
Producers	Pip Smart
	Judy Thompson
	Kim Baldwinson
Advertiser	McDonald's, "Staying Up"

In New Zealand, the 2012 Olympics were broadcast live in the middle of the night. A young lad keeps sneaking down to watch the Games when he's supposed to be in bed. No matter which room he tries, his dad turns off the TV every time. He's reduced to donning headphones and building an elaborate tent of sheets to mask the screen. His dad appears again – this time bearing a meal from McDonald's. They huddle up for a night of watching the Games together. McDonald's: proud supporters of all those staying up.

FISHING (CONSEQUENCES)

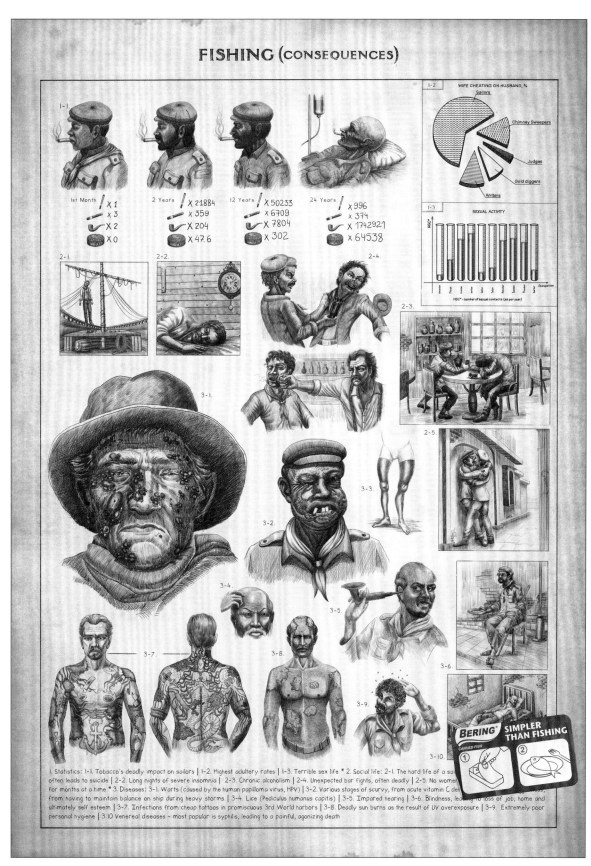

I. Statistics: 1-1. Tobacco's deadly impact on sailors | 1-2. Highest adultery rates | 1-3. Terrible sex life * 2. Social life: 2-1. The hard life of a sailor often leads to suicide | 2-2. Long nights of severe insomnia | 2-3. Chronic alcoholism | 2-4. Unexpected bar fights, often deadly | 2-5. No women for months at a time * 3. Diseases: 3-1. Warts (caused by the human papilloma virus, HPV) | 3-2. Various stages of scurvy, from acute vitamin C deficiency from having to maintain balance on ship during heavy storms | 3-4. Lice (Pediculus humanus capitis) | 3-5. Impared hearing | 3-6. Blindness, leading to loss of job, home and ultimately self esteem | 3-7. Infections from cheap tattoos in promiscuous 3rd World harbors | 3-8. Deadly sun burns as the result of UV overexposure | 3-9. Extremely poor personal hygiene | 3.10 Venereal diseases ~ most popular is syphilis, leading to a painful, agonizing death

Agency	BBDO, Moscow
Creative Director	Mihai Coliban
Copywriters	Artem Mukhin
	Andrey Sivkov
Art Directors	Oleg Panov
	Maxim Kitaev
	Mihai Coliban
Illustrator	Nishikant Palande
Art Buying	Giuliana Giora
Account Manager	Ekaterina Konovalova
Advertiser	Bering Canned Fish, "Simpler than Fishing"

TAKE AWAY. ALWAYS AT BURGER KING® CENTRAL STATION.

TASTE IS KING™

28 Food

Agency	Shout Advertising, Gothenburg
Copywriter	Pontus Caresten
Art Director	Niclas Fors
Illustrator	Robert Melander
Final Art	Malin Svensson
Account Mgr.	Stefan Gustafsson
Production Mgr.	Jeanette Åberg
Advertiser	Burger King, "Bags"

Agency	Leo Burnett, Chicago
Global CCO	Mark Tutssel
CCO	Susan Credle
Executive CD	John Montgomery
Creative Directors	Avery Gross
	Brian Shembeda
Copywriters	Rene Delgado
	Alex Esseveld
Art Directors	Rene Delgado
	Alex Esseveld
Producers	Ross Greenblat
	Samantha Howes
Advertiser	McDonald's, "Fry Lights"

To launch the Best Fries on the Planet campaign, a billboard across the street from a Chicago McDonald's resembled the top of a giant box of fries. The fries themselves were represented by a row of searchlights (made up of 200,000 individual lumen lights) casting their yellow beams into the night sky. They were visible from three miles away on a clear night, so nocturnal strollers had no excuse to go hungry.

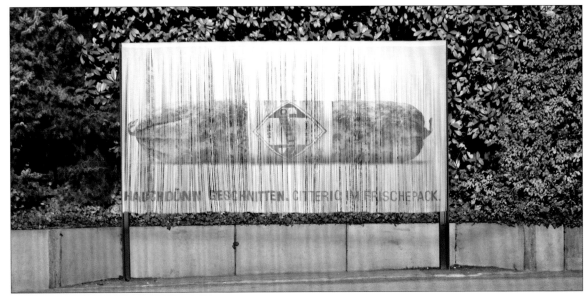

Agency	Advico Y&R, Zurich
Creative Directors	Dominik Oberwiler
	Martin Stulz
Copywriter	Julia Brandstätter
Art Director	Fabienne Marcolin
Photographer	Markus Weber
Graphic Design	Annik Weber
Account Manager	Carmela Dias
Advertiser	Citterio Meat,
	"Cut Into
	Finest Slices"

A conventional billboard was replaced by a curtain of individual strips. The salami appeared almost exactly the way it does in a pack of Citterio: cut into thin slices.

Aldi.
Like brands.
Only cheaper.

aldi.co.uk

Agency	McCann, Manchester
Creative Directors	Dave Price
	Neil Lancaster
Copywriter	Neil Lancaster
Art Director	Dave Price
Advertiser	Aldi Supermarkets,
	"Chocolate Bunnies"

We're back in the world of Aldi, whose own-label products are like big brands – only cheaper. A little girl in a furry rabbit costume, her face smeared with chocolate, contemplates a chocolate bunny from Lindt (£2). "I like this chocolate bunny," she says. Then she looks at the empty gold wrapping of a bunny from Aldi (99p). "But I don't know where this one's gone. I think the pixies has eaten it." Aldi: like brands – only cheaper.

Agency	BBDO, Kiev
Creative Director	Rytis Juodeika
Copywriter	Anna Pochtarenko
Art Director	Anna Krasnozhon
Photographer	Sergey Poznanskyi
Retouching	Vlad Petrusevich
Account Director	Anna Rybalka
3D Designer	Yuryi "Gary" Gorbach
Advertiser	Wrigley Orbit, "Strawberrynana"

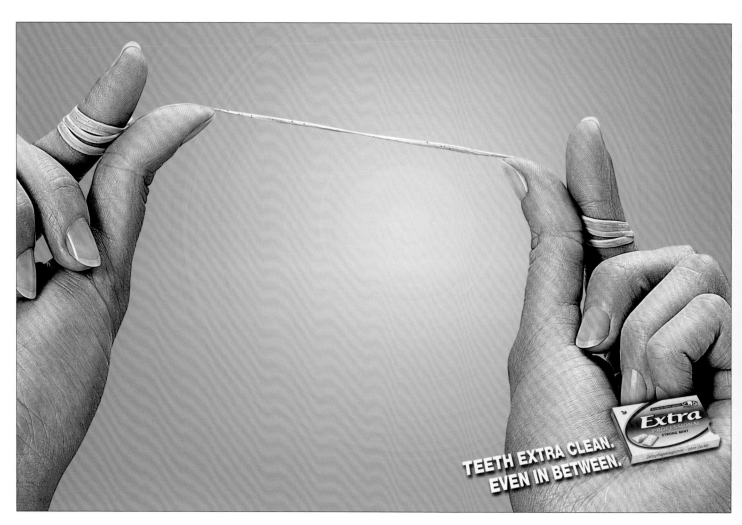

TEETH EXTRA CLEAN.
EVEN IN BETWEEN.

32   **Confectionery & Snacks**

Agency	DDB & Tribal, Amsterdam
Creative Directors	Joris Kuijpers
	Dylan De Backer
Copywriter	Menno Schipper
Art Director	Nils Taildeman
Production	Electric Zoo, Amsterdam
Director	Hans Knaapen
Producers	Maarten van Hemmen
	Nikki Haighton
Advertiser	Autodrop Liquorice Candy, "Secret Portal"

When a guy in an office plunges his hand into a packet of Autodrop candy, his arm disappears up to its elbow. He seems to have found a bottomless supply! One of his colleagues hastens to test it out. We cut to a scene of workmen in their hut, who are astonished to see a hand emerging from a candy bag to forage among their own stash of sweets. Back at the office, the boss wants his turn. But when his hand emerges in the parallel dimension, a workman is ready with his shovel…Autodrop candy is "absurdly delicious".

Agencies	BBDO Proximity, Hamburg & Düsseldorf
CCO	Wolfgang Schneider
Executive CD	Volker Waesch
Creative Director	Michael Plueckhahn
Copywriters	Daniel Hoffmann
	Claudia Janus
Art Directors	Claudia Janus
	Mona Morsch
Photographer	Maik Rositzki
Advertiser	Wrigley
	Extra Professional, "Dental Floss"

Agency	BAR, Lisbon
Creative Directors	Diogo Anahory
	José Bomtempo
Copywriter	Marco Pulido
Art Director	Luís Nora
Producer	Nuno Calado
Development	Nuno Moura
Creative Solution	Fernando Fonseca
Advertiser	Gorila Vintage
	Chewing Gum,
	"Cassette Tape" &
	"Delorean"

Agency	TBWA\España, Barcelona
Creative Directors	Ramón Sala
	Joan Vidal
	Fer García
Copywriter	Joan Vidal
Art Director	Fer García
Photographer	Pep Ávila
Post Production	Patrick Bras
	Eclipse, Barcelona
Advertiser	Chupa Chups
	with Gum

Agency   Gitam BBDO,
         Tel Aviv
CCO   Guy Bar
Executive CD   Shani Gershi
Creative Director   Karmel Abuzalaf
Copywriter   Arnon Rotem
Art Director   Eitan Cohen
Illustrator   Miriam Moshinsky
Account Team   Yuval Vaingast
         Aviya Sagie
         Yael Meltzer
Advertiser   Hubba Bubba,
         "Myths"

SECURITY CAMERAS AROUND THE WORLD...

ALSO CAPTURE...

PEOPLE STEALING KISSES

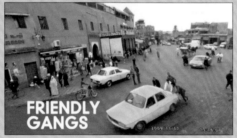

HONEST PICKPOCKETS

FRIENDLY GANGS

AND A FEW CRAZY HEROES.

LET'S LOOK AT THE WORLD A LITTLE DIFFERENTLY

Coca-Cola open happiness

Agency	Wunderman, Buenos Aires	
Creative Director	Martin Mercado	
Production	Landia, Buenos Aires	
Advertiser	Coca-Cola, "Security Cameras"	

Security cameras were designed to capture the nastier moments of city living. But as this spot demonstrates, the cameras also capture positive and funny things. Such as people stealing kisses, dancing to buskers, fencing with umbrellas and giving food to the homeless, as well as random acts of kindness, craziness, love and courage. Not to mention a dad buying his son a Coke. Let's look at the world differently. Coca-Cola: open happiness.

Large Coffee. 1,50 €.   i'm lovin' it

Large Coffee. 1,50 €.   i'm lovin' it

 Drinks **37**

Agency	DDB, Helsinki
Creative Director	Vesa Tujunen
Copywriter	Vesa Tujunen
Art Director	Jukka Mannio
Photographer	Marjo Tokkari
Illustrator	Fake Graphics
Graphic Design	Antti Salminen
Producer	Kirsi Pärni
Account Team	Jarno Lindblom
	Pia Eiro
	Niina Pankko
Advertiser	McDonald's,
	"Large Coffee"

Coca-Cola und die Konturflasche sind eingetragene Schutzmarken der The Coca-Cola Company. Coca-Cola ist koffeinhaltig.

38   Drinks

Agency	Publicis Conseil, Paris	**Music Production**	Sean Atherton	
Creative Director	Steve O'Leary		Sian Rogers	
Copywriter	Antonin Jacquot	**Sound Design**	Anthony Moore	
Art Director	Philippe d'Orgeville		Jon Clarke	
Production	Sonny/Première	**Post Production**	Antoine Daubert	
	Heure, Paris		Wam, Paris	
Director	Guy Manwaring	**Advertiser**	Coke Zero,	
Producers	Constance Guillou		"Unlock	
	Pierre Marcus		the 007 in You"	
	Guillaume Delmas			
	Timothe Rosenberg			

When a guy spots a pretty girl with her boorish boyfriend and hangers-on, sipping a Coke makes him feel as cool as James Bond. He hums the Bond theme as he approaches their table. The girl joins in. She's whisked away, but he continues humming the theme as he gives chase on foot and moped, leading to various Bond-style situations. Finally he rescues the girl and they clink Coke bottles to seal their relationship. Coca-Cola is an official Bond movie sponsor – and it might unlock the 007 in you.

Agency	McCann, Berlin
Creative Directors	Bill Biancoli
	Stefan Baechle
	Thorsten Adenauer
Copywriter	Tilo Endert
Art Director	Erik Gonan
Graphic Design	Lisa Marie Schröder
Account Team	Susanne Wenig
	Dennis Schwinn
Advertiser	Coca-Cola,
	"Open Happiness"

Agencies	McCann, Frankfurt & Geneva
Creative Director	Bill Biancoli
Copywriter	Bill Biancoli
Art Directors	Birol Bayraktar
	Michael Jacob
	Florian Fischkal
Illustrator	Yue-Shin Lin
Account Mgr.	Christiane Hahn
Advertiser	Coca-Cola, "Athletes"

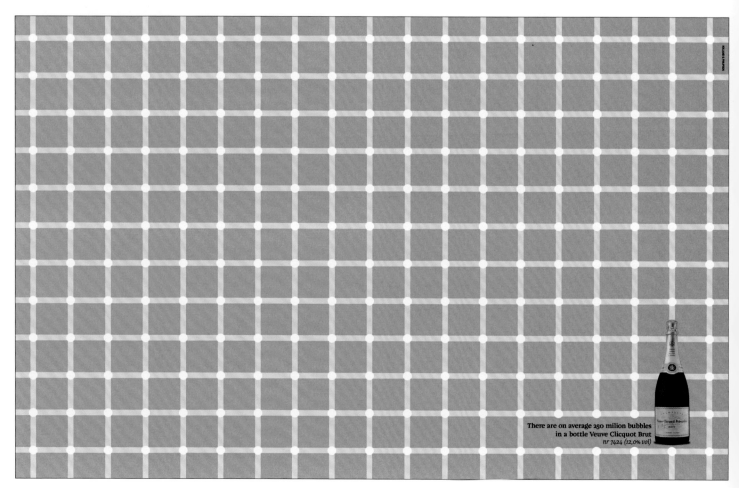

40   **Drinks**

Agency	Wieden+Kennedy, Amsterdam
Creative Directors	Mark Bernath
	Eric Quennoy
Copywriter	Dan Maxwell
Art Directors	Thijs Biersteker
	Adrien Bindi
Production	MJZ, London
Director	Matthijs Van Heijningen
Producers	Chris McBride
	Tony Stearns
	Niko Koot
Advertiser	Heineken, "The Express"

Heineken's man of the world gets more than he bargains for when he's mistaken for James Bond while boarding a Russian express. The villains pursue him through the train as he uses his skills to overcome unlikely obstacles – at one point he builds a house of cards in the shape of the Kremlin – until he finally bumps into Bond in the bar, accompanied by Bond girl Severine and a mysterious metallic case. Bond parachutes off the train, leaving our hero holding the bag.

Agency	Holland & Philipson, Stockholm
Creative Directors	Mats Holland
	Daniel Philipson
Copywriter	Sandra Malmgren
Graphic Design	Nina Mårtensson
Advertiser	Veuve Clicquot Champagne, "Bubbles"

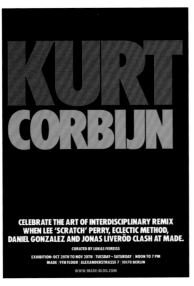

KURT CORBIJN

CELEBRATE THE ART OF INTERDISCIPLINARY REMIX
WHEN LEE 'SCRATCH' PERRY, ECLECTIC METHOD,
DANIEL GONZALEZ AND JONAS LIVERÖD CLASH AT MADE.

CURATED BY LUKAS FEIREISS

EXHIBITION: OCT 28TH TO NOV 28TH | TUESDAY – SATURDAY | NOON TO 7 PM
MADE | 9TH FLOOR | ALEXANDERSTRASSE 7 | 10178 BERLIN

WWW.MADE-BLOG.COM

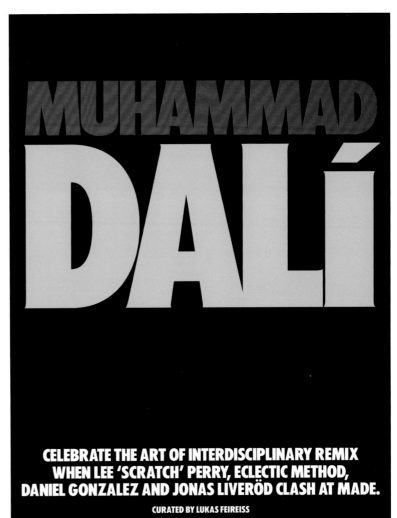

MUHAMMAD DALÍ

CELEBRATE THE ART OF INTERDISCIPLINARY REMIX
WHEN LEE 'SCRATCH' PERRY, ECLECTIC METHOD,
DANIEL GONZALEZ AND JONAS LIVERÖD CLASH AT MADE.

CURATED BY LUKAS FEIREISS

EXHIBITION: OCT 28TH TO NOV 28TH | TUESDAY – SATURDAY | NOON TO 7 PM
MADE | 9TH FLOOR | ALEXANDERSTRASSE 7 | 10178 BERLIN

WWW.MADE-BLOG.COM

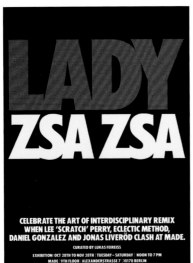

LADY ZSA ZSA

CELEBRATE THE ART OF INTERDISCIPLINARY REMIX
WHEN LEE 'SCRATCH' PERRY, ECLECTIC METHOD,
DANIEL GONZALEZ AND JONAS LIVERÖD CLASH AT MADE.

CURATED BY LUKAS FEIREISS

EXHIBITION: OCT 28TH TO NOV 28TH | TUESDAY – SATURDAY | NOON TO 7 PM
MADE | 9TH FLOOR | ALEXANDERSTRASSE 7 | 10178 BERLIN

WWW.MADE-BLOG.COM

TYRA BANKSY

CELEBRATE THE ART OF INTERDISCIPLINARY REMIX
WHEN LEE 'SCRATCH' PERRY, ECLECTIC METHOD,
DANIEL GONZALEZ AND JONAS LIVERÖD CLASH AT MADE.

CURATED BY LUKAS FEIREISS

EXHIBITION: OCT 28TH TO NOV 28TH | TUESDAY – SATURDAY | NOON TO 7 PM
MADE | 9TH FLOOR | ALEXANDERSTRASSE 7 | 10178 BERLIN

WWW.MADE-BLOG.COM

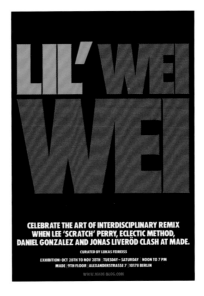

LIL' WEI WEI

CELEBRATE THE ART OF INTERDISCIPLINARY REMIX
WHEN LEE 'SCRATCH' PERRY, ECLECTIC METHOD,
DANIEL GONZALEZ AND JONAS LIVERÖD CLASH AT MADE.

CURATED BY LUKAS FEIREISS

EXHIBITION: OCT 28TH TO NOV 28TH | TUESDAY – SATURDAY | NOON TO 7 PM
MADE | 9TH FLOOR | ALEXANDERSTRASSE 7 | 10178 BERLIN

WWW.MADE-BLOG.COM

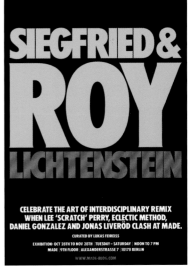

SIEGFRIED & ROY LICHTENSTEIN

CELEBRATE THE ART OF INTERDISCIPLINARY REMIX
WHEN LEE 'SCRATCH' PERRY, ECLECTIC METHOD,
DANIEL GONZALEZ AND JONAS LIVERÖD CLASH AT MADE.

CURATED BY LUKAS FEIREISS

EXHIBITION: OCT 28TH TO NOV 28TH | TUESDAY – SATURDAY | NOON TO 7 PM
MADE | 9TH FLOOR | ALEXANDERSTRASSE 7 | 10178 BERLIN

WWW.MADE-BLOG.COM

Agency	TBWA\Berlin	Photographers	Niels Krueger
Creative Directors	Philip Borchardt		Robert Wunsch
	Nico Zeh	Graphic Design	Ricardo Mueller
	Tadi Rock		Kim Mueller
	Dirk Henkelmann		Moni Eckey
Copywriters	Andrew Morgan	Typographers	Andrew Morgan
	Philip Borchardt		Kim Mueller
	Nico Zeh		Ricardo Mueller
Art Directors	Andrew Morgan		Moni Eckey
	Philipp Migeod	Producer	Katrin Dettmann
	Stefano de Luccia	Advertiser	Absolut Vodka, "MADE Scratch'n'Cut"

Agencies	Fred & Farid, Paris & Shanghai
Creative Directors	Fred Raillard
	Farid Mokart
Production	Gorgeous, London
Director	Peter Thwaites
Producers	Anna Hashmi
	Kate Taylor
Advertiser	Martini Royale, "Luck Is an Attitude"

The ad's crowd-sourced star Yuri Buzzi – cast via a talent search on Facebook – shows us what happens when you follow the Martini philosophy and embrace life. In a split screen film we see one charming, confident Yuri following up every opportunity and flirting with all the ladies, while his alter ego takes a more down at heel approach. We follow the two Yuris to a hip nightclub. But a twist at the end shows the more introvert Yuri taking the initiative when it really counts. Luck is an attitude.

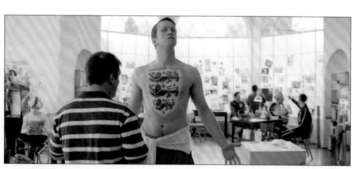

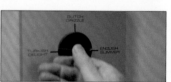

42   **Drinks**

Agency	Selmore, Amsterdam
Creative Director	Diederick Hillenius
Copywriter	Thomas Reinhold
Art Director	Tibor Van Ginkel
Production	Bonkers, Amsterdam
Director	Jonathan Herman
Producers	Saskia Kok
	Marga Bierema
DOP	Glynn Speeckeart
Editor	Gert Van Berckelaer
Post Production	Hectic Electric
Advertiser	Bavaria, "Charlie Sheen - Rehab"

"We don't want to see you back here," says the director of a rehab clinic to wild-living actor Charlie Sheen. "Don't worry," says Charlie, "let's not have a drink some time." But driving home, he's amazed to see a pregnant woman drinking beer. Construction workers, taxi drivers, gym-goers, even cops – they're all drinking beer. Is he hallucinating? When he arrives home, everyone is drinking beer. "What the…?" He scurries inside to hide until someone drops a beer though the cat flap and he examines its label. It's Bavaria's alcohol-free beer. Cheers!

Agency	Fold7, London
Creative Director	Ryan Newey
Copywriters	Ryan Newey
	John Yorke
Art Director	Ryan Newey
Production	Academy Films, London
Director	Peter Cattaneo
Producers	Sam Balderstone
	Sally-Ann Houghton
Advertiser	Carlsberg, "Fan Academy"

Legendary soccer commentator Des Lynam welcomes a trio of hopefuls to the Fan Academy, where fans of the England team are honing their skills for Euro 2012. Applying patriotic body paint, queuing for the loo, braving penalty shoot-outs and the torrential rain of an English summer – the fans are tested on all these and more. But for those who graduate, there's the ultimate reward – a pint. Giving your all for England? That calls for a Carlsberg.

Agency	DDB, Helsinki	Agency	MedinaTurgul DDB,
Creative Director	Vesa Tujunen		Istanbul
Copywriter	Jani Tynnilä	Creative Director	Kurtcebe Turgul
Art Director	Jukka Mannio	Copywriter	Arda Erdik
Photographer	Perttu Saksa	Art Director	Baris Sarhan
Illustrator	Saddington & Baynes,	Illustrators	Baris Sarhan
	London		Onur Aynagoz
Graphic Design	Antti Salminen	Advertiser	Sek Milk
Producer	Kirsi Pärni		
Account Team	Jarno Lindblom		
	Inka Karvonen		
Advertiser	McDonald's,		
	"The Real Milkshake"		

Agency	Ogilvy France, Paris
CCO	Chris Garbutt
Creative Director	Thierry Chiumino
Copywriters	Baptiste Clinet
	Nicolas Lautier
	Florian Bodet
Art Directors	Baptiste Clinet
	Nicolas Lautier
	Florian Bodet
Production	Soixante Quinze, Paris
Director	Johan Renck
Producers	Annabelle Fournier
	Jeanne Marie de La Fontaine
	Laure Bayle
Post Production	Mikros Image
DOP	Simon Chaudoir
Advertiser	Perrier, "The Drop"

As a beautiful woman arrives at an international conference, we see that the sun has become so hot that the entire world is melting. The woman turns out to be an astronaut. She's sent into space with a bottle of Perrier to refresh the sun – but at the last moment she gulps down the whole lot. Fortunately, the one last drop is refreshing enough to quench the sun's rays. Imagine what a whole bottle could do for you?

44   **Drinks**

Agency	DDB, Paris
Creative Directors	Nick Bell
	Pierrette Diaz
	Matthieu Elkaim
Copywriter	Pierre-Antoine Dupin
Art Director	Frédéric Lahache
Production	Gorgeous, London
Directors	Stacy Wall
	Lucinda Ker
Advertiser	Lipton Ice Tea, "Slap"

On a hot and dusty plain, actor Hugh Jackman is rehearsing a scene that requires an actress to slap him. The director thinks she's not putting her back into it, so he shows her how it's done. "OK," says Hugh after a couple of stinging slaps. But the rest of the crew lines up to slap him too. Calling for time out, the actor sips an ice tea and then coolly drops an ice-cube down the actress's back. She slaps him – hard! The scene is in the can. "One more time," says the director. Lipton Ice Tea: never lose your cool.

Agency	Publicis, Milan
Creative Directors	Bruno Bertelli
	Cristiana Boccassini
Copywriters	Rachele Proli
	Michela Talamona
Art Director	Fabrizio Tamagni
Production	Sonny, London
Director	Fredrik Bond
Producers	Alicia Richards
	Mariella Maiorano
DOP	Mattias Montero
Editor	Patrick Ryan
Advertiser	Heineken, "The Sunrise"

A good-looking guy enters a club where the ravishing DJ Audrey Napoleon is playing. The guy accepts a beer and even a shot, but as the night wears on he switches to water. His moderation pays off when the clubbers start to get legless while he still has plenty of energy left for dancing. Plus, he's got Audrey's attention. When the night ends, she comes looking for him and they step out into the dawn together. Sunrise belongs to moderate drinkers.

Agency	Leo Burnett, Sydney
Creative Director	Andy DiLallo
Copywriter	Mike Felix
Art Director	Matt Swinburne
Photographer	Andreas Smetana
Typographer	Jason Young
Advertiser	Bundaberg Red, "Catfish" & "Pig"

46 **Drinks**

Agency	BAR, Lisbon
Creative Directors	Diogo Anahory
	José Bomtempo
Copywriter	Diogo Anahory
Art Director	Eduardo Tavares
Photographer	Masayuki Kondo
Production	Heitor Estúdio
Advertiser	Blue Soft Drink,
	"Orange" & "Mango"

Agency	MK Norway, Bergen
Creative Director	Armando Zuniga
Copywriter	Jon Hjørnevik
Art Directors	Doffen Trellevik
	Ole Færøvik
	Armando Zuniga
Photographer	Adam Taylor
Graphic Design	Ole Færøvik
	Pedro Moreira
Account Director	Britt Hege Karlsen
Advertiser	Schweppes,
	"Your Taste"

Everybody on the ground!

This is a robbery!

What do you think you're doing?

Oh... but I thought you said,
"Everybody on the ground"

I mean everybody except
for those wearing hoods...

and those wearing stockings
and holding a gun.

except for those
do the robbing!

Let's get organized
and carry out a serious robbery

WIND
για όλους

48 **Communication Services**

Agency	The Newtons Laboratory, Gerakas	**DOP**	Christos Voudouris	
Creative Director	Sorotos Giannis	**Editor**	Yiorgos Mavropsaridis	
Copywriter	Vassilis Klissouras	**Account Team**	Dimitris Belecos	
Art Director	Paris Godenopoulos		Mirella Bairaktari	
Production	Filmiki Productions	**Planner**	Kostas Verveniotis	
Director	Dennis Iliadis	**Project Manager**	Andreas Gregoriadis	
Producer	Kaiti Alevitsovitou	**Advertiser**	Wind Hellas,	
Creative Head	Andreas Gregoriadis		"Bank Robbery"	

"OK – everybody on the ground!" says a bank robber. When even his fellow robbers throw themselves to the floor, he adds irritably: "Except those wearing hoods." A couple of kids wearing hoodies get up. "I mean except those wearing stockings," he says. Most of the women stand up. Furious by now, he says: "Except those wearing stockings and carrying a gun!" An old woman pulls a huge revolver from her purse. "Except those doing the robbing!" All the bank's employees rise. When mobile carrier Wind says it will offer free airtime to everybody, it really means everybody.

The post office now sells coffee.

Communication Services   **49**

Agency	Spillmann/Felser/ Leo Burnett, Zurich
Creative Directors	Peter Brönnimann Patrick Suter
Copywriter	Reto Vogler
Art Directors	Natasha La Marca Sebastian Krayer
Advertiser	Swiss Post, "Coffeestamp"

Agency	BBH India, Mumbai
Creative Director	Russell Barrett
Copywriters	Nikhil Panjwani
	Malhaar Rao
	R.Venkatraman
Art Director	Kunal Sawant
Production	Eeksaurus Films
Director	E.Suresh
Producers	Nilima Eriyat
	Sushma Joseph
Advertiser	Google Chrome,
	"Tanjore"

This ad for Google Chrome tells the real story of Tanjore resident G. Rajendran and how he kept the region's ancient art tradition alive. A cunning stage performance shows us how he set up his own website and used Google to promote himself. The spot demonstrates how the oldest Indian art form used the most modern marketplace to keep itself relevant.

50   **Communication Services**

Agency	Spillmann/Felser/
	Leo Burnett, Zurich
Creative Director	Peter Brönnimann
Copywriter	Johannes Raggio
Art Director	Pablo Schencke
Production	Cobblestone,
	Hamburg
Director	Axel Laubscher
Producer	Suzana Kovacevic
Advertiser	Tutti.ch,
	"Spinning" &
	"Wallpaper"

During a "spinning" class at his gym, a young guy on a cycling machine has his eyes firmly on the butts of the girls in front of him. Cut to a picture of his mountain bike – for sale. If there's something you don't want to use any more, advertise it on Tutti.ch, one of the biggest classified advertising sites in Switzerland.

In another spot for the site, a husband returns home to find that his wife has been decorating. He looks dismayed by the "pretty" wallpaper covering every surface. Next we see his movie projector advertised on Tutti.ch.

Agency	Forsman & Bodenfors, Gothenburg	
Copywriters	Martin Ringqvist	
	David Lundgren	
Art Directors	Kim Cramer	
	Lars Elfman	
Production	Acne, Stockholm	
Producers	Kalle Schröder	
	Alexander Blidner	
Designers	Icka Samrin	
	Marc Eastmond	
Account Team	Jerk Zander	
	Erica Berghagen	
Advertiser	Tele2, "The Christening"	

Telecom operator Tele2's brand spokesman is Frank, a black sheep. On the same day as the christening of Sweden's new crown princess, Frank christened his own baby on prime time TV. A choir and full orchestra accompanied Frank as he sung the contemporary hymn "You Raise Me Up" (written by Secret Garden's Rolf Løvland with lyrics by Irish novelist Brendan Graham). A majestic church, hundreds of blazing candles and a priest holding the swaddled lamb added up to an extravaganza that must have brought a tear to the eye of many a viewer.

Agency	BBDO, New York	Line Producer	Pete Vitale
CCO	David Lubars	DOP	Guillermo Navarro
Executive CDs	Greg Hahn	Editing House	Mackenzie Cutler
	Ralph Watson	Editors	Ian Mackenzie
Creative Director	Mike Sweeney		Nick Divers
Production	Smuggler, Hollywood	Flame Artists	Jimmy Hayhow
Director	Randy Krallman		Brendan Hogan
Producers	Patrick Milling Smith	Sound Design	Sam Shaffer
	Brian Carmody	Advertiser	AT&T,
	Lisa Rich		"Speed Dating" &
	Anthony Curti		"Romantic Dinner"
	Diane McCann		

Superfast downloading can have its downsides. Take this gentleman for instance – a lothario on the prowl at a speed dating session. He claims he's ready to settle down, but by checking his profile online, his potential partner can see that his relationship status says: "Never getting married." And his personal motto is: "Here for a good time, not for a long time." And as for the video in which he compares himself to "a wild stallion"... Download three times faster with AT&T.

"It's so nice to spend time together, just you and me..." says a woman during a romantic dinner. "I know," says her partner, briefly glancing downwards. "Wait," she asks him, "did you just check the game on your phone?" The guy denies such a thing is even possible. But while she's talking he flinches painfully. She frowns. Then he cheers – quietly. "Yessss!" AT&T's network lets your iPhone download three times faster. So you can watch the game wherever.

The Post goes online.
With the *E POSTBRIEF*.

Deutsche Post

52 **Communication Services**

Agency	Jung von Matt, Hamburg	Agency	BBDO, Moscow
Executive CDs	Mathias Stiller	Creative Directors	Luis Tauffer
	Thomas Schwarz		Andres Vergara
Creative Directors	Boris Schwiedrzik	Copywriters	Luis Tauffer
	Markus Ewertz		Andres Vergara
Copywriter	Adrian Staehelin	Art Director	Luis Tauffer
Art Director	Daniel Ahrens	Photographer	Carioca Studio
Photographer	Sebastian Burgold	Art Buying	Giuliana Giora
Art Buying	Marjorie Jorrot	Advertiser	DHL,
Account Team	Ilan Schaefer		"Express Delivery"
	Julia Kottowski		
	Annika Dahmen		
Advertiser	Deutsche Post		

Agency	Publicis Conseil, Paris
Creative Director	Olivier Altmann
Copywriter	Marc Rosier
Art Directors	Jean-Marc Tramoni
	Julien Didier
Production	Soixante Quinze, Paris
Director	Jonathan Herman
Producers	Emmanuel Guiraud
	Marie Wallet
	Felicie Crosnier
	Maylis Pajot
	Alice Pigeon
	Pierre Marcus
	Patrick Pauwels
	Guillaume Delmas
Post Production	Alain Le Borgne
	Quentin Martin
	Raimbaut Gaffier
DOP	Joost Van Gelder
Advertiser	Orange, "4G"

In a restaurant, a young woman working on a laptop sees a man spill a few drops of soup on his shirt. Catching his eye, she turns her screen and shows him a slapstick video of a man covered in green gunk. As their romance takes flight, they use images and videos to flirt with one another. Soon a neighbouring diner and the waiters are in on the act. The suave neighbour tries to steal the show but the nice guy wins the battle. Thanks to Orange, downloading has never been so fast.

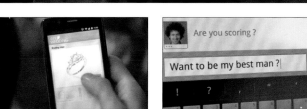

Communication Services 53

Agency	Publicis Yorum, Istanbul
Creative Director	Cevdet Kizilay
Copywriter	Zafer Kulunk
Art Director	Erkut Terliksiz
Production	Soda Film, Istanbul
	PSB Films, Kiev
Director	Gurkan Kurtkaya
Producers	Yalcin Kilic
	Arzu Koksal
	Armagan Kuscu
DOP	Maher Maleh
Post Production	1000 Volt, Istanbul
Advertiser	Turk Telekom

A narrator relates a scene from Dostoyevsky's "Crime and Punishment" as the events take place on screen: the killer Raskolnikov leaves his apartment, passing the doorway of a man in modern dress, who seems to be watching his every move. But we soon learn that the man is blind – and that he's listening to the novel courtesy of Turk Telecom's "talking books" service. Great books can make even the most serious problems disappear.

Agency	Publicis Conseil, Paris
Creative Director	Olivier Altmann
Copywriter	Marc Rosier
Art Directors	Jean-Marc Tramoni
	Julien Didier
Production	Irene, Paris
Director	Mega Force
Producers	Guillaume De Bary
	Pierre Marcus
	Guillaume Delmas
Advertiser	Orange Intel, "The Kiss"

At a packed party, a young man is delighted when a pretty girl leans in for a kiss. So delighted that he gets straight to work on his phone, instantaneously changing his relationship status, sending a picture of the girl to his mother, buying a family car and even a wedding ring. Just across the room, his best pal receives a text: "Want to be my best man?" Thanks to Orange and Intel, you can now surf as fast you think.

Agency	Midttrafik Kommunikation/
	Thomas Falkenberg, Aarhus
Copywriter	Thomas Falkenberg
Production	M2Film, Aarhus
Director	Marc Wilkins/RARE
Producers	Ronni Madsen
	Jan P.
Advertiser	Midttrafik, "The Bus"

Remember when you thought being a bus driver would be pretty cool? Now the bus is cool again, thanks to this witty parody of a movie trailer. Waiting passengers are ecstatic when the conveyance of their dreams arrives at the bus stop. As they wallow in its luxuries, a gravel-voiced narrator lists its advantages: comfy seats; panoramic views; designer bells with cool functions. It even has its own lane. Plenty of slow motion and a handbrake turn complete the action movie ambience. And as for the driver – of course, he's still cool.

Dreaming of a holiday?

KiELO TRAVEL

Agency	New Moment New Ideas Company Y&R, Belgrade
Creative Director	Svetlana Copic
Copywriters	Slavisa Savic
	Svetlana Copic
Art Director	Slavisa Savic
Photographer	Nemanja Spoljaric
Advertiser	Kielo Travel Agency, "Pool"

Agency	Spillmann/Felser/
	Leo Burnett, Zurich
Creative Director	Peter Brönnimann
Copywriter	Patrick Suter
Art Directors	Reto Clement
	Simon Staub
Photographer	Oliver Nanzig
Advertiser	Switzerland Tourism,
	"Saint Bernard"

Agency	Spillmann/Felser/
	Leo Burnett, Zurich
Creative Directors	Peter Brönnimann
	Simon Staub
	Diana Rossi
Copywriter	Diana Rossi
Art Director	Simon Staub
Production	Stories, Zurich
Director	Michael Fueter
Producers	Yves Bollag
	Suzana Kovacevic
Advertiser	Switzerland Tourism,
	"Summer Holiday"

Swiss mountaineers turned brand ambassadors Sebi and Paul help the country's tourism industry prepare for a busy summer season. We observe them as they meticulously trim grass, clean streams, test parasols and wax their colleagues into buff perfection. They check that the boats on the lake are shipshape and even vacuum a sunbathing deck. In fact they do everything to ensure a perfect summer holiday, Swiss style.

Agency	Spillmann/Felser/
	Leo Burnett, Zurich
Creative Directors	Peter Brönnimann
	Diana Rossi
	Simon Staub
Copywriter	Fabian Windhager
Art Directors	Niels Schäfer
	Marco Donada
Production	Stories, Zurich
Director	Michael Fueter
Producers	Yves Bollag
	Suzana Kovacevic
Advertiser	Switzerland Tourism

Switzerland is so determined to ensure that visitors have a relaxing vacation that it has abolished time. So the country's two most famous ambassadors – mountaineers Sebi and Paul – travel around the land of precision timepieces removing or disabling all watches and clocks. A cuckoo clock is nailed shut and even a crowing cockerel is ordered to shut its beak. Switzerland is the home of real holidays.

the fastest cruise ferries in Greece

 MINOAN LINES

Agency	Ogilvy & Mather, London
Creative Director	Gerry Human
Copywriter	Laura Rogers
Art Director	Trevallyn Hall
Illustrator	Keita Sagaki
Typographer	Trevallyn Hall
Art Buying	Brigitte Martin
Acct. Director	Stephen Hillcoat
Advertiser	Expedia City Breaks, "Moscow" & "Paris"

Agency	Spot JWT, Athens
Creative Directors	Takis Liarmakopoulos Alexandros Tsoutis
Copywriter	Anastasios Lessis
Art Director	Alexis Alifragkis
Advertiser	Minoan Lines, "Dolphin"

Agency	BETC, Paris
Creative Directors	Rémi Babinet
	Florence Bellisson
Copywriter	Véronique de Surmont
Art Director	Marie-Eve Schoettl
Production	Caviar, Paris
Director	Angelin Preljocaj
Producer	Fabrice Brovelli
Advertiser	Air France, "L'Envol"

A couple dressed in pristine white embrace and perform an intimate ballet on a vast mirror that perfectly reflects the empty blue sky above them. They resemble birds – or perhaps an elegant aircraft. Air France is still making the sky the best place on earth.

400 horse power.

10877 horse power.

Do it again.

DB GERMAN RAIL

58   **Transport & Tourism**

Agency	Ogilvy, Frankfurt
CCO	Stephan Vogel
Copywriter/AD	Stephan Vogel
Production	Jo!Schmid, Berlin
Director	Martin Schmid
Producers	Michael Schmid
	Jennifer Porst
DOP	Peter Meyer
Editor	Marty Schenk
Post Production	Slaughterhouse, Berlin
Music	Pearls Music, Frankfurt
Advertiser	DB (German Rail),
	"Hard to Impress"

A smooth guy sidles up to a woman at a bar. Plonking down his car keys, he tries to impress her by boasting about his vehicle. "400 horse power…236 top speed. Tomorrow, 7pm?" The woman parries by plonking down an even bigger set of keys. "10,877 horse power…330 top speed. Tomorrow morning, 8.43am, platform 7." The woman is the real life driver of a high-speed train for German Rail.

Agency	McCann, Oslo
Copywriter	Stein Simonsen
Art Director	Torstein Greni
Production	4 ½, Oslo
Director	Marius Holst
Producers	Magnus Castracane
	Beril Holte Rasmussen
Project Manager	Camilla von Borcke
DOP	John Andreas Andersen
Account Dir.	Janne Espevalen
Advertiser	Wideroe Airline,
	"Grandpa's Magic Trick"

On a Norwegian farm, a little boy stands rapt in front of his grandfather, who has clearly just performed a magic trick. "Do it again!" asks the boy. The grandfather refuses. "Just one more time!" The old man bides his time. "Please!" Suddenly the grandfather begins rubbing his hands together, faster and faster. He cups them to his mouth, turns his head to one side – and appears to blow out a tiny aeroplane, silhouetted on the sky behind him. The trick is possible because Norwegian airline Wideroe has such frequent and punctual flights.

Agency	DLKW Lowe, London
Executive CDs	Dave Henderson
	Richard Denney
Creative Directors	Christian Sewell
	Andy McAnaney
Copywriters & ADs	Ben McCarthy
	Seb Housden
Typographer	Rob Carew
Digital Artwork	Rob Carew
Art Buying	Bel January
Advertiser	Legoland Windsor Resort, "Mini Breaks"

The Legoland resort in Windsor, UK, offers short breaks called Mini Breaks. In order to capture the "mini" idea and play on the scaled-down world of Lego, these mini poster sites were visible at a lower level than usual. Built from real Lego bricks, the installations were scaled-down versions of real poster formats. The low signs were placed in high profile locations such as train stations, roadsides and pedestrian areas throughout the UK.

Agency	Ingo, Stockholm	Agency	DDB DM9JaymeSyfu, Manila
Creative Director	Björn Ståhl		
Copywriter	Helena Thorsell	Creative Directors	Merlee Jayme
Art Director	Helena Thorsell		Louie Sotto
Photographer	Stefan Jellheden	Copywriter	Louie Sotto
Typographer	Fredrik Casservik	Art Directors	Herbert Hernandez
Account Team	Nina Widemar		Allan Montayre
	Anna Östergren	Illustrator	Allan Montayre
Planner	Thomas Weigle	Advertiser	Philippines Tourism,
Advertiser	Apollo Travel,		"Just as Beautiful"
	"Local Weather"		

Agency	Gitam BBDO, Tel Aviv
Agency	Gitam BBDO, Tel Aviv
CCO	Guy Bar
Executive CD	Danny Yakobowitch
Creative Director	Igal Ezra
Copywriter	Ronni Azulay
Art Director	Moshe Saikevich
Graphic Design	Alex Melik
	Hagai Shaked
Account Team	Elika Merhavi
	Shiran Haimovtich
Advertiser	Natour, "Organized Tours to Hectic Destinations"

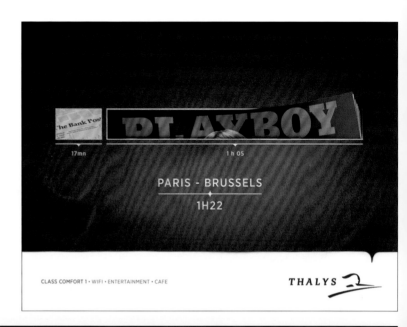

Agency	Gitam BBDO,		Agency	Rosapark, Paris
	Tel Aviv		Creative Directors	Jean-François Sacco
Executive CD	Danny Yakobowitch			Gilles Fichteberg
Creative Director	Igal Ezra		Copywriters	Jean-Christophe Royer
Copywriter	Ronni Azulay			Jamie Standen
Art Director	Noga Kara		Art Directors	Eric Astorgue
Illustrator	Noga Kara			Mark Forgan
Account Team	Elika Merhavi			Benoît François
	Asaf Viskin			Valentin Blondel
	Daniela Gardiner		Photographer	Yves Bagros
Advertiser	Diesenhaus		Planner	Gauthier Berdeaux
	Travel Services,		Art Buying	Chloé Bartoletti
	"Circle"		Advertiser	Thalys, "Timelines"

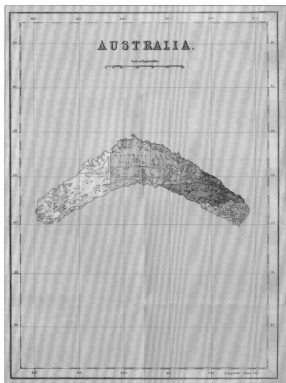
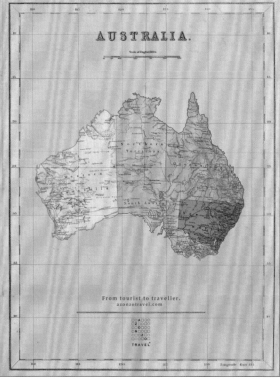

Agency	Publicis, Frankfurt	Agency	Young & Rubicam, Milan
Creative Director	Diana Sukopp	**Executive CD**	Vicky Gitto
Copywriter	Felix Seiffert	**Copywriter**	Matteo Lazzarini
Art Director	Anne Henkel	**Art Director**	Cristian Comand
Photographer	Marc Wuchner	**Illustrators**	Stefano Torresani
Account Mgr.	Claudia Giese		Cristian Comand
Advertiser	B&B Hotels, "Bed & Breakfast"	**Post Production**	Post:Atomic
		Advertiser	Azonzo Travel Agency, "Travel Maps"

64 **Retail Services**

Agency	Creative Artists Agency, Los Angeles	This now-famous animated tale features a farmer who slowly transforms his family farm into an industrialised animal factory. But then he has a crisis of conscience and decides to go "back to the start". Brilliantly accompanied by Willie Nelson's version of the Coldplay song "The Scientist", the film promotes the brand's commitment to sustainable food sources.
Production	Nexus Productions, London	
Director	John Kelly	
Producer	Liz Chan	
Music	Coldplay, "The Scientist"	
Singer	Willie Nelson	
Advertiser	Chipotle, "Back to the Start"	

Make Billy our problem
Have your kid's birthday party at McDonald's. Call us on 086 000 0040 to book.

Make Theodore our problem
Have your kid's birthday party at McDonald's. Call us on 086 000 0040 to book.

Make Tiffany our problem
Have your kid's birthday party at McDonald's. Call us on 086 000 0040 to book.

Agency	DDB, Johannesburg
Creative Director	Grant Jacobsen
Copywriter	Andre Vrdoljak
Art Director	Hital Pandya
Photographer	Carioca
Illustrator	Carioca
Typographer	Hital Pandya
Advertiser	McDonald's, "Monsters"

Aldi.
Like brands.
Only cheaper.

Agency	McCann, Manchester
Creative Directors	Dave Price
	Neil Lancaster
Copywriter	Neil Lancaster
Art Director	Dave Price
Advertiser	Aldi Supermarkets, "Like Brands" Campaign

Customers enjoy Aldi's low-price products just as much as famous brands. For instance, a fat guy thinks Aldi's low fat cereal is as good as Special K. "Mind you, this dress is still a bit tight." Even more bizarrely, two middle-aged men in romper suits discuss the merits of washing powder aimed at babies. "Fancy a pint?" says one, producing a bottle of milk. Next we meet a dinner lady. "The kids like these cheesy triangles. They also like these," she says, indicating Aldi's product. Then she confides: "I don't like cheese. I don't like kids." Aldi: like brands – only cheaper.

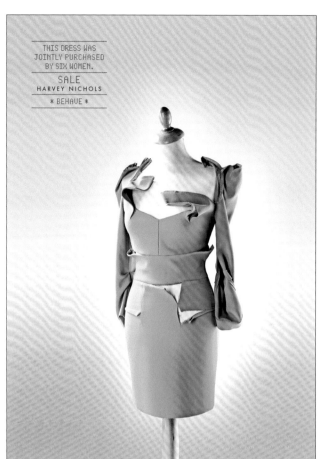

THIS DRESS WAS
JOINTLY PURCHASED
BY SIX WOMEN.
SALE
HARVEY NICHOLS
* BEHAVE *

THIS JACKET IS
NOW JOINTLY OWNED
BY THREE MEN.
SALE
HARVEY NICHOLS
* BEHAVE *

SALE
HARVEY NICHOLS
STARTS 1ST JUNE

Agency	Y&R, Dubai
Creative Director	Shahir Zag
Copywriter	Shahir Zag
Art Director	Kalpesh Patankar
Photographer	James Day
Illustrator	Kalpesh Patankar
Typographer	Kalpesh Patankar
Producer	Amin Soltani
Account Team	Line Hajjar
	Soulaf Tahtah
Client	Madhu Chibber
Advertiser	Harvey Nichols, "Behave"

Agency	Y&R, Dubai
Creative Directors	Shahir Zag
	Kalpesh Patankar
Copywriter	Shahir Zag
Art Director	Kalpesh Patankar
Photographer	The Remix Studio
Graphic Design	Kalpesh Patankar
Producer	Amin Soltani
Account Team	Zaakesh Mulla
	Line Hajjar
	Nazek Fawaz
Client	Madhu Chibber
Advertiser	Harvey Nichols, "Pelicans"

Agency	Selmore, Amsterdam
Copywriter	Niels Westra
Art Director	Jakko Achterberg
Production	Xsaga, Amsterdam
Directors	Clara Van Gool
	Nanine Linning
Producers	Patrick Roubroeks
	Hein Scheffer
	Marga Bierema
DOP	Nils Post
Editor	Kevin Whelan
Music	Sizzer
Choreography	Nanine Linning
Acct. Supervisor	Rina Verweij
Clients	Robert Bohemen
	Bianca Koot
Advertiser	De Bijenkorf Department Store, "Crazy Dance"

Every year the de Bijenkorf department store in Amsterdam holds its Thee Crazy Days of sales. The consumer hysteria generated by the event is depicted here in a wild ballet, as a dancer attempts to grab a pair of jeans while others try to snatch the coveted leg-wear from her. Finally she whips off her skirt and manages to slip into the jeans. They fit perfectly and the other dancers raise her up in admiration.

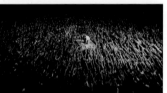

68   Retail Services

Agency	Heimat, Berlin
Creative Director	Guido Heffels
Copywriter	Alescha Lechner
Art Director	Hendrick Schweder
Production	Stink, Berlin
Director	Martin Krejci
Producers	Jan Dressler
	Kerstin Heffels
DOP	Stepan Kucera
Account Team	Matthias von Bechtolsheim
	Mark Hassan
	Maik Richter
Advertiser	Hornbach, "Festival"

Home improvements can seem like a personal challenge. Here's a guy building a shed in his garden. He misses a nail with his hammer – once, then twice. Now he's mad. Determination is etched on his face as he lifts the hammer. The world goes into slow motion. Animals in a forest glade pause to watch him. Angels look on from heaven. Now he's centre stage at a rock festival. The hammer connects. The crowd roars in approval. No-one feels it like you do – except maybe the folk at Hornbach home improvement stores.

Agency	Spillmann/Felser/ Leo Burnett, Zurich
Creative Director	Peter Brönnimann
Copywriters	Reto Vogler
	Johannes Raggio
Art Directors	Moritz Stillhard
	Pablo Schencke
Production	Pumpkin Film, Zurich
Director	Alex Feil
Producer	Suzana Kovacevic
Advertiser	Micasa, "Shredder"

"Children love playing on the grass," explains the narrator, as a bunch of scientists feed turf into a chipper. "They play in the woods a lot," he continues, while a pine tree is dumped into the machine. "They're out in all kinds of weather." Rainwater and leaves are added to the mix. "Then they come home." The techs turn on the chipper, which blasts a massive splotch of wet earth into a fake living room they've set up. Now we see why the Micasa California sofa has a stain-resistant cover. Micasa is made for living.

Agency	Ogilvy, Frankfurt
CCO	Stephan Vogel
Creative Directors	Matthias Storath
	Helmut Meyer
Copywriters	Martin Gillan
	Stephan Vogel
	Matthias Storath
Art Directors	Helmut Meyer
	Asae Tanaka
Photographer	Asae Tanaka
	Marco Perdigones
Art Buying	Valerie Opitz
Advertiser	Fleurop, "Text Campaign"

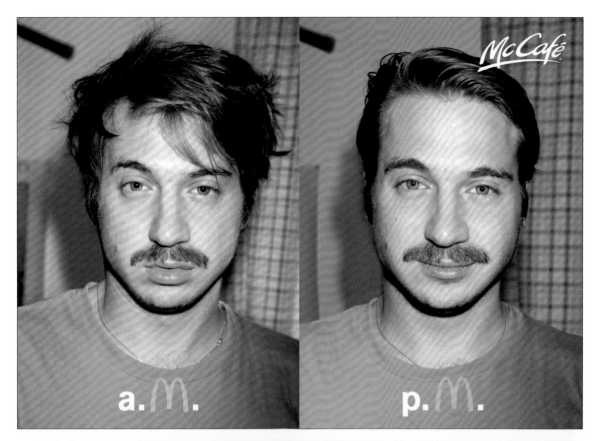

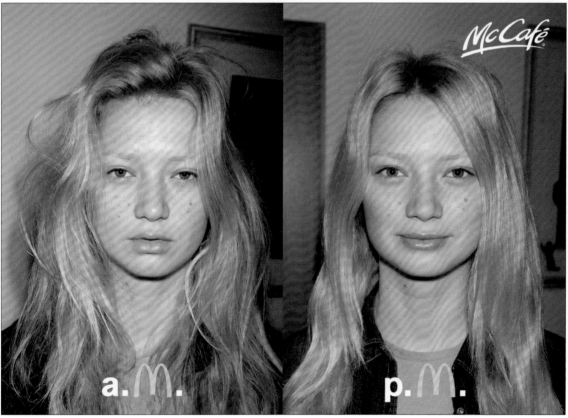

70 **Retail Services**

Agency	DDB Tribal, Vienna
CCO	Eric Schoeffler
Creative Directors	Lukas Grossebner
	Dian Warsosumarto
	Hannes Böker
Copywriter	Christoph Schönbäck
Art Director	Peter Mayer
Photographer	Lukas Gansterer
Account Team	Philipp Krumpel
	Lele Pittman
	Karin Zörner
Client	Andreas Schmidlechner
Advertiser	McDonald's, "AM/PM"

Agency	DDB Tribal, Vienna
CCO	Eric Schoeffler
Creative Directors	Werner Celand
	Hannes Böker
Copywriter	Antonia Kiefhaber
Art Directors	Marian Grabmayer
	Hannes Böker
Photographer	Vienna Paint
Acct. Director	Philipp Krumpel
Client	Andreas Schmidlechner
Advertiser	McDonald's, "Catapult"

Agency	Leo Burnett, London
Creative Director	Justin Tindall
Copywriter	Richard Ince
Art Director	Ed Tillbrook
Advertiser	McDonald's,
	"Next Stop,
	McDonald's"

Agency	Ruf Lanz, Zurich	Agency	Voskhod, Yekaterinburg	A pan-Asian café called Aziatage was about
Creative Directors	Markus Ruf	Creative Director	Andrey Gubaydullin	to open in Yekaterinburg. In order to promote
	Danielle Lanz	Copywriters	Alexander Parkhomenko	the venue, a street art project was developed
Copywriter	Andreas Hornung		Anton Kotovski	to dovetail with the March 8 opening date
Art Director	Isabelle Hauser		Andrey Chernay	and the Chinese Dragon Festival – the day
Photographer	Aschmann Klauser	Art Director	Vladislav Derevyannykh	on which all wishes come true! A billboard
Acct. Supervisor	Doelkar Monkhar	Graphic Design	Dmitry Maslakov	with 11,000 holes in it was installed near the
Advertiser	Hiltl Vegetarian		Yana Akhmetshina	café. Pairs of chopsticks were handed out.
	Restaurant, "Tongues"	Production	StreetArt	The idea was to split the two sticks and push
		Advertiser	Aziatage	one into the board. The other, branded stick
			Pan-Asian Café,	gave you a discount at the café. In just under
			"Chopsticks Dragon"	six hours a dragon was born.

Agency	DDB&Co, Istanbul
Creative Director	Karpat Polat
Copywriter	Melih Edis
Art Director	Cihangir Gumus
Retouching	Selim Sahin
Advertiser	Dank!, Second-Hand Furniture, "Boxes Campaign"

74 **Retail Services**

Agency	Ogilvy, Frankfurt
CCO	Stephan Vogel
Creative Director	Peter Strauss
Copywriter	Peter Strauss
Art Director	Ute Sonntag
Photographer	Susanne Walström
Jr. Creative	Sophia Metzler
Planning	Larissa Pohl
	Sabina Pal
Art Buying	Nathalie Schulz
Account Mgr.	Larissa Kleemann
Client	Bettina Peetz
Advertiser	Jako-O, "Let Kids be Kids"

OUCH

OOPS

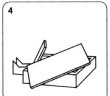

Get yourself furniture that is truly easy to assemble. **mömax** Finally a new furniture store.

Get yourself furniture that is truly easy to assemble. **mömax** Finally a new furniture store.

Agency	adam&eveDDB, London	Agency	Demner, Merlicek & Bergmann, Vienna
Creative Director	Jeremy Craigen		
Copywriters & ADs	Nikki Lindman	Creative Directors	Alistair Thompson
	Toby Brewer		Rene Pichler
Photographer	Alan Clarke	Copywriter	Patrick Hein
Designer	Peter Mould	Art Director	Rene Pichler
Art Buying	Daniel Moorey	Illustrators	Aron Cserveny
Planner	Elizabeth Jamot		Lukas Hueter
Account Team	Paul Billingsley	Final Art	Sarah Spanring
	Charlotte Evans	Account Team	Andrea Kliment
Advertiser	Harvey Nichols		Magdalena Draeger
	Summer Sale,		Siegfried Kaufmann
	"Excitement"	Advertiser	Mömax Furniture Store

DNB
The Norwegian Bank

Agency	Try/Apt, Oslo
Copywriter	Janne Brenda Lyso
Art Director	Stian Johansen
Production	Bacon, Oslo
Director	Martin Werner
Producer	Magne Lyngner
Account Team	Monika Augustsson
	Kristin Berge Jahr
Client	Kjetil Skogly
Advertiser	DNB Bank,
	"The Treasure"

Pirates board a navy galleon. A pirate holds his cutlass at the throat of a sailor. "Where's the treasure?" he snarls. But other sailors have already escaped in a longboat with the treasure chest. They arrive at an island and bury the treasure on the beach. Hundreds of years later, a pretty girl-next-door type accidentally stumbles on the hoard. We soon realise she's the girl who "accidentally" married George Clooney in last year's spot. Some people have all the luck. But you probably don't – so consider pension plans from DNB Bank.

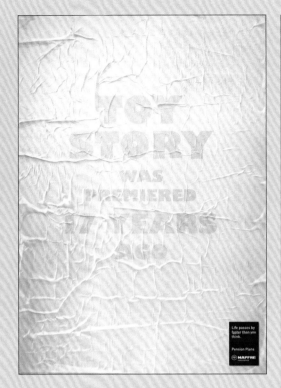

 Financial Services 77

Agency	Zapping/M&C Saatchi, Madrid
Executive CDs	Uschi Henkes
	Manolo Moreno
	Urs Frick
Copywriter	Jorge Campaña
Art Directors	Ana Delgado
	Alvaro Moragón
Photographer	Alfonso Herránz
Advertiser	Mapfre, "Life Passes By"

Just call us.

Centraal beheer | achmea

The insurance company
in Apeldoorn. (055) 579 800

CREDIT SUISSE

OXYGEN'S ELECTRIC SCOOTERS ARE LEAVING THE FOSSIL FUEL ERA BEHIND.

Credit Suisse is helping the company evolve.

credit-suisse.com/clients

---

78   Financial Services

Agency	DDB & Tribal, Amsterdam
Creative Directors	Joris Kuijpers
	Dylan De Backer
Production	Bonkers, Amsterdam
Director	Hein Mevissen
Producers	Jan Jinek
	Saskia Kok
	Yuka Kambayashi
DOP	Ueli Steiger
Editor	Martin Heijgelaar
Advertiser	Centraal Beheer, "Speedboat"

A young idiot with preposterous hair is showing off to a pretty blonde as he skippers a speedboat. He drives it with no hands, one foot, both feet. Then he lets the girl drive – while he stands a little too close behind. When he puts his hands on her waist, she jumps out of her skin and knocks them both overboard. The motorboat speeds on towards the horizon…with the couple's parasailing pal still attached. Just call Centraal Beheer insurance.

Agency	Havas Worldwide, London
Creative Director	Gerry Moira
Copywriter	Tim Langford
Art Directors	Dave Burn
	Phil Beaumont
Photographers	Erik Almas
	Andy Glass
	John Offenbach
Advertiser	Credit Suisse, "Oxygen"

Friday. German style.

Banking. German style.
www.forum.ua

BANK FORUM
Commerzbank Group

Agency	Ogilvy & Mather, Kiev
Creative Director	Will Rust
Copywriter	Alexandra Doroguntsova
Art Director	Taras Dzendrovskii
Producer	Irina Pigal
Planner	Martin Alles
Account Team	Alexandra Savonik
	Svetlana Polyakova
	Svetlana Korytko
Advertiser	Bank Forum, "Friday"

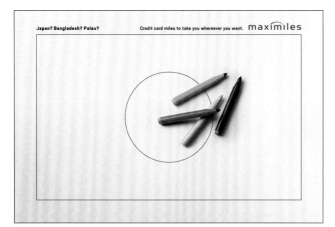

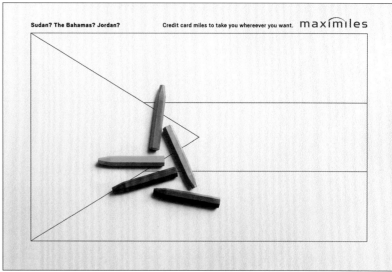

80 **Financial Services**

Agency	MedinaTurgul DDB, Istanbul
Creative Director	Kurtcebe Turgul
Copywriter	Talha Yuksel
Art Director	Mert Kunc
Illustrator	Fethi Izan
Advertiser	Maximiles Credit Card, "Flags Campaign"

Agency	Concept, Istanbul
Creative Directors	Kerem Ozkut
	Can Pehlivanli
Copywriter	Ertug Tugalan
Art Director	Namik Ergin
Photographer	Nejat Talas
Advertiser	Sekerbank,
	Home Loans,
	"Homeless Campaign"

82 **Homes, Furnishings & Appliances**

Agency	adam&eveDDB, London	**Producers**	Ben Link Matt Craigie	Christmas Day is not far away – but for this little boy it feels like an eternity. He whiles
Creative Directors	Ben Priest	**Planner**	David Golding	away his time with one eye on the advent
	Ben Tollett	**Editor**	Joe Guest	calendar. He makes a wizard's outfit and
	Emer Stamp		Final Cut, London	tries to magic the clock forwards. Finally, it's
Copywriters	John Long	**Sound Design**	Factory, London	the big night. He bolts his dinner and jumps
	Matt Gay	**Post Production**	MPC, London	into bed. He gets up early. To our surprise,
Art Directors	John Long	**Acct. Supervisor**	Tammy Einav	he ignores his own presents and takes an
	Matt Gay	**Client**	Craig Inglis	inexpertly wrapped gift from his wardrobe.
Production	Blink, London	**Advertiser**	John Lewis,	As he enters his parents' room, we realise
Director	Dougal Wilson		"The Long Wait"	he's been waiting to give them a present.
				John Lewis – for gifts you can't wait to give.

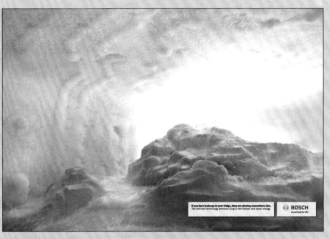

Homes, Furnishings & Appliances 83

Agency	DDB Tribal, Berlin	**Digital Artwork**	Michail Paderin
CCO	Eric Schoeffler	**Planner**	Jonas Pöhlmann
Creative Directors	Bastian Meneses von Arnim	**Art Buying**	Susanne Kreft
	Daniel Bödeker	**Idea**	Mario Loncar
Copywriters	Daniel Bödeker	**Account Team**	Britta Posner
	Mario Loncar		Azade Toygar
Art Directors	Veit Moeller	**Advertiser**	Bosch NoFrost Technology,
	Mario Loncar		"Icebergs" Campaign
Photographer	Szymon Plewa		

You know when it's PROTEK

PROTEK
Live monitoring security

You know when it's Protek

PROTEK
Live monitoring security

84   Homes, Furnishings & Appliances

Agency	Havas Worldwide, Tunis
Creative Director	Jean-François Fournon
Copywriters	Mehdi Klibi
	Haythem Derbel
Art Directors	Mehdi Klibi
	Haythem Derbel
Production	Not'Prod, Tunis
Director	Mehdi Klibi
Producers	Makrem Abdellatif
	Yosr Hmam
Planner	Sara Zebouchi
Advertiser	Protek,
	"Camera Campaign"

Protek security cameras have the power to change behaviour. In the first of two films, we see four guys attacking a young man. They've got him on the ground when the guy keeping watch notices the security camera and alerts them. Suddenly they pick up their victim and hoist him aloft as if celebrating his birthday. Then they set him on his feet, embrace him – and run away.

In the second spot a robber runs towards the victim holding a big stick with the intention of stealing his mobile phone. Then he notices the camera and abruptly changes his behaviour. He starts dancing with the stick, imitating the dabka, a Lebanese dance.

Agency	Leo Burnett, Mumbai
Creative Directors	K. V. Sridhar
	Nitesh Tiwari
	Vikram Pandey
Copywriter	Vikram Pandey
Art Director	Brijesh Parmar
Photographer	Amol Jadhav
Advertiser	Bajaj Exhaust Fans,
	"Get it Back" Campaign

① Unpack.
② Change Bulb.
③ Repeat in 20 years.

IKEA®

Agency	JWT, Warsaw
Creative Director	Mariusz Pitura
Copywriter	Joanna Sroka
Art Director	Bartosz Palasek
Advertiser	Ikea, "Bulb"

Agency	Havas 360, Paris
Executive CDs	Thomas Derouault
	Hugues Pinguet
Creative Director	Stephane Morel
Copywriter	Stephane Le Frapper
Art Director	Quentin Delachaux
Retouching	Quentin Delachaux
	Adrien Bénard
	Jean-Philippe Camus
Art Buying	Isabelle Baud
Acct. Supervisor	Arnaud Thizy
Advertiser	Spit, "Extra Strong Fixation"

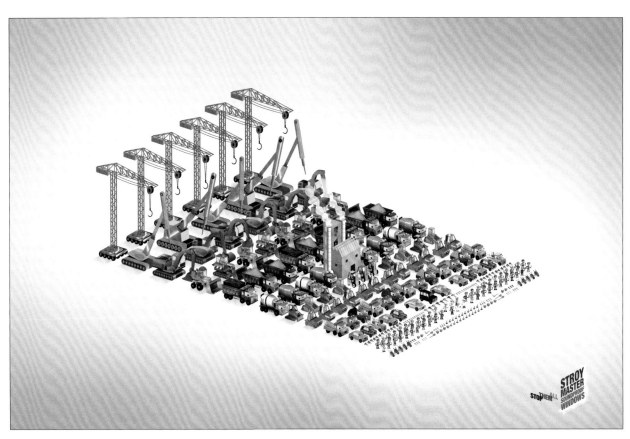

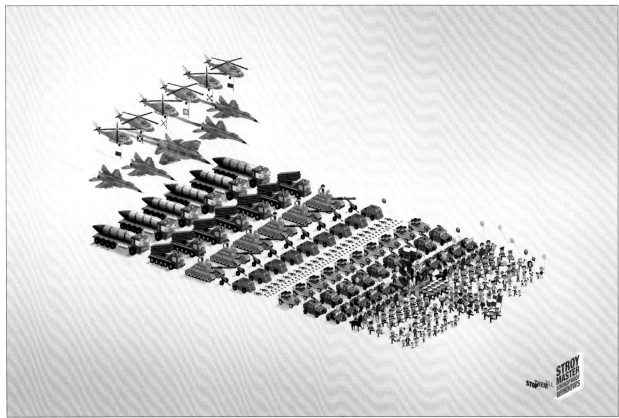

Homes, Furnishings & Appliances **87**

Agency	BBDO, Moscow
Creative Director	Mihai Coliban
Copywriters	Mihai Coliban
	Alexander Cherkashin
Art Director	Mihai Coliban
Illustrator	Cristian Turdera
Art Buying	Giuliana Giora
Acct. Manager	Ekaterina Konovalova
Advertiser	Stroy Master
	Soundproof Windows,
	"Stop them All"

"Snail", chocolate syrup and cherry compote on wood floor, Emma 2011   WMF would like to thank all the children for 125 years of unrestrained enjoyment.   125 years of children's cutlery from

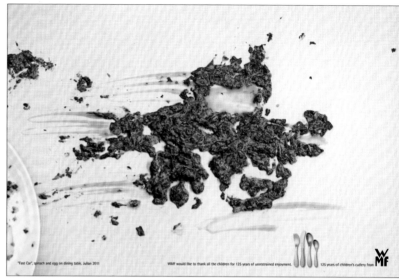

"Fast Car", spinach and egg on dining table, Julian 2011   WMF would like to thank all the children for 125 years of unrestrained enjoyment.   125 years of children's cutlery from

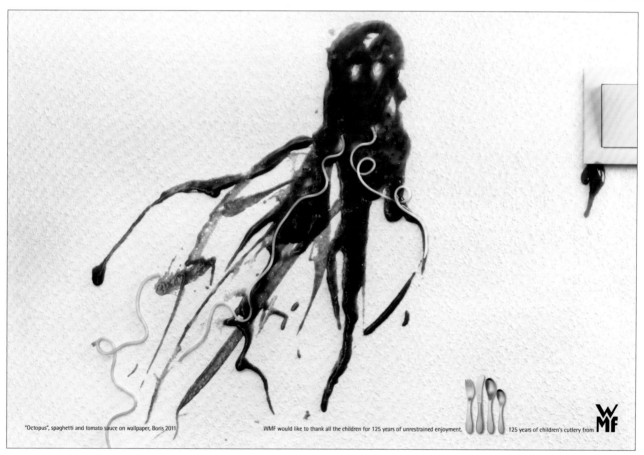

"Octopus", spaghetti and tomato sauce on wallpaper, Boris 2011   WMF would like to thank all the children for 125 years of unrestrained enjoyment.   125 years of children's cutlery from

88   **Homes, Furnishings & Appliances**

Agency	KNSK, Hamburg
Creative Directors	Tim Krink
	Ansgar Böhme
	Ulrike Wegert
Copywriters	Ulrike Wegert
	Ansgar Böhme
Art Director	Tim Krink
Illustrator	Ricarda Morgan
Advertiser	WMF, "125 Years of
	Children's Cutlery"

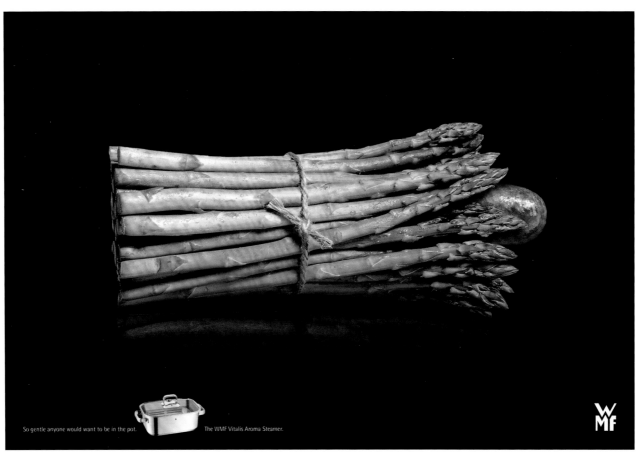

Homes, Furnishings & Appliances **89**

Agency KNSK, Hamburg
Creative Directors Tim Krink
Ansgar Böhme
Ulrike Wegert
Copywriters Ulrike Wegert
Ansgar Böhme
Art Directors Tim Krink
Julian Heidt
Advertiser WMF,
"Smuggled In"

90 **Household Maintenance**

Agency	DLKW Lowe, London
Creative Directors	Richard Denney
	Dave Henderson
Copywriter	Theo Bayani
Art Director	Miguel Gonzalez
Production	Outsider, London
Director	Jorn Threlfall
Producers	Tex Travi
	Abigail Tarrant
Advertiser	Omo Laundry Detergent, "Set Free"

We follow the experiences of a little girl as she sets a series of animals and insects free: a frog is returned to a pond, a moth released from a lamp, a spider rescued from the bathtub, an injured bird released back into the wild. Finally it's the girl's turn, as her mother drives her to the park and lets her run wild with her pet dog. The mother realises that if you love something, you set it free. It's all part of Omo's core message: dirt is good.

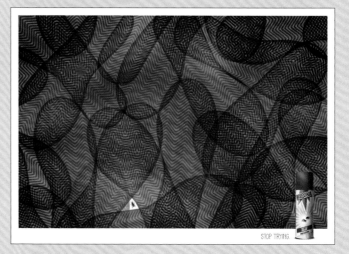

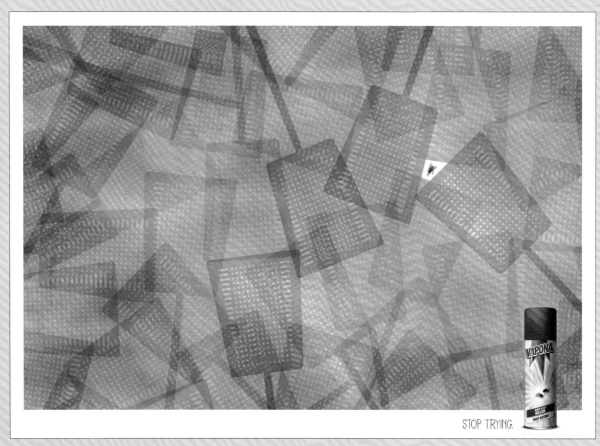

 **Household Maintenance** **91**

Agency	Herezie, Paris
Creative Director	Andrea Stillacci
Copywriters	Daniel & Mattia
Art Directors	Daniel & Mattia
Illustrator	Hojiro
Final Art	Capucine Lhermitte
Planning	Luc Wise
Advertiser	Vapona Insecticide, "Stop Trying"

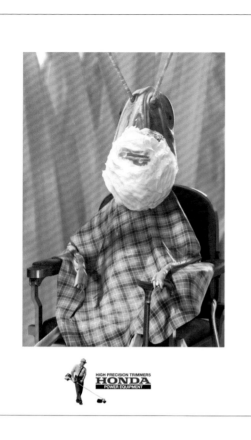

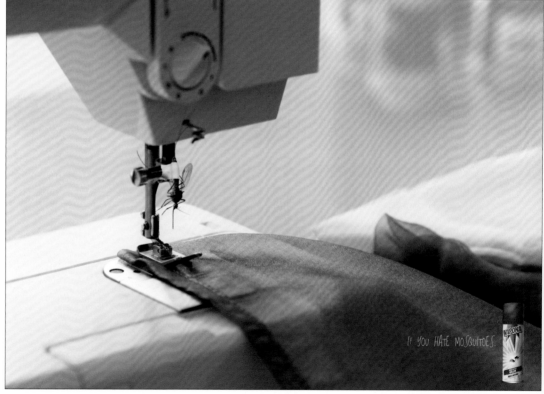

Household Maintenance

Agency	Ogilvy, Frankfurt	Agency	Herezie, Paris
Creative Directors	Tim Stuebane	Creative Director	Andrea Stillacci
	Birgit van den Valentyn	Copywriter	Céline Lescure
	Stephan Vogel	Art Director	Julian Brice
Art Director	Matthias Bauer	Art Buying	Marine Azzouz
Illustrators	Heinrich Eisele	Retouching	Antoine Merot
	Maximilian Baberg	Final Art	Capucine Lhermitte
Graphic Design	Arne Felgendreher	Planning	Luc Wise
	Christoph Hubrich	Advertiser	Vapona,
Art Buying	Valerie Opitz		"Torturing Mosquitoes"
Account Mgr.	Iskra Velichkova		
Client	André Neumann		
Advertiser	Honda Trimmers		

Agency	DLKW Lowe, London
Creative Directors	Dave Henderson
	Richard Denney
Copywriter	Theo Bayani
Art Director	Miguel Gonzalez
Photographer	Dario Mitidieri
Typographer	Jamie Craven
Project Mgr.	Gary Wallis
Head of Art	Christian Sewell
Head of Design	Jamie Craven
Advertiser	Omo Laundry Detergent, "Dirt is Good"

94 **Household Maintenance**

Agency	Heimat, Berlin	**Agency**	Grey, Dubai
Creative Director	Guido Heffels	**Creative Director**	Alisdair Miller
Copywriter	Mirjam Kundt	**Copywriter**	Mohanad Shuraideh
Art Director	Susanna Fill	**Art Director**	Mohanad Shuraideh
Photographer	Taylor James	**Photographer**	Graham Tooby
Graphic Design	Martijn Koster	**Digital Artwork**	Loupe Imaging
Typographer	Taylor James	**Advertiser**	Fresh Carpet
Digital Artwork	Taylor James		Odor Eliminator,
Clients	Frank Sahler		"Sheep" & "Sewage"
	Julia Ziegelmann		
Advertiser	Hornbach, "Roots"		

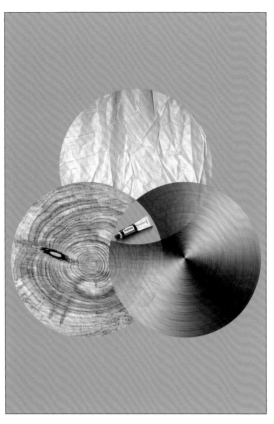

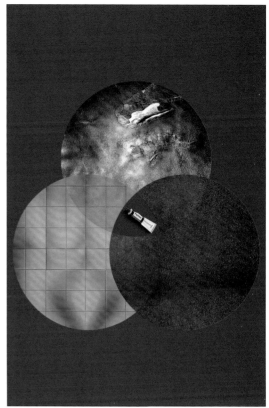

Agency	DDB&Co, Istanbul		**Agency**	TBWA\Central Asia & Caucasus, Almaty
Creative Director	Karpat Polat		**Creative Director**	Juan Pablo Valencia
Copywriter	Karpat Polat		**Copywriter**	Juan Pablo Valencia
Art Director	Lucas Zaiden		**Art Director**	Juan Pablo Valencia
Advertiser	Pattex, "Circles Campaign"		**Illustrator**	Marat Kumekov
			Graphic Design	Yulia Shevchik
			Advertiser	Persil Expert, "Reading the Wrong Story"

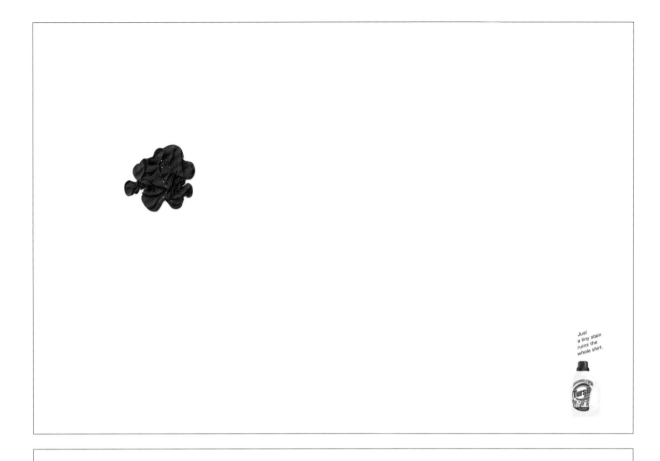

Just
a tiny stain
ruins the
whole shirt.

Just
a tiny stain
ruins the
whole blouse.

96   **Household Maintenance**

Agency	TBWA\Istanbul
Creative Directors	Ilkay Gurpinar
	Volkan Karakasoglu
Copywriters	Bahadir Peksen
	Gokhan Akca
Art Directors	Guney Soykan
	Zeynep Orbay
Photographer	Ilkay Muratoglu
Advertiser	Tursil, "Stain Clothes"

Agency	DDB Tribal, Vienna	**Account Team**	Ivana Kulenkampff-Thomann
CCO	Eric Schoeffler		Karin Löfler
Creative Directors	Bernhard Rems		Shila Cassini
	Hannes Böker	**Client**	Thomas Hauser
Copywriter	Antonia Kiefhaber	**Advertiser**	Pattex,
Art Director	Marian Grabmayer		"Inner Cinema" Campaign
Photographer	Friendly Fire		
Graphic Design	Andra Dehelean		
	Gabriel Haberl		

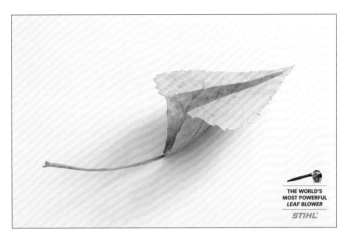

98 **Household Maintenance**

Agency	Publicis Conseil, Paris	**Retouching**	Fred Perrot
CCO	Olivier Altmann	**Account Team**	Stephane Gaillard
Creative Director	Frederic Royer		Benjamin Merllie
Copywriter	Mathieu Degryse		Sylvie Tavares
Art Director	Yves-Eric Deboey		Adeline Blanc
Assistant AD	Fanny Chevalier	**Clients**	Regis Guimont
Photographer	Yann Le Pape		Gilles Olleris
Art Buying	Jean-Luc Chirio	**Advertiser**	Stihl, "Airplanes"
	Aurelie Lubot		

Agency	DDB, Hong Kong	Agency	Falck & Co, Stockholm
Creative Directors	Jeffry Gamble	**Creative Director**	Svante Heiding
	May Wong	**Copywriters**	Angelica Lindgren
	Asawin Phanichwatana		Magnus Abelin
Copywriter	Joshua Wong	**Art Directors**	Daniel Backman
Art Directors	Leslie Wong		Annki Andersson
	Tony Cheung	**Graphic Design**	Helén Kvarnlöf
Photographer	Nok Remix Studio		Pia Towers
Illustrator	Anuchai Srijarunputong	**Digital Artwork**	Bildrepro
Producer	Annie Tong	**Planner**	Anders Frisk
Account Team	Simone Tam	**Account Team**	Lennart Lundquist
	Alexis Chiu		Camilla Donar
Advertiser	Glad Cling Wrap	**Advertiser**	Esstack Adhesive

100   **Household Maintenance**

Agency	Beacon Communications, Tokyo	**Digital Artwork**	Sunao Sakurai
Creative Directors	Jon King	**Producers**	Kozo Nagashima
	Keizo Mugita		Makiko Okada
	Shuji Matsumura	**Ceramic Artist**	Yasuko Hasegawa
Copywriter	Minoru Hongo	**Chef Pâtissier**	Hideki KaWamura
Art Director	Norihiro Sasa	**Stylists**	Asako Kijima
Photographer	Fumio Doi		Masato Okamura
Graphic Design	Chizuru Horikawa	**Advertiser**	Ariel,
	Yuichiro Yoshino		"Dine Dangerously"

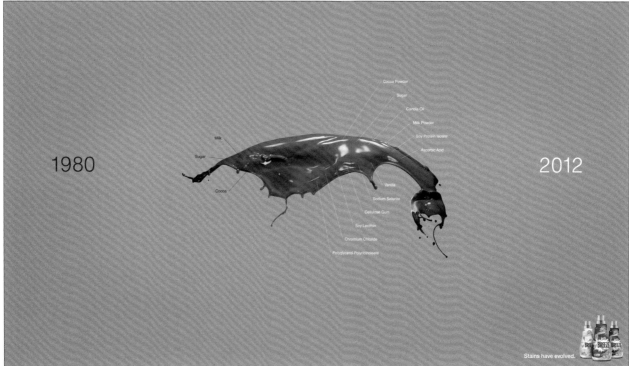

1980

2012

Agency	Gitam BBDO, Tel Aviv	**Agency**	Lowe, Singapore
CCO	Guy Bar	**Creative Directors**	Dominic Stallard
Executive CD	Danny Yakobowitch		Clinton Manson
Copywriter	Tomer Abramovitch		Lisa Glasgow
Art Director	Noga Kara	**Art Directors**	Liong Khoon Kiat
Photographer	Iior Nordman		Loh Seow Khian
Producer	Noga Sagi	**Photographer**	Jeremy Wong
Account Team	Elika Merhavi	**Planners**	Ranjit Jathanna
	Idit Zemmer		Brent Gosling
	Naeema Tahori	**Art Buying**	Dionne Yau
Advertiser	Nikol Window Wipes	**Advertiser**	Breeze Washing
			Detergent, "Evolution"

102 **Public Interest**

Agency	Wander, Los Angeles
Creative Director	Max Joseph
Copywriter	Max Joseph
Art Director	Max Joseph
Production	Wander, Los Angeles
Director	Max Joseph
Producer	Aaron Weber
Advertiser	Rainforest Alliance, "Follow the Frog"

If you want to help the rainforest, there are lots of things you can do. But as the narrator explains, here's what you're not going to do: you're not going to quit your job, travel to the heart of the forest, ingratiate yourself with tribesmen and lead them in an epic uprising against evil loggers. This guy tries all that – and it doesn't end well. Instead, just follow the frog. Look for the frog logo on Rainforest Alliance Certified Products.

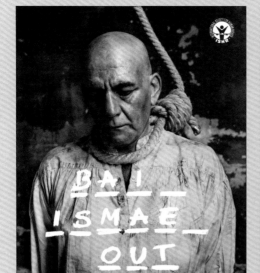

▲ **Public Interest** 103

Agency	BBDO Proximity, Düsseldorf
CCO	Wolfgang Schneider
Creative Director	Michael Plueckhahn
Copywriter	Dominique Becker
Art Directors	Sven Knaebel
	Nicoletta Kiermanzek
Photographer	Robert Eikelpoth
Producer	Bernhard Burg
Art Buying	Birgit Paulat
Account Team	Liselotte Schwenkert
	Judith Hillebrand
Advertiser	ISHR "Hangman Campaign"

Agency	Ogilvy, Beijing
Creative Directors	Graham Fink
	Bill Chan
	Kweichee Lam
	Rain Yu
Copywriters	Doug Schiff
	Jackie Bai
Art Directors	Rain Yu
	Xinyan Liu
Production	Camis Image
	Crystal Education
Director	Rain Yu
Producers	Feng Gao
	Yunsong Liu
	Rong Ma
	Ning Sun
	Jeff Wong
DOP	Kai Chen
Illustrator	Xinyan Liu
Editor	Sa Xiao
Lighting	Yu Liu
Animation	Feng Gao
	Lucy Lee
Account Mgr.	Henry Ho
Advertiser	PETA, "Skin"

A bizarre animated fashion show begins. The creatures parading in couture creations look like aliens. Then one of them unzips a mask to reveal that he's a fox. We realise we're watching animals dressed in clothes made from human skin and organs. The camera moves backstage to show us horrific scenes of body parts and a terrified child prisoner. Now how do you feel about wearing fur? Animal protection charity PETA asks: "Who's the animal?"

Agency	Memac Ogilvy Label, Tunis
CD	Nicolas Courant
Copywriters	Ali Mokdad
	Steve Hough
	Asma Kanzari
Art Director	Gerald Heraud
Production	Not'Prod, Tunis
Director	Xavier Mairesse
Producers	Ahmed Hassi
	Makrem Abdellatif
	Moez Nemsi
	Aziz M'Bazaia
Advertiser	ATFD, "Women's Vote"

In Tunisian Arabic, "voice" and "vote" are the same word. In these two films, women in Tunisia open their mouths to speak. But their voice boxes have been taken over by men, who spout sexist drivel. The older woman: "Since when is beating your wife a crime? If you ask me they deserve it." And so on.

The younger one: "I think women who work should give their salaries to their husbands…Stay at home, raise the kids and shut up!" Don't let anyone take your voice. Vote in the Tunisian elections.

Agency	Lyle Bailie International, Belfast
Creative Directors	David Lyle
	Julie Anne Bailie
Copywriters & ADs	David Lyle
	Julie Anne Bailie
Production	Lyle Bailie International
Director	Syd Macartney
Producer	Sonia Laughlin
DOP	Dennis Crossan
Advertiser	Department of the Environment, "Just Because"

A series of people narrowly escape traffic accidents. "Just because I'm a pedestrian, it doesn't mean I'm nobody," says a woman. "Just because I'm a driver, it doesn't mean I can see you," a man points out. "Just because you're at the speed limit," says a small boy out with friends, "doesn't mean you're not dangerous." Pedestrians and drivers all behave in an irresponsible manner and get away with it – until an old man who doesn't look before crossing the street is run down. Just because you use the road, doesn't mean you own it. Respect everyone's journey.

Agency	Havas Worldwide, Helsinki
Creative Director	Marko Vuorensola
Copywriter	Annu Terho
Art Director	Marko Vuorensola
Production	Sauna@Grillifilms
Director	Mikko Lehtinen
Exec. Producer	Petteri Lehtinen
Producers	Paul Earl
	Hana Kovic
DOP	Jure Verovsek
Post Production	Post Control
Advertiser	Fragile Childhood

We see close-ups of children's faces. They look scared and confused. Then we see their parents – who have the faces of contorted monsters. A hellish hare with bloodshot eyes, a cloaked Grim Reaper, a zombie, an eerie clown, a sinister Santa and a masked serial killer – each one is more terrifying than the last. But that's how kids see drunken parents. Fragile Childhood is combating parental alcohol abuse.

Agency	McCann Worldgroup, Helsinki
Creative Directors	Jyrki Poutanen
	Timo Silvennoinen
Production	Ragnar Jansson Productions, Stockholm
Director	Ragnar Jansson
Producers	Yrjö Haavisto
	Jyrki Poutanen
Graphic Design	Kari Mikkonen
	Piia Seppälä
	Kim Takala
Advertiser	AIDS Council Finland

One of two spots showing both sides of an erotic clinch. It's a steamy scene shot in black and white, featuring an amorous couple with hot bodies. Their breathing quickens as their excitement grows. But when the woman begins to ease off her panties, something unexpected pops up. It's a GPS tag – and a list of all the people who've "checked in" there. The same happens when the guy slides off his drawers in the second spot. Ever wondered who's checked in there before you? Better to play safe.

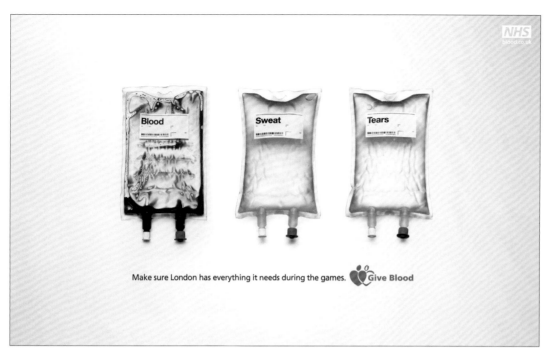

Agency	DLKW Lowe, London
Executive CDs	Richard Denney
	Dave Henderson
Creative Directors	Phil Cockrell
	Graham Storey
Copywriter	Matt Lever
Art Director	Helen Rhodes
Producer	Gary Wallis
Design	Jamie Craven
Project Manager	Irene Gross
Advertiser	National Health Service, "Blood, Sweat & Tears"

Agency	Forsman & Bodenfors, Gothenburg
Copywriters	Marcus Hägglöf
	Jacob Nelson
Art Director	Johanna Hofman-Bang
Production	Acne, Stockholm
Producer	Magnus Kennhed
Post Production	The Chimney Pot
Account Team	Andreas Engstrand
	Johanna Bringefält
Advertiser	Unicef, "Santa"

Santa is checking the toys that are about to leave his workshop when he stumbles on a package of Unicef "gifts". Every Christmas the charity sells vaccines, medicine, nutrition and school materials destined for children in need. Those who buy them get a gift card commemorating the good deed to give to their friends. But Santa isn't happy. "All this stuff goes to poor kids? I don't do poor countries!" Santa is the perfect symbol of inequality. But Unicef goes where he doesn't.

Agency	TBWA\Paris
Creative Directors	Eric Holden
	Rémi Noël
Copywriter	Benoit Leroux
Art Director	Philippe Taroux
Production	Henry de Czar
Director	Joe Vanhoutteghem
Producers	Jean-Luc Bergeron
	Jean Ozannat
	Maxime Boiron
DOP	Sebastian Blenkov
Editor	Manu Van Hove
Advertiser	Amnesty International

Banknotes float in a polluted river. They cover the body of a journalist killed on the street. They're stuck to the victim of an Abu Ghraib-style torture. They obscure scenes of a beheading and mask child soldiers. Money can hide terrible things. That's why Amnesty International refuses money from governments and multinational corporations. Its actions are supported only by individual donations – from people like you and me.

SERVE
A CULL
CANS
HER

BUR
REST
CAN
SUR

COAL
INK
AND
SIR

THE EARLIER IT'S RECOGNIZED, THE BETTER YOUR ODDS.
ontario.ca/screenforlife

Ontario

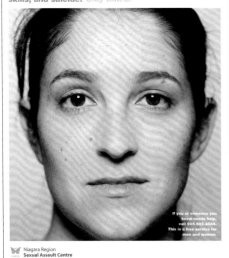

Susan Etienne, 28, was sexually abused as a child, but never received help. She is now much more likely to struggle with alcoholism, drug abuse, depression, anxiety, abusive relationships, eating disorders, self-mutilation, anger issues, poor overall coping skills, and suicide. Stay tuned.

If you or someone you know needs help, call 905.682.4584. This is a free service for men and women.

Niagara Region
Sexual Assault Centre

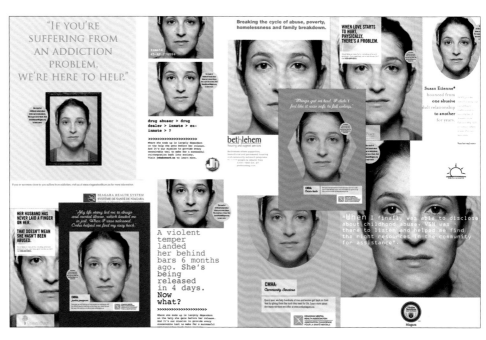

Agency	BBDO, Toronto		Cancer can now be detected in its early stages as pre-cancer cells. This dramatically increases the odds of survival. These posters show different forms of cancer masquerading as other words to let people detect the disease themselves.
Creative Directors	Peter Ignazi		
	Carlos Moreno		
Copywriters	Frank Macera		
	Craig McIntosh		
Art Directors	Jonathan Guy		
	Jaimes Zentil		
Production	SGL Studios		
Planner	Yvette Thornley		
MD	Lori Davison		
Advertiser	Ministry of Health, Cancer Awareness, "Early Detection"		

Agency	BBDO, New York		People who are sexually abused are more likely to fall into depression, violence, drug abuse and petty crime. To dramatize this, sexual abuse charity CARSA contacted ten other charities and asked them to use the same young woman featured on its posters in their own campaigns. A yellow circle in the corner of each poster directed viewers back to the original campaign. Sexual abuse victims can become the "poster children" of society's problems.
CCO	David Lubars		
Creative Director	James Clunie		
Copywriters	James Clunie		
	Chris Beresford-Hill		
Art Director	James Clunie		
Photographer	Billy Siegrist		
Designer	James Clunie		
Advertiser	CARSA, "Face of PSA Poster Project"		

Agency	Publicis Conseil, Paris	**Account Team**	Emmanuelle Henry Debora Guarachi
CCO	Olivier Altmann	**Clients**	Eric Molinie
Creative Director	Veronique Sels		Stefania Parigi
Art Directors	Bastien Grisolet		Valerie Coton
	Alexandra Offe	**Advertiser**	Samusocial,
Photographer	Marc Paeps		"A Woman's
Retouching	Adrien Bénard		Nightmare"
Producers	Jean-Luc Chirio		
	Charly Forain		

A homeless 16-year-old lives in your neighbourhood bus shelter.
The horrible part is, now you have to wait out in the cold.

Learn. Support. Act at
Facebook.com/RaisingtheRoof

RAISING THE ROOF HOMELESS YOUTH HAVE NOTHING, BUT POTENTIAL.

A 16-year-old homeless girl and her dog live under a bridge.
Most people who see this will help by calling animal services.

Learn. Support. Act at
Facebook.com/RaisingtheRoof

RAISING THE ROOF HOMELESS YOUTH HAVE NOTHING, BUT POTENTIAL.

If a 16-year-old is abused, hungry or alone, people feel the urge to help.
If that 16-year-old also happens to be homeless, people think he should get a job.

Learn. Support. Act at
Facebook.com/RaisingtheRoof

RAISING THE ROOF HOMELESS YOUTH HAVE NOTHING, BUT POTENTIAL.

Ever walk past a 17-year-old homeless boy and think 'Somebody else will stop to help him'?
Don't feel bad. Everyone thinks that way.

Learn. Support. Act at
Facebook.com/RaisingtheRoof

RAISING THE ROOF HOMELESS YOUTH HAVE NOTHING, BUT POTENTIAL.

Agency	Leo Burnett, Toronto
CCO	Judy John
Creative Directors	Judy John
	Lisa Greenberg
Copywriter	Steve Persico
Art Director	Anthony Chelvanathan
Photographer	Anthony Chelvanathan
Producer	Kim Burchiel
Account Team	Natasha Dagenais
	Jeremy Farncomb
Advertiser	Raising the Roof, "Nothing But Potential"

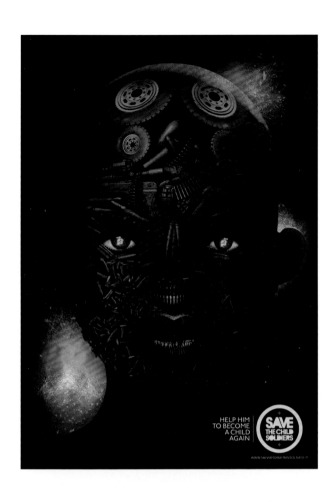

HELP HIM
TO BECOME
A CHILD
AGAIN

SAVE
THE CHILD
SOLDIERS

SMS.MMS.RIP
Don't text and drive

Brake
stopping the carnage
supporting the victims

DYING 2 SND
A REPLY?
Don't text and drive

Brake
stopping the carnage
supporting the victims

110   **Public Interest**

Agency	McCann, Milan	**Agency**	Blue Hive, London
Creative Director	Alex Brunori	**Creative Directors**	Greg Burke
Copywriter	Francesca Pagliarini		Karin Onsager-Birch
Art Director	Gaetano Del Pizzo	**Copywriter**	Nigel Edginton-Vigus
Illustrator	Davide Bianca	**Art Director**	Peter Hvid
Digital Artwork	Saizen Media	**Photographer**	James Day
Advertiser	Save the Child Soldiers,	**Graphic Design**	Kevan Ansell
	"Weaponized"	**Digital Artwork**	Chris Parsons
		Retouching	Dennis Tuffnell
		Project Mgr.	Mark Doyle
		Advertiser	Brake, "Don't Text and Drive"

Agency	BETC, Paris
Creative Director	Stéphane Xiberras
Copywriters	Julien Deschamps
	Arnold Zalluram
Art Director	Jordan Lemarchand
Photographer	Roman Jehanno
Graphic Design	T@ng
Advertiser	Victimes & Citoyens,
	"Wrong Place" Campaign

WHEN JOURNALISTS ARE TARGETED, THE TRUTH STAYS HIDDEN.

This is the affidavit of journalist Tara Singh Hayer. It details what he uncovered about the bombing of Air India flight 182. When he was murdered, his statement became inadmissible in court. And the truth died with him.

CJFE CANADIAN JOURNALISTS FOR FREE EXPRESSION

Defend the right to free expression at cjfe.org.

Agency	Juniper Park, Toronto
Executive CDs	Terry Drummond
	Alan Madill
	Barry Quinn
Copywriter	Matt Hubbard
Art Director	Mike Schonberger
Illustrators	Ryan Teixeira
	Nabil Elsaddi
	Mike Schonberger
Producers	Mark Prole
	Toby Sime
Advertiser	Canadian Journalists for Free Expression, "Cover Up"

Agency	DDB Tribal Group, Düsseldorf	**Agency**	Advico Y&R, Zurich
CCO	Eric Schoeffler	**Creative Directors**	Daniel Bieri
Executive CD	Dennis May		Thomas Engeli
Creative Directors	Jan Propach	**Copywriters**	Dieter Boller
	Holger Scheuermann		Kevin Bloch
Copywriter	Christian Ole Puls		Florian Tillmann
Art Directors	Florian Zwinge	**Graphic Design**	Vincent Schaublin
	Dominika Zajac	**Advertiser**	Reporters Without
Photographer	Michael Hägele		Borders, "Putin"
Illustrator	Bernd Ertl		
Graphic Design	Sybille Rybczynski		
Advertiser	Reporters Without Borders,		
	"The Power of Pencils"		

114 **Public Interest**

Agency	Memac Ogilvy Label, Tunis
Creative Director	Nicolas Courant
Copywriters	Asma Kanzari
	Mehdi Lamloum
	Yosri Mimouna
Art Directors	Gerald Heraud
	Yassine Boughaba
Advertiser	Engagement Citoyen, "The Return of Dictator Ben Ali"

Tunisians had finally overthrown Ben Ali after decades of dictatorship. But when the time came to vote in their first ever free elections, polls showed only 55% would turn out. Engagement Citoyen, a non-profit organization encouraging Tunisians' democratic awakening, needed to convert apathy into action. So it placed a giant poster of Ben Ali in the centre of town – as if the dictator had returned. Angry onlookers were shocked, then outraged, then furious. They tore the poster down. When they did, they discovered another poster underneath: "Beware, dictatorship can return. On October 23rd, vote."

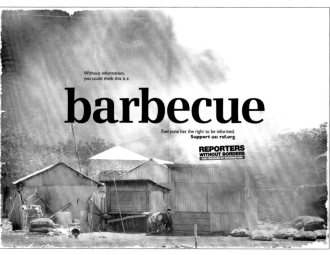

Agencies	McCann, Berlin & Geneva
Creative Directors	Bill Biancoli
	Erik Gonan
	Tilo Endert
Copywriter	Philipp Gloyer
Art Director	David Morales
Digital Artwork	Uta Pätzold
MD	Carole Massanes
Account Team	Nathalie De Valleuil
	Lilia Naydenova
Advertiser	Reporters Without
	Borders, "Irritating Opinions"

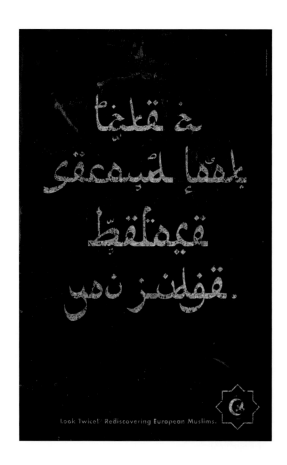

BEHIND BEGGARS THERE ARE PEOPLE MAKING FORTUNES.
Don't encourage begging! Help responsibly at www.politiacapitalei.ro/printsicersetor

BEHIND BEGGARS THERE ARE PEOPLE MAKING FORTUNES.
Don't encourage begging! Help responsibly at www.politiacapitalei.ro/printsicersetor

116   **Public Interest**

Agency	Demner, Merlicek & Bergmann, Vienna
Creative Directors	Francesco Bestagno
	Alexander Hofmann
Copywriter	Alexander Hofmann
Art Director	Claudia Strauss
Final Art	Aron Cserveny
Producer	Cornelia Huber
Account Mgt.	Lisa Benischek
Advertiser	Steirischer Herbst, "Look Twice"

Agency	Publicis, Bucharest
Creative Director	Razvan Capanescu
Copywriter	Otilia Coman
Art Director	Irina Stoleru
Photographer	Carioca Studio
Advertiser	Bucharest City Police, "Beggars" Campaign

Agency	DDB, Lagos
Creative Directors	Chuma Obumselu
	Babatunde Sule
Copywriter	Maurice Ugwonoh
Art Director	Abolaji Alausa
Illustrator	Abolaji Alausa
Advertiser	Girl Hub Advocacy for
	Female Empowerment,
	"Speechless"

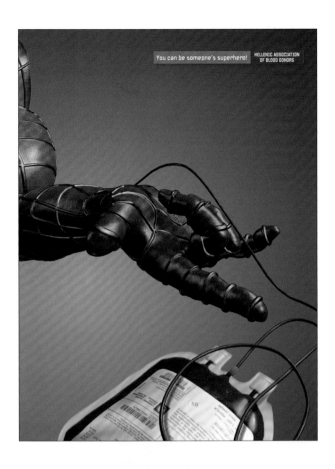

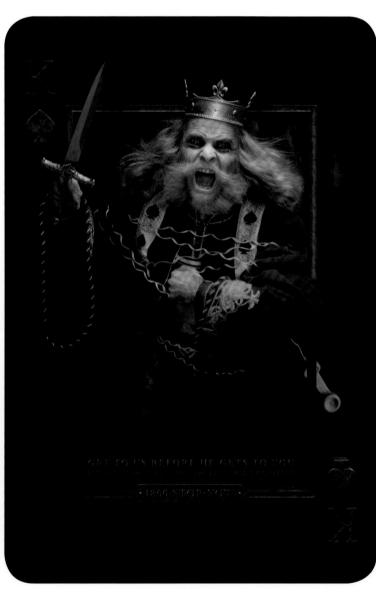

118   **Public Interest**

Agency	Spot JWT, Athens		**Agency**	Leo Burnett Group, Singapore	Gambling addiction has become a big problem in Singapore since the country's first casinos opened in 2010. There's a saying among Singaporean gamblers, "The winners go home by taxi, the losers take the bus." So these giant playing cards were strategically placed in bus shelters outside casinos to let gamblers know that they don't have to fight their addiction alone.
Creative Directors	Takis Liarmakopoulos			
	Alexandros Tsoutis		**Creative Director**	Chris Chiu	
Copywriter	Anastasios Lessis		**Copywriter**	Colin Koh	
Art Director	Alexis Alifragkis		**Art Director**	Jae Soh	
Advertiser	Hellenic Association		**Photographer**	Jeremy Wong	
	of Blood Donors,			Nemesis Pictures	
	"Spiderman"		**Advertiser**	Ray of Hope	

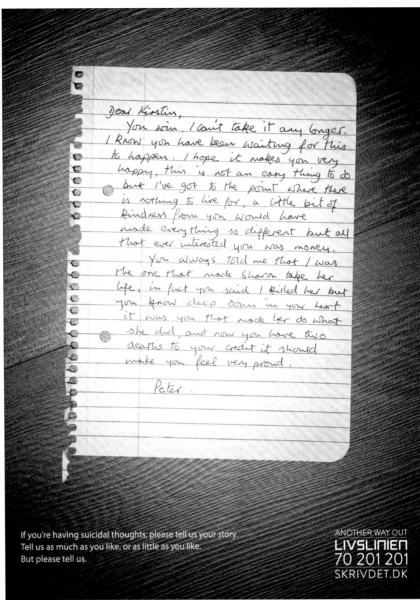

Agency	Adpeople Worldwide, Copenhagen	Agency	Publicis, Amsterdam
Creative Director	Jonathan Lowth	Creative Directors	Marcel Hartog
Copywriter	Jonathon Taylor		Jeroen van Zwam,
Art Director	Søren Møller	Production	In Case of Fire
Photographer	Martin Juul	Director	Olaf van Gerwen
Advertiser	Livslinien, "Another Way Out"	Producers	Arjan Oosterveer
			Marja Borkus
			Ron Townsend
		Editors	Kim Hinrichs
			Michael Horvers
		Sound Design	Robin Schlösser
		Post Production	Condor Video
		Advertiser	ALS Foundation, "Joep"

A pleasant man named Joep Coebben introduces himself. He tells us that on September 1st 2009 he was diagnosed with the wasting disease ALS (or Lou Gehrig's Disease) – a death sentence. He urges us to support the ALS Foundation as more research is needed into the cause of this merciless disease. But it's not for Joep's sake, because "I have already died." In all, nine ALS patients agreed to appear in ads that would be aired after they had died as part of a highly effective awareness campaign.

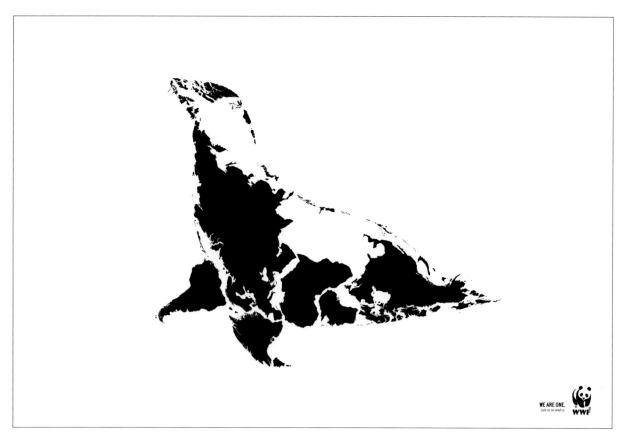

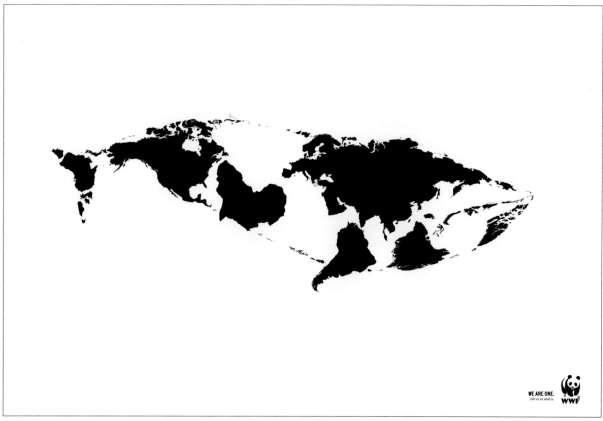

120 **Public Interest**

Agency	BBDO, Moscow
Creative Directors	Luis Tauffer
	Andres Vergara
Copywriters	Luis Tauffer
	Andres Vergara
Art Directors	Andres Vergara
	Luis Tauffer
Illustrator	Kentaro Nagai
Advertiser	WWF, "We are One"

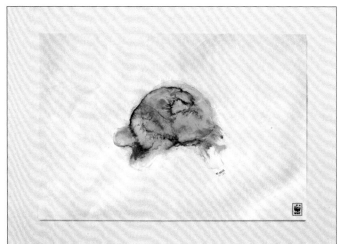

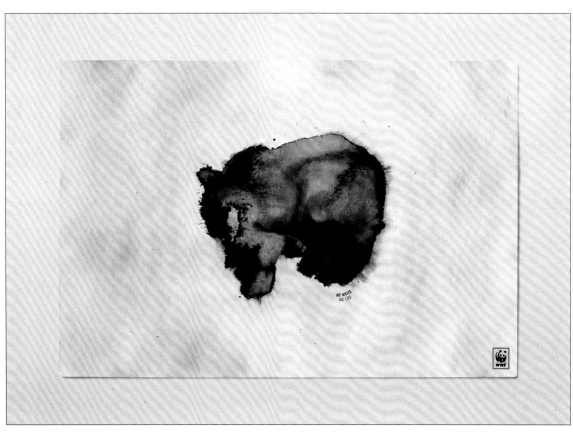

Agency	Contrapunto BBDO, Madrid
Creative Directors	Félix del Valle
	Carlos Jorge
Copywriters	Aurora Hidalgo
	Raúl López
Art Directors	Aurora Hidalgo
	Raúl López
Photographer	Alberto Escudero
Illustrator	Lucía Ares
Art Buying	Javier Luján
Advertiser	WWF,
	"Water Colours"

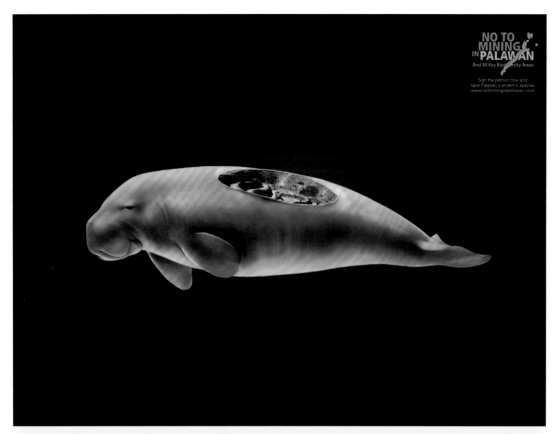

Public Interest

Agency	DDB DM9JaymeSyfu, Manila
Creative Directors	Merlee Jayme
	Eugene Demata
	Jerry Hizon
Copywriter	Jerry Hizon
Art Director	Dee Taar
Illustrators	Josh Galvez
	Blane Rosales
Advertiser	Save Palawan Movement, "Wounds Campaign"

Agency	TBWA\Paris
Creative Directors	Eric Holden
	Rémi Noël
Copywriter	Benoit Leroux
Art Director	Philippe Taroux
Photographer	Marc Gouby
Art Buying	Julie Champin
Retouching	Janvier
	Kilato
	La Retoucherie
Advertiser	Amnesty International, "Independence" Campaign

124   **Health & Beauty**

Agency	Havas Worldwide, London	An Amish village is holding its annual pageant. It's a sombre affair: the male performers wear black waistcoats and grey trousers, the female audience grey dresses and white bonnets. The "talent round" features tool sharpening and tap-dancing. Backstage, a young man reaches for his VO5 styling gel. He steps into the spotlight with immaculately styled hair – and is immediately banished. A girl in the audience stands and throws aside her bonnet to reveal equally extravagant locks. They run off into the countryside together. VO5 Extreme Style – break the mould.
Executive CD	Mick Mahoney	
Creative Director	Dom Gettins	
Copywriter	Harry Stanford	
Art Director	Mike Insley	
Production	Blink, London	
Director	Adam Hashemi	
Producers	Jo Charlesworth	
	Ben Mann	
Advertiser	VO5, "Pageant"	

Agency Publicis Comunicación
España, Madrid
Creative Director Alexandre Okada
Copywriter Manu Mazzaro
Art Director Manu Mazzaro
Advertiser Visionlab,
"Prescription Glasses"

Agency	Havas Worldwide, London
Executive CD	Mick Mahoney
Creative Director	Brendan Wilkins
Production	Academy Films
Directors	Si & Ad
Producers	Katy Dell
	Lucy Gossage
Advertiser	Durex, "Durex Vinyl"

Two records – one pink with a female symbol on the label, one blue with a male symbol – spin on a mixing desk. Although they're both playing the same smooth Marvin Gaye number ("Let's Get It On"), they're totally out of synch: the female disc is playing way too slow, while the male one is a speeded-up babble. The DJ makes some adjustments – and now the discs are in perfect harmony. Durex Performax Intense. Livens her up. Slows him down.

126 **Health & Beauty**

Agency	Herezie, Paris
Creative Director	Andrea Stillacci
Group Head	Jean-Laurent Py
Copywriter	Edouard Dorbais
Art Director	Rémi Arnaud
Production	OPC, Toronto
Director	Jon Barber
Producers	Dennis Beier
	Barbara Vaira
Planners	Luc Wise
	Celine Choueri
DOP	Christopher Collette
Advertiser	Optifog, "Risky Moments"

You can get yourself in all sorts of trouble when your spectacles steam up. For instance, this young man is on a date. The food involves some steamed vegetables. As a result, he can't see a thing. Which explains why he's seductively caressing his date's fish instead of her hand. Foggy moments can be risky. Stop the fog with Optifog anti-mist lenses.

Agency	DDB, Paris
Executive CD	Alexandre Hervé
Copywriter	Alexis Benoit
Art Director	Paul Kreitmann
Production	Les Télécréateurs, Paris
Director	Perlorian Brothers
Producers	Sophie Megrous
	Emilie Talpaert
Planner	Fabien Leroux
Sound Design	The, Paris
Advertiser	Playboy Fragrances, "Press to Play"

This campaign for Playboy's fragrance imagines what could happen when you "press to play". A young woman in the back seat of a limo presses the button to lower the divider. Several different scenarios unfold. In the first, the driver is incredibly sexy. In the second, he's incredibly sexy and allergic to clothes. Or maybe there are two naked drivers. Or she's on a Venetian gondola. Or the driver is a secret agent. Or best of all, he's trained a dog to drive so he can be with her on the back seat. Anything can happen when you "press to play".

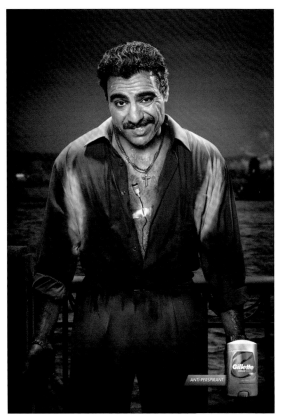

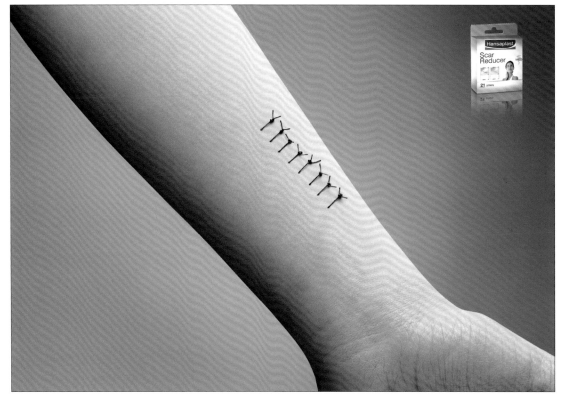

Agency	BBDO, New York	Agency	TBWA\España,
CCO	David Lubars		Barcelona
Executive CD	Toygar Bazarkaya	Creative Directors	Ramón Sala
Creative Directors	Raj Kamble		Joan Vidal
	Paul Vinod		Fer Garcia
Copywriter	Apoorva Kale	Copywriter	Joan Vidal
Art Director	Daniel Aykurt	Art Directors	Fer Garcia
Photographer	Matt Barnes		Ferran Mestre
Account Team	Ben Griffiths		David Pastor
	Seshadri Sampath	Photographer	Felipe Mena
Advertiser	Gillette Odor Shield	Advertiser	Hansaplast Scar
	Anti-Perspirant,		Reducer, "Stiches"
	"Dry Armpits" Campaign		

Agency	Y&R, Prague
Creative Director	Jaime Mandelbaum
Copywriter	Daniel Joseph
Art Director	Matthew Edwards
Illustrator	Marek Motalik
Head of Art	Marco Antonio do Nascimento
Retouching	Furia
Advertiser	Betadine, "Bike" & "Running"

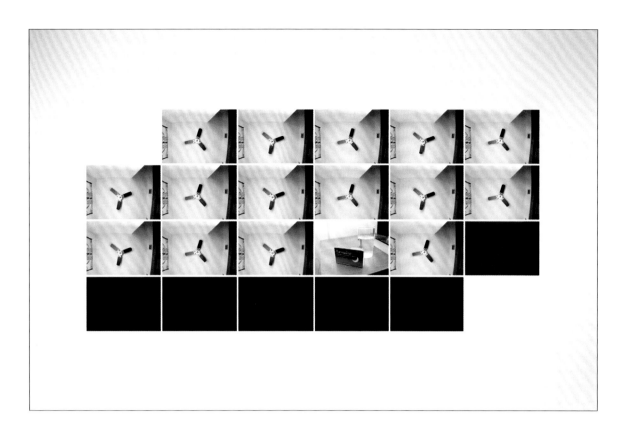

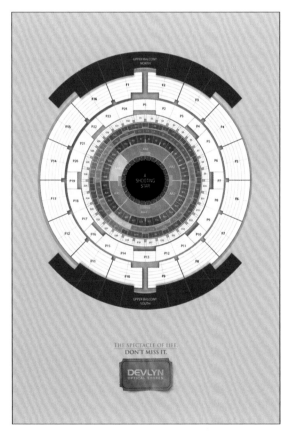

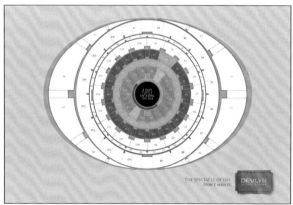

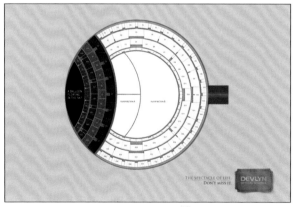

Agency	Havas Worldwide, Madrid	**Agency**	BBDO Mexico, Mexico City
Creative Directors	Mariano Duhalde Haitz Mendibil Ekhi Mendibil	**Creative Directors**	Luis Ribó Sebastián Corti
		Copywriters	Ariel Soto
Copywriters	Marta Fiallo Mariano Duhalde Ekhi Mendibil		Octavio Navarro
		Art Directors	Antonio García Jorge Martínez
Art Directors	Daniel Arenal Haitz Mendibil	**Illustrator**	Jorge Martínez
Advertiser	Dormidina, "Insomnia - Bedroom"	**Advertiser**	Devlyn Optical Stores, "Eyes"

Health & Beauty

Agency	Herezie, Paris
Creative Director	Andrea Stillacci
Copywriter	Anthony Clouet
Art Director	Léo Aram
Illustrator	Vaïnui De Castelbajac
Planner	Luc Wise
Producer	Capucine Lhermitte
Advertiser	Aloelub Lubricant, "Make it Possible"

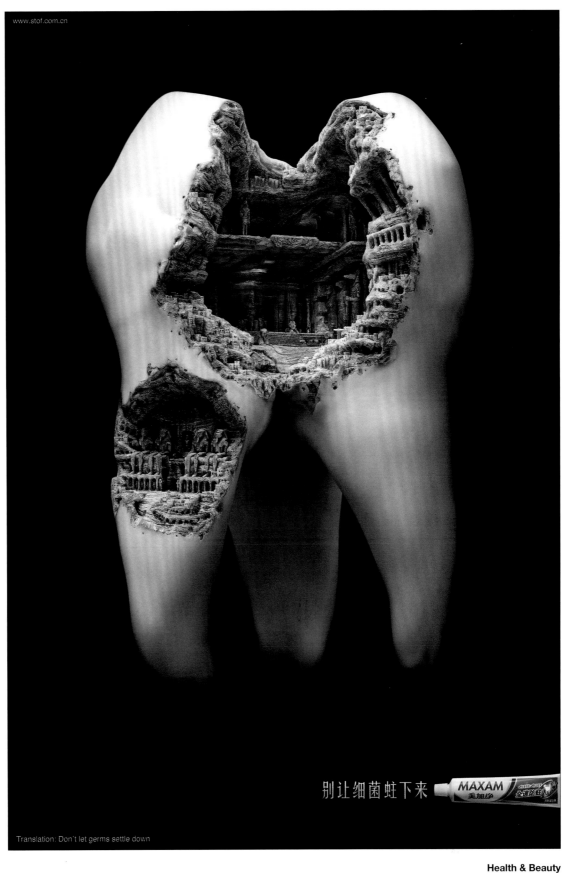

別让细菌蛀下来

Translation: Don't let germs settle down

Agency	JWT, Shanghai	**Production**	Illusion, Bangkok
Creative Directors	Yang Yeo	**Producers**	Somsak Pairew
	Elvis Chau		Anotai Panmongkol
	Hattie Cheng	**Print Production**	Liza Law
Copywriter	Chanfron Zhao		Joseph Yu
Art Directors	Danny Li		Isaac Xu
	Haoxi Lv		Chivel Miao
Photographers	Surachai Puthikulangkura	**Client Service**	Carol Ma
	Kingkong	**Advertiser**	Maxam Toiletries,
Illustrators	Surachai Puthikulangkura		"Civilization-Egypt"
	Supachai U-Rairat		

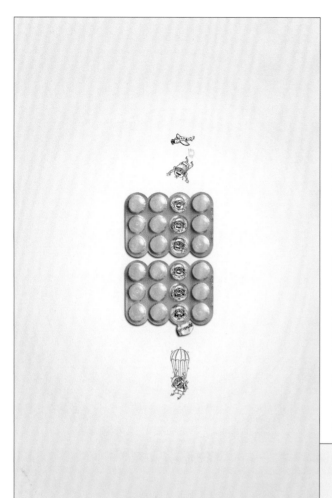

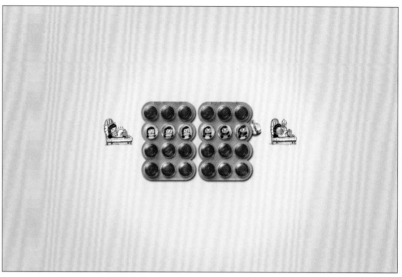

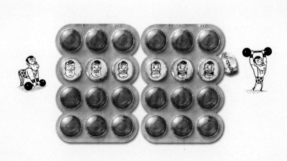

132   **Health & Beauty**

Agency   Havas Worldwide, Madrid
Creative Directors Mariano Duhalde
                        Haitz Mendibil
                        Ekhi Mendibil
Copywriter   Fernando Rodríguez
Art Director   Jacobo Concejo
Illustrator   Dario Adanti
Advertiser   Strepsils,
                        "Shoooout" Campaign

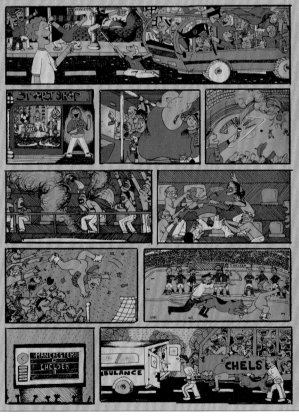

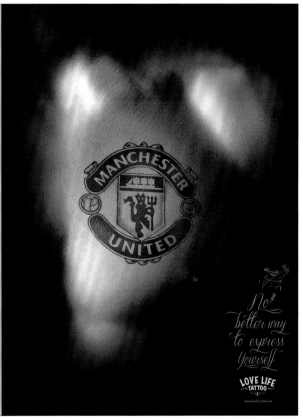

Agency	BBDO, Moscow
Creative Directors	Luis Tauffer
	Andres Vergara
Copywriters	Luis Tauffer
	Franck Vinchon
	Andres Vergara
Art Directors	Luis Tauffer
	Artiom Gelvez Kostenko
Photographer	Dima Gushchin
Illustrator	Maria Cecilia Lopez
Advertiser	Love Life Tattoo Studio,
	"Express Yourself"

134 **Health & Beauty**

Agency	DDB DM9JaymeSyfu, Manila
Creative Directors	Merlee Jayme
	Eugene Demata
	Jerry Hizon
	Louie Sotto
Copywriter	EJ Galang
Art Director	Miko Quiogue
Illustrator	Allan Montayre
Digital Artwork	Pinoy Reyes
Advertiser	Pharex Carbocisteine, "Center of Attention" Campaign

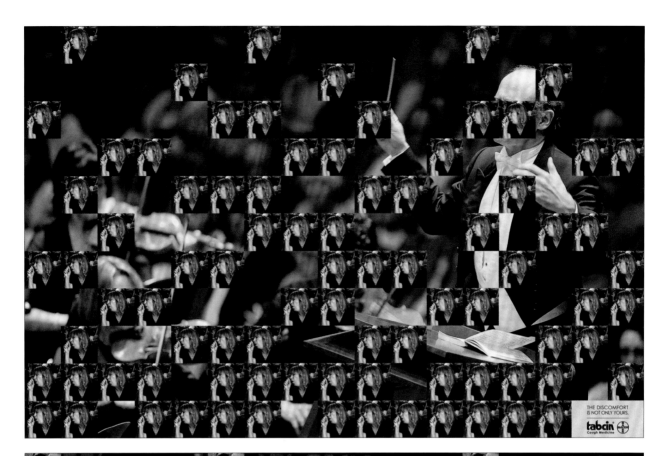

Agency	Young & Rubicam, Buenos Aires
Creative Directors	Martin Mercado
	Diego Tuya
	Darío Rial
	Martín Goldberg
	Daniel Oliveira
Copywriter	Juan Ignacio Galardi
Art Director	Gonzalo Fernandez
Photographer	El Negro Pizzorno
Producer	Fernando Costanza
Advertiser	Tabcin, "Interruptions"

136   **Health & Beauty**

Agencies	Fred & Farid, Paris & Shanghai
Creative Directors	Fred & Farid
Copywriter	Feng Huang
Art Directors	Feng Huang Pierre Jouffray
Photographer	Rankin
Art Buying	Carmela Guiragossian
Advertiser	Weight Watchers, "Treat Yourself Better"

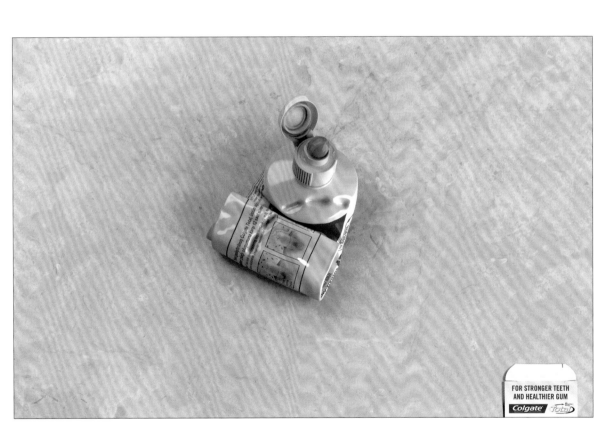

Agency	Contrapunto BBDO, Barcelona	**Agency**	Young & Rubicam, Istanbul
Creative Directors	Tomás Oliva Jofre Biscarri Carlos de Javier	**Creative Directors**	Ozan Varisli Ergin Koyluceli
Copywriter	Sergi Pros	**Copywriter**	Cumhur Gucer
Art Director	Jesus Navas	**Art Director**	Aren Selvioglu
Photographer	Xavier Pastor	**Illustrator**	Ahmet Arif Eken
Advertiser	Reflex Spray, "Marathon" Campaign	**Advertiser**	Colgate Total Toothpaste, "Strong Teeth"

Let kids be kids.

Agency	Ogilvy, Frankfurt	**Music Production**	Andreas Bruhn
CCO	Stephan Vogel		Michi Besler
Creative Director	Peter Strauss	**Creative Assistant**	Sophia Metzler
Copywriter	Peter Strauss	**Planners**	Larissa Pohl
Art Director	Ute Sonntag		Sabina Pal
Production	Jo!Schmid, Berlin	**Account Mgr.**	Larissa Kleemann
Director	Martin Schmid	**Client**	Bettina Peetz
Producers	Anne Baeker	**Advertiser**	Jako-O,
	Claudia Vaternahm		"The Schedule"
Editor	Toni Froschhammer		

Two little girls are sitting on the front steps of their school, perhaps waiting for the bus. "Want to play today?" says one, in a gloomy tone, as if she already knows the answer. The other replies wearily: "Piano lesson. Tomorrow?" "Ballet. Wednesday?" "Yoga. Thursday?" "French. And the weekend?" "Speech therapy and pottery class." "Uh-huh?" "Yeah." Cut to scenes of kids dressing up, painting, playing outdoors and swinging in hammocks. Let kids be kids. That's the policy of kids' clothing and toys brand Jako-O.

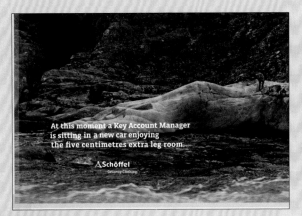

At this moment a Key Account Manager is sitting in a new car enjoying the five centimetres extra leg room.

△Schöffel
Getaway Clothing.

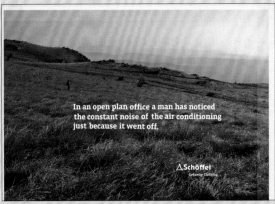

In an open plan office a man has noticed the constant noise of the air conditioning just because it went off.

△Schöffel
Getaway Clothing.

Right now in a fitness studio a man is watching himself in the mirror running on the spot and sweating.

△Schöffel
Getaway Clothing.

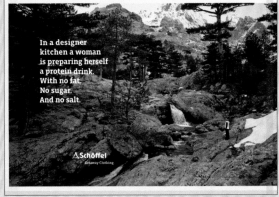

In a designer kitchen a woman is preparing herself a protein drink. With no fat. No sugar. And no salt.

△Schöffel
Getaway Clothing.

In a temperature controlled conference room a meeting about »Workload Efficiency Management« is just starting.

△Schöffel
Getaway Clothing.

Agency	Ogilvy, Frankfurt	**Photographer**	Uli Wiesmeier
CCO	Stephan Vogel	**Planners**	Thomas Strerath
Creative Directors	Helmut Meyer		Larissa Pohl
	Nico Ammann		Magnus Höltke
	Lothar Mueller	**Account Team**	Christian von Dewall
Copywriters	Lothar Mueller		Sarah Nawroth
	Martin Gillan	**Client**	Corinna Umbach
Art Directors	Nico Ammann	**Advertiser**	Schoeffel Outdoor Clothing,
	Till Schaffarczyk		"Campaign with a View"

140 **Clothing, Footwear & Personal Accessories**

Agency	Spillmann/Felser/ Leo Burnett, Zurich
Creative Directors	Martin Spillmann Johannes Raggio Pablo Schencke
Copywriters	Johannes Raggio Diana Rossi
Art Director	Pablo Schencke
Photographers	Michael Nager Ebo Fraterman
Art Buying	Suzana Kovacevic
Advertiser	Victorinox, "Fan Letters" Campaign

Mojave desert, CA, 1937

NEVER HIDE Ray-Ban
GENUINE SINCE 1937

Long Island, NY 1992

NEVER HIDE Ray-Ban
GENUINE SINCE 1937

Agency	Marcel, Paris	**Art Buying**	Jean-Luc Chirio
International CD	Erik Vervroegen		Lauriane Dula
Creative Directors	Erik Vervroegen		Thomas Geffrier
	Eric Jannon	**Planner**	Rob Klingensmith
	Dimitri Guerassimov	**Producer**	Ruth Levy
Copywriter	Martin Rocaboy	**Costume Design**	Arianne Philips
Art Directors	Bastien Grisolet	**Set Design**	Rick Floyd
	Anaïs Boileau	**Account Team**	Alberto Scorticati
	Souen Le Van		Shannon Eddy
Photographer	Mark Seliger		Julie Amen
Digital Artwork	Asile	**Client**	Erika Ferszt
		Advertiser	Ray-Ban Legends,
			"75 Years of Legends"

Agency	BBH India, Mumbai
Executive CD	Russell Barrett
Creative Director	Russell Barrett
Copywriters	Russell Barrett
	Abhiruchi Chand
Art Director	Kunal Sawant
Production	Ramesh Deo Productions
Director	Abhinay Deo
Producers	Apurba Sengupta
	Sushma Joseph
Advertiser	World Gold Council,
	"Diwali"

During Diwali, India's biggest festival, people traditionally bought gold jewellery for their loved ones, but lately they've been buying domestic appliances instead. The situation is dramatized when a woman promises her daughter-in-law a special gift, originally given by the woman's husband "on our first Diwali together". The girl thinks she's going to get a gold necklace, but the mother-in-law presents her with: an ancient TV set. If only he had invested in jewellery all those years ago. This Diwali, says the World Gold Council, make the right choice.

Agency	Publicis Conseil, Paris
CCO	Olivier Altmann
Creative Director	Frederic Royer
Copywriter	Roland Martin
Art Director	Charles Morand
Photographers	Cesar Ancelle-Hansen
	Jacques Demarcillac
Producers	Charles Denis
	Stéphanie Perrot
Art Buying	Anne Traonouil
Clients	Yann Dalibot
	Matthieu Barat
Advertiser	Sooruz, "Flexible Wetsuits"

Agency	DLV BBDO, Milan
Creative Directors	Stefania Siani
	Federico Pepe
Copywriter	Dennis Casale
Art Director	Matteo Pozzi
Illustrator	Davide Calluori
Advertiser	Cam Baby Products,
	"Curiosity" Campaign

Agency	BETC, Paris	Agency	Young & Rubicam, Prague
Creative Directors	Rémi Babinet	Creative Director	Jaime Mandelbaum
	Florence Bellisson	Copywriter	Martina Vesela
Copywriter	Valérie Chidlovsky	Art Directors	Marco Antonio do Nascimento
Art Director	Jane Giard		Atila Martins
Photographer	Boo George	Illustrator	Marek Motalik
Advertiser	Aigle, "Family"	Retouching	Furia
		Advertiser	Coleman Sleeping Bags, "Beach" & "Forest"

Agencies	Fabrica, Treviso
	72andSunny, Amsterdam
Creative Directors	Erik Ravelo
	Carlo Cavallone
	Paulo Martins
	Robert Nakata
Copywriter	Carlo Cavallone
Art Directors	Paulo Martins
	Robert Nakata
Graphic Design	Wendy Richardson
Advertiser	Benetton, "Unhate"

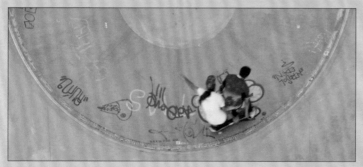

146 **Automobiles**

Agency	Weapon7, London	The Smart Fortwo is a nippy little city car
Executive CD	Jeremy Garner	that only has two seats. To bring its fun and
Creative Directors	Jason Cascarina	agile character to life, top skateboarders
	Anthony McGinty	Kilian Martin and Alfredo Urbon perform
Copywriter	Jason Cascarina	tricks as a tandem on a single skateboard.
Art Director	Anthony McGinty	The hypnotic results are amped up by
Production	Pulse Films, London	the raw blue-rock guitar riffs of Hanni El
Director	Ben Newman	Khatib's track "You Rascal You".
Producers	Oliver Roksill	
	Adam Walker	
Account Director	Rich Moloney	
Head of Planning	Dan Bowers	
Advertiser	Smart Fortwo	

Park Assist technology from Volkswagen.

Das Auto.

Park Assist technology from Volkswagen.

Das Auto.

Park Assist technology from Volkswagen.

Das Auto.

Agency	DDB, Sydney	**Producers**	Grant Navin
Executive CD	Dylan Harrison		John Wood
Creative Directors	Steve Wakelam	**Art Buying**	Leesa Murray
	Nick Pringle	**Management**	Nicole Taylor
Copywriters	Steve Wakelam		Dave Murphy
	Nick Pringle	**Clients**	Jutta Friese
Art Directors	Steve Wakelam		Peter Stewart
	Nick Pringle		Loren Elsegood
Photographer	Andreas Bommert	**Advertiser**	Volkswagen,
Retouching	Matt Bright		"Park Assist
			Technology"

Agency	DDB, Sydney
Executive CD	Dylan Harrison
Creative Directors	Steve Wakelam
	Nick Pringle
Copywriter	Malcolm Caldwell
Art Director	Ian Broekhuizen
Production	Soma Films, Sydney
Director	Sean Meehan
Producers	Sam McGarry
	Victoria Bennett
Editor	Drew Thompson
	Method Studios
Sound Design	Simon Kane
	Song Zu
Music	Elliot Wheeler
	Turning Studios
Post Production	Method Studios
Planner	Nick Andrews
Management	Nicole Taylor
	Josette Addinall
Clients	Jutta Friese
	Peter Stewart
	Loren Elsegood
Advertiser	Volkswagen Tiguan, "Cross Country"

A woman awakes in a hotel bed. Noticing the time, she wakes her partner in a panic. They jump into their clothes and go down for a fast breakfast. Still rushing, they load up on buffet food and dash out to their Volkswagen Tiguan. Then begins a hair-raising ride through the countryside. They park the car in a lane, dash across a muddy field and dive into the rear of a tent. Then they emerge from the front, where their buddy from a neighbouring tent is cooking breakfast, oblivious to their night in the posh hotel. You can get used to high quality.

148   Automobiles

Agency	DDB, Torino
Creative Director	Aurelio Tortelli
Copywriters	Michela Grasso
	Beatrice Furlotti
Art Directors	Daniele Ricci
	Maddalena Giavarini
Production	Movie Magic, Milan
Director	John Immesoete
Advertiser	Volkswagen Polo, "Cost Reduction" Campaign

Meet Bill Right, a well-meaning American in the wrong job. He has to convince Volkswagen engineers to cut corners in order to save costs. But the dour engineers constantly reject his cheery yet inappropriate suggestions.

Lose a bolt on the wheels? A 20% cost reduction, but less safety. Lose one of the double gaskets on the doors? More noise. "That's not noise," Bill protests. "That's the world embracing you!" The engineers walk away. Another leaves the room when Bill moots removing the car's under-body protection. And forget replacing the adjustable steering wheel with a comfy cushion. Others may cut corners – not Volkswagen.

Precision Parking.
Park Assist by Volkswagen.

Mean made meaner.
The Golf GTI Edition 35. Now with 235 horsepower.

Das Auto.

Agency	DDB Tribal, Berlin		**Agency**	DDB Tribal, Berlin
CCO	Eric Schoeffler		**CCO**	Eric Schoeffler
Creative Directors	Maged Nassar		**Creative Directors**	Marc Isken
	Ali Ali			Nils Haseborg
Copywriters	Maged Nassar		**Copywriter**	Christian Anhut
	Ali Ali		**Art Director**	Jack Christensen
Illustrator	The Operators, London		**Illustrator**	Sebastian Hudert
Art Buying	Susanne Kreft		**Account Mgr.**	Christina Mueller
Account Team	Susanne Plümecke		**Clients**	Cornelia Kabelitz
	Catrin Schmid			Giovanni Perosino
Advertiser	Volkswagen Park Assist,		**Advertiser**	Volkswagen Golf GTI 35,
	"Hedgehog and Fish"			"Crocodile Boots"

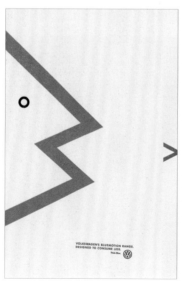

150 **Automobiles**

Agency	adam&eveDDB, London	**Management**	Jonathan Hill
Creative Director	Jeremy Craigen		Jason Lusty
Copywriter	Jonathan John	**Account Team**	Paul Mitcheson
Art Director	David Mackersey		Harriet Bates
Illustrator	Peter Mould	**Clients**	Giovanni Perosino
Typographer	Peter Mould		Cornelia Kabelitz
Designer	Peter Mould	**Advertiser**	Volkswagen BlueMotion,
Project Mgrs.	Tim Walther		"Think Blue Logo Campaign"
	Craig Neilson		

It's back.

The 21st Century Beetle.
The classic shape of the '60s love bug has returned. But unlike its predecessor, the new 21st Century Beetle has the ability to accelerate from 0 to 100 in an almost disconcerting 7.5 seconds. And to reflect this new found power, the new body has been given a more masculine, leaner look. It also comes with all the obligatory state of the art 21st Century kit. Like an up to the nanosecond Fender sound system, xenon lights, keyless access and a panoramic sunroof. Things its more basic '60s self could not even have imagined in its most psychedelic dreams. And the front? Well you'll see that looming large in your rear view mirror, moments before it overtakes. www.beetle.com

Volkswagen
Das Auto.

Sharan.
More space, less fights.

Volkswagen
Das Auto.

Agency	adam&eveDDB, London	Agency	DDB, Brussels
Creative Director	Jeremy Craigen	Creative Director	Peter Aerts
Copywriters	Patrick McClelland	Copywriters	Rom & John
	Jonathan John	Art Directors	John & Rom
Art Directors	Grant Parker	Photographer	Frieke Janssens
	Feargal Ballance	Graphic Design	Benjamin Hiffe
	David Mackersey	Producer	Brigitte Verduyckt
Photographer	Nick Meek	Retouching	Paul Roberts
Typographers	Peter Mould	Production	Initials LA
	Oliver Watts	Advertiser	Volkswagen Sharan
	Andrew Walsh		
Art Buying	Daniel Moorey		
Advertiser	Volkswagen Beetle		

Agency	adam&eveDDB, London
Creative Director	Jeremy Craigen
Copywriter	Tom Chancellor
Art Director	Luke Flynn
Production	Pulse, London
Directors	Will Lovelace
	Dylan Southern
Producers	Mark Harbour
	Natalie Hill
	Sarah Browell
Planner	Tom Lloyd
DOP	Martin Ruhe
Editor	Leo Scott
Music	Sniffy Dog
Post Production	Oliver Bersey
	Framestore, London
Advertiser	Volkswagen Polo, "Dad"

Fathers are protective of their daughters. Here we see a relationship evolving over the years, from the moment dad arrives home from the hospital with mum and new baby, sheltering them from the rain with his coat. He's there when his daughter takes her first steps, learns to swim and ride a bike. He shields her eyes from scary movies – and makes meaningful eye contact with her first boyfriend. When she leaves home, he gives her the keys to a shiny new Volkswagen Polo. He wants her to be in safe hands.

Agency	RKCR/Y&R, London
Creative Directors	Martin Davey
	Martin Casson
Copywriter	Martin Davey
Art Director	Martin Casson
Production	Gorgeous, London
Director	Vince Squibb
Producers	Alicia Richards
	James Miller
Advertiser	Land Rover Discovery, "Dry-Cleaner"

A drycleaner is surprised when a couple drop off a pile of clothes that have clearly been worn in the desert – sand is still spilling out of them. On the couple's next visit, they leave two squelchy parkas full of melted snow. The drycleaner looks bemused. When they return, he looks positively apprehensive. This time the clothes seem to have spent time in the jungle. As the pair leave, he sees them drive off in a Land Rover Discovery. Comprehension dawns on his face. Been anywhere interesting lately?

Agency	H, Puteaux
Creative Directors	Gilbert Scher
	Marco Venturelli
	Luca Cinquepalmi
Copywriter	Marco Venturelli
Art Director	Luca Cinquepalmi
Production	Bandits, Suresnes
Director	Scott Lyonthat
Producers	Philippe Dupuis-Mendel
	Christopher Thiery
	Julie Malet
Advertiser	Citroën C3, "Paris Rome"

The fuel-saving advantages of the new C3 are demonstrated in a simple but effective way. As a man fills the car at the garage, images of landscapes begin rotating on the screen like a petrol pump display. We start with the Arc de Triomphe in Paris. Then roads, pylons, fields and other scenes from a journey roll by. We finish at the Coliseum, over 1,400 kilometres later. The Citroën C3 can cover the entire distance on a single tank.

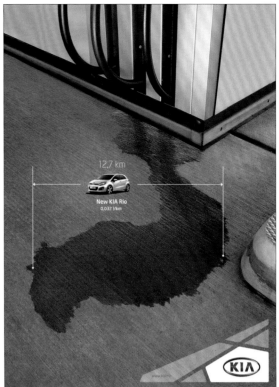

WITH THE NEW VOLVO V70 VOUS POUVEZ CONDUIRE TRÈS LOIN OHNE ZU STOPPEN UND ZU TANKEN NEANCHE UNA VOLTA.

VOLVO V70. 1550 KILOMETERS ON ONE TANK.

Agency	Innocean Worldwide, Madrid	**Agency**	Forsman & Bodenfors, Gothenburg
Executive CD	Stephen Ward	**Copywriters & ADs**	Agnes Stenberg-Schentz
Creative Director	Stephen Ward		Jeremy Phang
Copywriter	Jan Pfiffer	**Designer**	Mikko Timonen
Art Director	Igor Karpalov	**Account Team**	Anders Bothén
Photographer	Mert Dürümoglu		Anna Levegård
Retouching	Claudia Kupp	**Client**	Bengt Junemo
Account Team	Jorge López	**Advertiser**	Volvo V70,
	Estefanía Villaespesa		"1550 Kilometers
Client	Ricardo De Diego		on One Tank"
Advertiser	Kia Rio,		
	"Kia Spill" Campaign		

154 Automobiles

Agency	Publicis Conseil, Paris	Agency	Contrapunto BBDO, Madrid
Creative Director	Olivier Altmann	Creative Directors	Félix del Valle
Copywriter	Mathieu Degryse		Carlos Jorge
Art Director	Yves-Eric Deboey	Copywriters	Félix del Valle
Photographer	David Gill		Paco Castillo
Planning	Hélène Duvoux-Mauguet	Art Directors	Carlos Jorge
Art Buying	Jean Luc Chirio		David Albardonedo
	Gael Cheval	Art Buying	Javier Luján
	Soone Riboud	Advertiser	Smart, "Mupi"
Advertiser	Renault F1, "Red is Dead"		

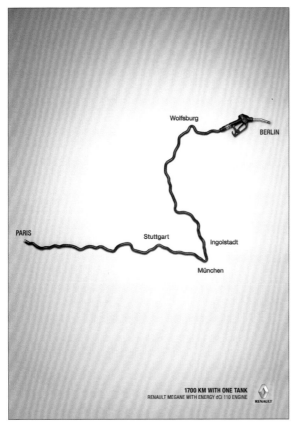

1700 KM WITH ONE TANK
RENAULT MEGANE WITH ENERGY dCi 110 ENGINE

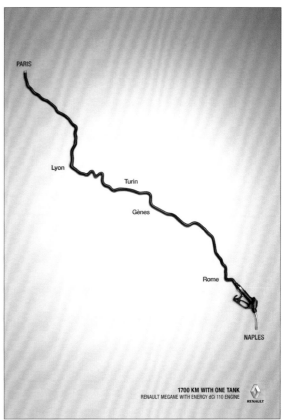

1700 KM WITH ONE TANK
RENAULT MEGANE WITH ENERGY dCi 110 ENGINE

NEW MEGANE DCI 130
ONLY 3,5L / 100 KM

Agency	Publicis Conseil, Paris	Agency	Publicis Conseil, Paris
Creative Director	Olivier Altmann	CCO	Olivier Altmann
Copywriter	Didier Aerts	Creative Director	Herve Riffault
Art Director	Alexandra Offe	Copywriter	Alexandre Hildebrand
Photographer	Nicolas Descottes	Art Director	Martin Darfeuille
Art Buying	Jean-Luc Chirio	Assistant AD	Antoine Dezes-Richard
	Marion Venot	Photographer	Will Sanders
Advertiser	Renault Mégane DCI, "Petrol Pumps"	Planner	Anouk Benlolo
		Retouching	Eye Dream
		Advertiser	Renault Mégane DCI, "Homeless Cars"

NEW CITROËN C3 PICASSO SPACEBOX. A COMPACT CAR NEVER FELT SO SPACIOUS.

CRÉATIVE TECHNOLOGIE

NEW CITROËN C3 PICASSO SPACEBOX. A COMPACT CAR NEVER FELT SO SPACIOUS.

CRÉATIVE TECHNOLOGIE

156 **Automobiles**

Agency	Bold Ogilvy & Mather, Athens	Agency	H, Puteaux
Executive CD	Yiannis Sideris	Creative Directors	Gilbert Scher
Creative Director	Lazaros Nikiforidis		Marco Venturelli
Copywriter	Lazaros Nikiforidis		Luca Cinquepalmi
Art Director	Vangelis Tolias	Copywriter	Marco Venturelli
Illustrator	Juan Carlos Paz	Art Director	Luca Cinquepalmi
Account Team	Rebecca Salmona	Photographer	Alberto Callari
	Maggie Adamou	Art Buying	Nadia Curti
Advertiser	Ford Fiesta, "Keyless"	Advertiser	Citroën C3 Picasso, "Spacebox" Campaign

Agency	Exxtra Kommunikation, Zurich	Always keeps enough distance: Audi A7 with adaptive cruise control.	**Agency**	DDB DM9JaymeSyfu, Manila
Creative Directors	Markus Gut		**Creative Director**	Louie Sotto
	Dominik Oberwiler		**Copywriter**	Louie Sotto
	Martin Stulz		**Art Director**	Herbert Hernandez
Copywriter	Sven Rufer		**Illustrator**	Allan Montayre
Art Director	Lukas Wietlisbach		**Digital Artwork**	Pinoy Reyes
MD	Susan Baumgartner		**Advertiser**	Mini Cooper,
Advertiser	Audi, "Side Assist"			"Rollercoaster"

UNOPENED HIGHWAY /VRGORAC, CROATIA

158 **Automotive & Accessories**

Agency	Forsman & Bodenfors, Gothenburg	**Planner**	Tobias Nordström
		Designer	Jerry Wass
Copywriters	Martin Ringqvist	**Account Team**	Olle Victorin
	Björn Engström		Cilla Glenberg
Art Directors	Anders Eklind		Alison Arnold
	Sophia Lindholm		Britta Malmberg
Production	Smuggler, Los Angeles	**Advertiser**	Volvo FH Truck,
Producer	Ray Leaky		"The Ballerina Stunt"
	Alexander Blidner		

How do you demonstrate the precision handling of the new Volvo FH truck? You get two of them to speed down a deserted highway with a tightrope walker crossing a high wire between them. And she has to get across before the trucks enter a low tunnel. The tension is stretched to maximum as high wire record holder Faith Dickey inches gingerly across what seems like the endless space between the speeding trucks. She completes the walk just in time.

Automotive & Accessories   **159**

Agency	Scholz & Friends, Berlin
Creative Directors	Martin Pross
	Matthias Spaetgens
	Robert Krause
Copywriter	Christian Brandes
Art Director	Joerg Waschescio
Photographer	Alex Rank
Post Production	F. A. Cesar
Art Buying	Kirsten Rendtel
Account Team	Josef Hoehnow
	Anna Gabriel
Advertiser	Mercedes-Benz Vito,
	"Danger Doesn't Announce Itself"

TomTom does the Robot
Your Journey... now on Android

Look to the side without looking to the side.
Blind Spot Assist from Mercedes-Benz.

Mercedes-Benz
The best or nothing.

Automotive & Accessories

Agency	Khanna \ Reidinga, Amsterdam
Creative Director	Hesling Reidinga
Production	Czar, Amsterdam
Director	Gerrit Willemsen
Producer	Willem Bos
Editor	Amber Hooijmans
Music	Nobody Beats the Drums
Advertiser	TomTom Android, "TomTom Does the Robot"

An android is really just a robot. So when GPS navigation system TomTom became available for Android phones, the news was announced with a video showing the TomTom staff "doing the robot" – a funny machine-like dance – in their offices. First only one member of staff seems affected, but pretty soon they've all joined in.

Agency	Jung von Matt, Hamburg
CCOs	Dörte Spengler-Ahrens
	Jan Rexhausen
Creative Director	Felix Fenz
Copywriters	Andreas Hilbig
	David Wegener
Art Directors	Alexander Norvilas
	Michael Hess
Photographer	Klaus Merz
Typographers	Kürten & Lechner
Digital Artwork	Amina Warscheid
	Marius Schwiegk
Advertiser	Mercedes-Benz, "Look Twice"

Agency	BBDO Proximity, Berlin	Post Production	Sevengreen Picture
CCO	Wolfgang Schneider		Works, Hamburg
Creative Directors	David Mously	Account Team	Sebastian Schlosser
	Jan Harbeck		Jan Hendrik Oelckers
Copywriter	David Missing		Martin Vejdovsky
Art Director	Daniel Haschtmann		Joris Jonker
Photographer	Jan van Endert		Jana Valencikova
Typographer	Daniel Haschtmann	Advertiser	Mercedes-Benz,
Art Buying	Lynn Sutliff		"Night View Assist"

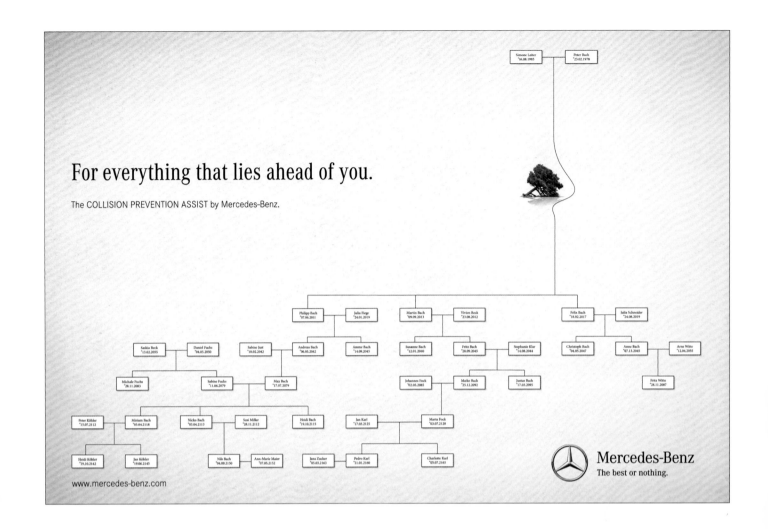

For everything that lies ahead of you.

The COLLISION PREVENTION ASSIST by Mercedes-Benz.

Mercedes-Benz
The best or nothing.

www.mercedes-benz.com

Detects hidden danger.

Detects hidden danger.

Detects hidden danger.
The new Active Brake Assist 2® for Mercedes-Benz Trucks.

Mercedes-Benz
Trucks you can trust

162   **Automotive & Accessories**

Agency	BBDO Proximity, Berlin
CCO	Wolfgang Schneider
Creative Directors	David Mously
	Jan Harbeck
Art Director	Daniel Haschtmann
Graphic Design	Anne Herrmann
Producer	Markus Kuhn
Art Buying	Lynn Sutliff
MD	Dirk Spakowski
Account Directors	Sebastian Schlosser
	Massimiliano Sacchetti
Advertiser	Mercedes-Benz,
	"Tree of Life"

Agency	Scholz & Friends, Berlin
Creative Directors	Martin Pross
	Matthias Spaetgens
	Michael Winterhagen
	Nils Busche
Copywriter	Michael Schoepf
Art Director	Walter Ziegler
Illustrator	Walter Ziegler
Advertiser	Mercedes-Benz Trucks,
	"Hidden Dangers"

THE · LEARNER · DRIVER   THE · OLD · LADY   THE · COURIER   THE · VAN · MAN

Volkswagen Front Assist. It knows what's ahead.

Look away.

Unless you are driving a Volkswagen with City Emergency Brake.

www.volkswagen.com

Please ignore.

Unless you are driving a Volkswagen with City Emergency Brake.

www.volkswagen.com

Don't look up here.

Unless you are driving a Volkswagen with City Emergency Brake.

www.volkswagen.com

Agency	adam&eveDDB, London		**Agency**	Grabarz & Partner, Hamburg
Creative Director	Jeremy Craigen		**Creative Directors**	Ralf Heuel
Copywriter	Matt Lee			Timm Weber
Art Director	Pete Heyes			Christoph Stricker
Photographer	Victoria Ling			Tobias Heinze
Illustrator	Jon Rogers		**Copywriter**	Sonja Schaefer
Digital Artwork	Gutenberg Networks		**Art Directors**	Kaloyan Yanev
Designer	Peter Mould			John-John Skoog
Art Buying	Daniel Moorey		**Digital Artwork**	Mareike Doerries
Retouching	Andrew Walsh		**Production**	Gabriel Dominik
Advertiser	Volkswagen, "Tarot"		**Advertiser**	Volkswagen, "Ignore" Poster Campaign

164   **Automotive & Accessories**

Agency	adam&eveDDB, London
Creative Director	Jeremy Craigen
Copywriter	Matt Lee
Art Director	Pete Heyes
Photographer	Sue Parkhill
Art Buying	Daniel Moorey
Account Team	Paul Billingsley Harriet Bates
Advertiser	Volkswagen, "Safe Distance" Campaign

Agency	adam&eveDDB, London
Creative Director	Jeremy Craigen
Copywriters	Sigrid Egedal
	Oliver Rimoldi
Art Directors	Sigrid Egedal
	Oliver Rimoldi
Photographer	Harry Cory-Wright
Art Buying	Daniel Moorey
Account Team	Paul Billingsley
	Harriet Bates
Advertiser	Volkswagen, "Bored Road Signs"

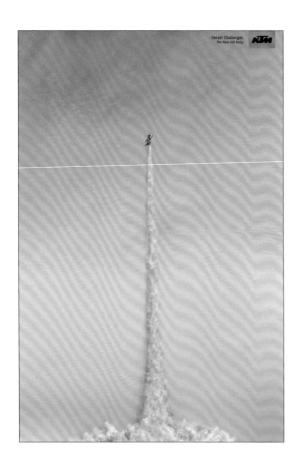

166 **Automotive & Accessories**

Agency	DDB&Co., Istanbul	Agency	Bold Ogilvy & Mather, Athens
Creative Director	Karpat Polat	Executive CD	Yiannis Sideris
Copywriter	Ali Hikmet Yavuz	Creative Director	Lazaros Nikiforidis
Art Directors	Asil Yildiz	Copywriter	Lazaros Nikiforidis
	Canhur Aktuglu	Art Director	Vangelis Tolias
Advertiser	KTM 450 Rally, "Rocket"	Photographer	Carioca, Bucharest
		Illustrator	Carioca, Bucharest
		Account Team	Rebecca Salmona
			Maggie Adamou
			Lena Belibassaki
		Advertiser	Ford Transit, "Shop Windows"

THE NEW VOLVO HAS ROOM FOR THE KING. AND HIS HORSE.

AIRING CUPBOARD AND BUNK BED. STANDARD IN THE NEW VOLVO.

World premiere for the new Volvo FH truck.

VOLVO

WATCH OUT! THIS IS NOT ENOUGH HEADROOM FOR THE NEW VOLVO.

World premiere for the new Volvo FH truck.

VOLVO

THE NEW VOLVO HAS ROOM FOR A PUSHCHAIR AND 40 TONS OF TIMBER.

World premiere for the new Volvo FH truck.

VOLVO

THE NEW VOLVO IS THIS LONG

World premiere for the new Volvo FH truck.

VOLVO

Agency	Forsman & Bodenfors, Gothenburg
Copywriters	Björn Engström
	Martin Ringqvist
Art Directors	Anders Eklind
	Sophia Lindholm
Designer	Jerry Wass
Planner	Tobias Nordström
Content Architect	Johan Wingård
Account Team	Olle Victorin
	Cilla Glenberg
	Britta Malmberg
Advertiser	Volvo FH Truck

Gothenburg is the home town of Volvo, so the launch of the new Volvo FH truck deserved a big outdoor campaign. It purpose was not only to launch the truck, but to strengthen the Volvo brand and highlight its role as a big local employer. The posters appeared in every single corner of the city, taking over 1600 sites. The playful copy first gave the impression that the new Volvo was a car with incredible capacity.

Agency	Try/Apt, Oslo	A man tells us that movies keep invading his life. We see him dipping a toe into his bath – only to hear the theme from Jaws. He finds an axe buried in his door, then a gangster tied up in the trunk of his car. He's forced to play chess with Death in a café. Out jogging, he's plunged into a costume drama. His car transforms into a robot. "The worst is Norwegian social realism from the 70s." And when a dinosaur peers through the window, we just have to believe him. Canal Digital: more movies than ever.
Copywriter	Lars Joachim Grimstad	
Art Director	Egil Pay	
Production	One Big Happy Family	
Director	Joachim Trier	
Producers	Mone Mikkelsen	
	Helene Hovda Lunde	
Account Team	Marte Heiersted	
	Lars Mitlid	
Advertiser	Canal Digital, "The Man Who Lived in a Film"	

HOW I
MET YOUR
MOTHER

TWO
AND A HALF
MEN

GOSSIP
GIRL

Media 169

Agency	Rafineri, Istanbul
Creative Directors	Ayse Bali
	Orkun Demirelli
	Ufuk Uslu
Copywriter	Serkan Soylem
Art Director	Can Guven
Advertiser	CNBC-E Turkey, "News & Series"

Agency	McCann Erickson, Tel Aviv
Creative Director	Rona Yakobi
Copywriters	Yoav Hebel
	Tal Perlmuter
Art Director	Sigal Abudy
Advertiser	Yes Satellite TV, "Yes Life is Short"

A gangster (Tony Soprano actor James Gandolfini) warns us that "life is short". He advises us to try something new everyday. Such as: "Dance!" We see Tony's henchmen shooting at a guy's feet. "Connect to the silence of the sea." A body bag is dumped into the ocean off a bridge. "Try to give your body a good rest." Someone is being buried. "Surprise an old friend…" Tony lurks in the backseat of a future victim's car. In fact all his advice is mirrored by violent gangster activity. Try new things – like all the new movies on Israel's Yes TV.

170   **Media**

Agency	RKCR/Y&R, London
Creative Director	Damon Collins
Copywriters & ADs	Ted Heath
	Jules Chalkley
	Paul Angus
	Nick Simons
Production	Passion Pictures
	Red Bee Media
Director	Pete Candeland
Producers	Sarah Caddy
	Lottie Hope
Advertiser	BBC, "Stadium UK"

The BBC gave everyone a front-row seat at the 2012 Olympic Games. So this magnificent animated film turns the British Isles into one huge arena: Stadium UK. We see a whole host of Olympians – sprinters on London streets, cyclists in quarries, weightlifters in dockyards and swimmers in Scottish lochs – preparing and then competing in Olympic sports throughout the land. All set to a rousing soundtrack by Elbow.

Agency	DDB Brasil, Sao Paulo
Creative Directors	Sergio Valente
	Marco Versolato
Copywriter	Caio Mattoso
Art Director	Rodrigo Mendes
Production	Ad Studio, Sao Paulo
Directors	Jarbas Agnelli
	Doug Bello
Producers	Rino Siveiro
	Gilberto Pires
Advertiser	Follow Magazine, "Is the New"

We all know that brown is the new black. This animated song for trendy magazine Follow tells us a few other things too. "Data is the new oil, talent is the new gold, sharing is the new currency. Freak is the new geek, geek is the new chic, weird is the new charming." Moreover: "Poor is the new rich, technology is the new cigarette, paper is the new vinyl." Not only that but: "Text message is the new love letter, unfollowing is the new defriending, privacy is the new luxury and used is the new new." Follow magazine. It's new.

Agency	CHI & Partners, London
Executive CD	Jonathan Burley
Creative Director	Jonathan Burley
Copywriter	Daniel Fisher
Art Director	Richard Brim
Art Buying	Emma Modler
Retouching	Rob Swainson
	Dave Turfitt
Planner	Ben Southgate
Account Team	William Leabeater
	Olivia Skone
Advertiser	The Sunday Times,
	"Rich List"

CLOSER TO NEWS

Agency	Havas Worldwide, Düsseldorf
Creative Directors	Felix Glauner
	Martin Breuer
	Martin Venn
Copywriter	Christian Kroll
Art Director	Ingmar Krannich
Production	Jotz! Filmproduktion, Düsseldorf
Producers	Jan Behrens
	Christoph vom Bauer
Editors	Martin Basan
	Jochen Becker
Sound Design	Studio Funk & Co., Düsseldorf
Post Production	Pirates ´n Paradise
Account Team	Harald Jaeger
	Simone Klinke
Clients	Cornelia Dienstbach
	Jasmin Hoehn
Advertiser	N-TV, "News App" Campaign

News channel N-TV's app for mobile devices puts the latest news at your fingertips. The first of three short spots shows German Chancellor Angela Merkel nodding off at a boring ceremony. The app user's giant finger nudges her awake. But the finger can be malicious too: at a windy memorial ceremony it knocks a wreath onto the Ukrainian prime minister. And in a third spot it causes Hillary Clinton to trip as she enters a plane. The N-TV app: news at your fingertips.

SHAW) EXO

shaw.ca

172 Media

Agency	BETC, Paris
Creative Directors	Stéphane Xiberras
	Damien Bellon
Copywriter	Damien Bellon
Production	Pop-Up Films, London
Director	Karen Cunningham
Producer	Julia Fetterman
Advertiser	Young Director Awards, "The Light is Your Friend"

A couple are trying to get amorous in bed one morning when their kid – a ginger geek in specs – bursts in. Much to their alarm, he begins "directing" the scene. "This is all wrong! When you kiss each other, make it feel like you've never met before. Daddy, I need more excitement, more passion, more conviction!" Some people were born to be directors, as this ad for the CFPE/Shots Young Directors Award suggests. "And remember," the boy tells his mother, "the light is your friend."

Agency	BBDO, Toronto
Creative Directors	Carlos Moreno
	Peter Ignazi
Copywriter	Craig McIntosh
Art Director	Jaimes Zentil
Production	Smuggler, LA
	Soft Citizen, Toronto
Director	Stylewar
Producer	Dena Thompson
DOP	Oliver Wood
Editor	Noah Herzog
Music	Human Worldwide
Advertiser	Shaw EXO, "Car Chase"

A Hollywood-style car chase has just begun when we notice a crucial difference. Instead of watching passively in front of their TV sets, the viewers are perched on top of the vehicles in their armchairs. So they viscerally experience every screech, skid, collision and stunt. When you watch TV on the new Shaw Exo network, it's so intense you feel as if you're there.

Agency	CHI & Partners, London
Executive CD	Jonathan Burley
Creative Director	Jonathan Burley
Copywriter	Rob Webster
Art Director	Alexei Berwitz
Photographer	Getty & Rex Features
Graphic Design	Dan Beckett
Retouching	Dave Turfitt
	Rob Swainson
Art Buying	Emma Modler
Planner	Ben Southgate
Acct. Supervisor	William Leabeater
Advertiser	The Times, "Jubilee" Campaign

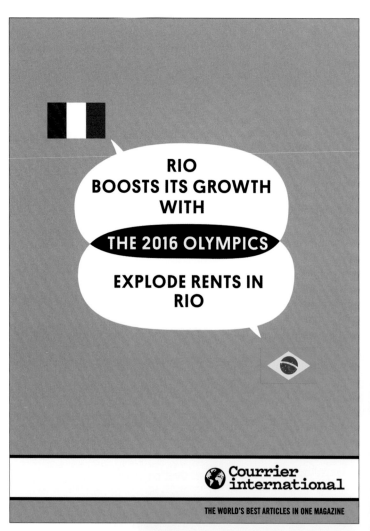

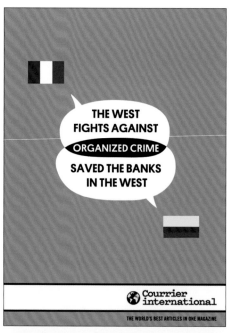

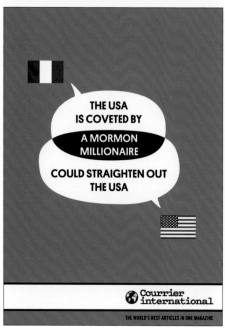

Media

Agency	BETC, Paris
Creative Director	Vincent Behaeghel
Copywriter	David Soussan
Art Director	Clémentine Allain
Advertiser	Courrier International, "Points of View"

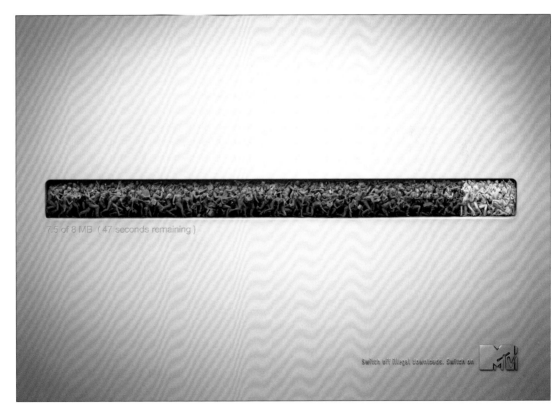

Agency	Spillmann/Felser/	Agency	Ogilvy, Frankfurt
	Leo Burnett, Zurich	CCO	Stephan Vogel
Creative Director	Peter Brönnimann	Creative Directors	Matthias Storath
Copywriter	Johannes Raggio		Helmut Meyer
Art Director	Pablo Schencke	Copywriter	Haiko Hoernig
Advertiser	WOZ Die Wochenzeitung,	Art Director	Patrick Ackmann
	"Always Critical"	Illustrators	Surachai Puthikulangkura
			Supachai U-Rairat
			Illusion, Bangkok
		Art Buying	Valerie Opitz
		Account Mgt.	Yves Rosengart
		Client	Robin Karakash
		Advertiser	MTV, "Downloadbar"

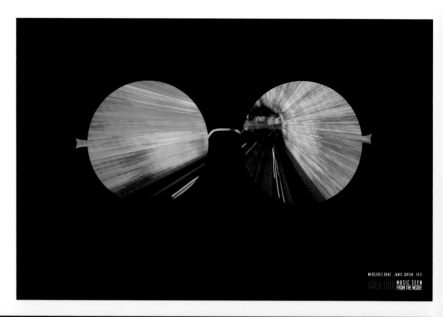

Agency	BDDP & Fils, Paris
Creative Director	Olivier Moine
Copywriter	Caroline Laumont
Art Director	Aurore De Sousa
Photographer	Olivier Foulon
Art Buying	Marie Ferrara
	Elise Kubler
Advertiser	Les Echos, "The Decision Maker"

Agency	Publicis Conseil, Paris
CCO	Olivier Altmann
Creative Director	Veronique Sels
Copywriter	Alexandre Girod
Art Director	Julien Vergne
Art Buying	Elysian Fields
Account Team	Cesar Croze
	Emmanuelle Henry
Clients	Olivier Thomas
	Philippe Budillon
Advertiser	Rock & Folk, "Closer to the Music"

THERE'S MORE LIFESTYLE IN YOUR NEWS NOW.
The sunday paper "Sonntagszeitung" now with the lifestyle-magazine encore!

THE INSIDE STORY

THERE'S MORE LIFESTYLE IN YOUR NEWS NOW.
The sunday paper "Sonntagszeitung" now with the lifestyle-magazine encore!

THE INSIDE STORY

Fresher

FOX MOVIES
NO COMMERCIAL BREAKS
foxmoviestv.com

Agency	Advico Y&R, Zurich	
Creative Directors	Martin Stulz	
	Dominik Oberwiler	
Copywriter	Julia Brandstätter	
Art Director	Matthias Kadlubsky	
Graphic Design	Annik Weber	
Consultants	Julia Kull	
	Christoph Schwarz	
Production	Scheffolz Vizner	
	Fluxif, Zurich	
Advertiser	Sonntags Zeitung,	
	"Encore Campaign"	

Agency	Leo Burnett, Dubai
CCO	Bechara Mouzannar
Regional ECD	Peter Bidenko
Creative Director	Mohamed Oudaha
Copywriter	Jaison Ben
Art Director	Mohammad Aram
Graphic Design	Ammar Safi
Traffic Manager	Gabriel Noronha
Account Team	Nadia Bedaywi
	Lara El Barkouki
Advertiser	Fox Movies,
	"Break-Free"

Advertising breaks can intrude on your movie-watching pleasure, which is why this channel shows movies without breaks. To advertise that fact, it printed scenes from movies on the double page spreads of magazines and inserted a torn fake ad between them, as if it had been ripped out to give the movie a full showing.

Agency	adam&eveDDB, London		**Agency**	Young & Rubicam, Milan
Executive CD	Jeremy Craigen		**Group CD**	Vicky Gitto
Creative Directors	Matt Lee		**Copywriter**	Davide Iacono
	Pete Heyes		**Art Director**	Alessandro Agnellini
Copywriters & ADs	Chris Lapham		**Photographer**	FM Photographers, Milan
	Aaron McGurk		**Advertiser**	Repubblica.it,
Art Buying	Julie Hughes			"The World Changes
Planner	Elaine Miller			in Seconds"
Designer	Aaron McGurk			
Retouching	Andrew Walsh			
Advertiser	Financial Times, "Seeing Stars"			

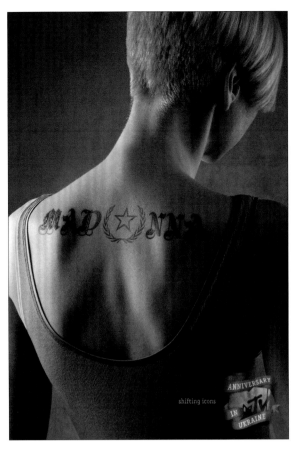

Agency	Leo Burnett Ukraine, Kiev	**Agency**	DDB, Paris
Creative Directors	Natalia Dundina	**Executive CD**	Alexandre Hervé
	Tatiana Fedorenko	**Copywriter**	Olivier Lefebvre
Copywriters	Konstantyn Kovalchuk	**Art Directors**	Benjamin Marchal
	Tatiana Fedorenko		Augustin Camus
Art Director	Ivan Akinin	**Art Buying**	Justine Bruneau
Photographer	Dmitriy Pochitalin	**Planner**	Sébastien Genty
Illustrator	Maxim Podolyanyuk	**Advertiser**	Le Mouv, "No,
Post Production	Bee Factory, Brussels		Not Everything
Advertiser	MTV "5th Anniversary		was Better Before"
	in Ukraine"		

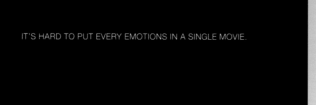

IT'S HARD TO PUT EVERY EMOTIONS IN A SINGLE MOVIE.

UGC

MORE MOVIES, MORE EMOTIONS.

Agency	TBWA\Paris	**DOP**	Laurent Tangy
Creative Directors	Philippe Simonet	**Editor**	Benjamin Favreul
	Eric Holden	**Music**	Sébastien Cortella
	Rémi Noël		La Rencontre
Copywriter	Benoit Leroux	**Sound Design**	Benoit Dunaigre
Art Director	Philippe Taroux	**Post Production**	Coralie Duarte
Production	Stink, Paris		Reepost, Paris
Director	Emma Luchini	**Account Team**	Gregoire Assemat-Tessandier
Producers	Greg Panteix		Laurence Borne
	Virginie Chalard	**Client**	Stéphanie Prince-Flandé
	Maxime Boiron	**Advertiser**	UGC, "Emotions"

A classic movie scenario: a man is reunited with the woman he loves. They look suitably moved. But then the director gets into the act. "Be more puzzled. More interrogative. More thoughtful…but friendly. Yet frightened at the same time." And so on. The actress's face becomes distorted with the effort. Even the crew get twitchy trying to keep up. When the director asks his assistant what he thinks of the scene, the man's face is a whirl of conflicting emotions. It's impossible to pack every emotion into one film. Luckily, there's a film for everyone at UGC cinemas.

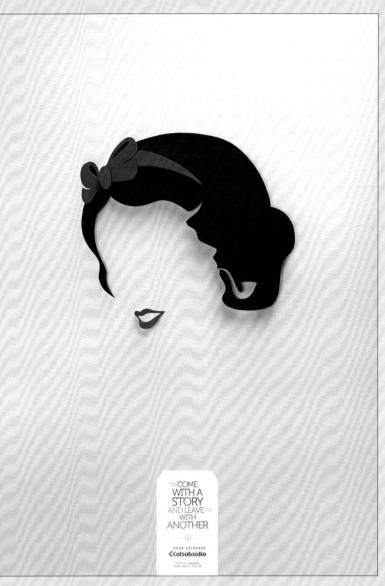

 Recreation & Leisure **181**

Agency	Lowe/SSP3, Bogotá
Creative Directors	José Miguel Sokoloff
	Gustavo Marioni
	Carlos Camacho
	Jaime Duque
Copywriter	Mario Lagos
Art Directors	Andrés Lancheros
	Sebastian Pelaez
	Guillermo Siachoque
Account Director	Carlos Obando
Advertiser	Colsubsidio Libraries, "Book Exchange"

Agency	BBDO, Toronto
Creative Directors	Peter Ignazi
	Carlos Moreno
Copywriters	Michael Clowater
	Craig McIntosh
Art Director	Linda Carte
Production	Sons & Daughters, Toronto
Director	Mark Zibert
Producers	Liane Thomas
	Andrew Sulliman
	Terry Kavanagh
DOP	Chris Mably
Editing House	PosterBoy Edit
Editor	Mark Paiva
Music/Sound	RMW Music
Visual Effects	Crush Inc.
Flame Artists	David Whiteson
	Andre Arevalo
CG Artists	Josh Clifton
	Leo Silva
Advertiser	Canadian Paralympic Committee, "Running"

One take. No special effects. Dozens of extras. And one amazing human being. In the first shot we see exertion on the face of an athlete running around a track. As he sprints around the circuit, he runs into his own past: retraining, an operation, hospital, and the accident that nearly killed him. Finally he's free of the past and running faster than ever on his prosthetic limb. Alister McQueen is "unstoppable", like all the competitors in the Paralympic Games.

182   Recreation & Leisure

Agency	Ogilvy & Mather, Vienna
Creative Director	Gerd Schulte Doeinghaus
Copywriters	Helge Haberzettl
	Karin Schalko
Art Directors	Gregor Ahman
	Michael Kaiser
Production	Balloonart, Vienna
	Sabotage Filmproduktion
Advertiser	Model Maker Fair, "Stratos Jump 1:350"

How to promote the Model Maker Fair in Vienna? Link it with the news. To be precise, daredevil Felix Baumgartner's free fall from the stratosphere. While the world waited for this frequently postponed event, the Model Maker Fair provided its own spectacular images, enacting the hair-raising adventure on a scale of 1:350 using Playmobil characters. Tiny – but still epic. YouTube viewers apparently loved the 122-metre skydive almost as much as the genuine stunt, with 8 million views in the first week. Mission accomplished.

Agency	Made by Vaculik, Bratislava
Creative Director	Dejan Galovic
Copywriter	Peter Blaho
Art Directors	Bohumil Dohnal
	Peter Hrevus
	Andrej Canecky
Production	Hitchhiker Films
Director	Roman Valent
Advertiser	Istropolitana Int'l Festival of Theater Schools, "You Must Die for It"

An aspiring young actor is auditioning on stage when the director tells him: "No! You must die for it!" The director climbs on stage to demonstrate the scene – only to die, quite literally, of a heart attack. The young actor mimics his every move, even to the point of being zipped up in a body bag and carted off in an ambulance. In the last scene we see him emerging from a graveyard, brushing earth from his shoulders and looking proud of himself. The 19th International Festival of Theatre Schools; featuring young actors who'd die for their art.

UNSTOPPABLE>>

>>PARALYMPIC.CA

Agency	BBDO, Toronto
Creative Directors	Peter Ignazi
	Carlos Moreno
Copywriter	Michael Clowater
Art Director	Linda Carte
Photographer	Mark Zibert
Digital Imaging	Jano Kirijian
CEO	Henry Storgaard
MD	Lori Davison
Account Director	Rebecca Flaman
Advertiser	Canadian Paralympic
	Committee, "Unstoppable"

Agency	Ogilvy, Frankfurt
Creative Director	Helmut Meyer
Copywriters	Lisa Reissner
	Stephan Vogel
Art Directors	Andreas Wagner
	Lisa Reissner
Photographer	Joachim Bacherl
Art Buying	Caroline Walczok
Account Mgr.	Michael Fucks
Client	Katrin Kahler
Advertiser	Matchbox,
	"Welcome Back Boy"

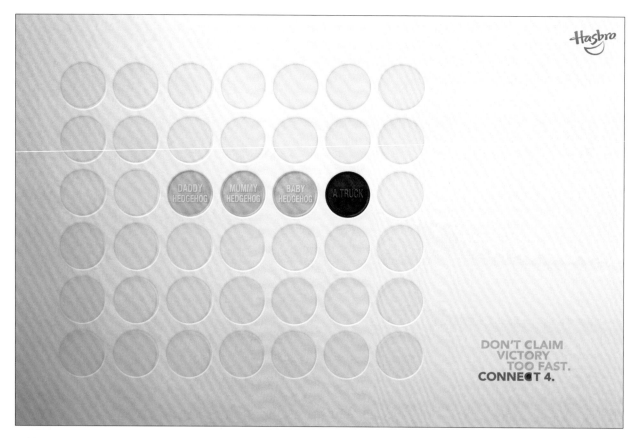

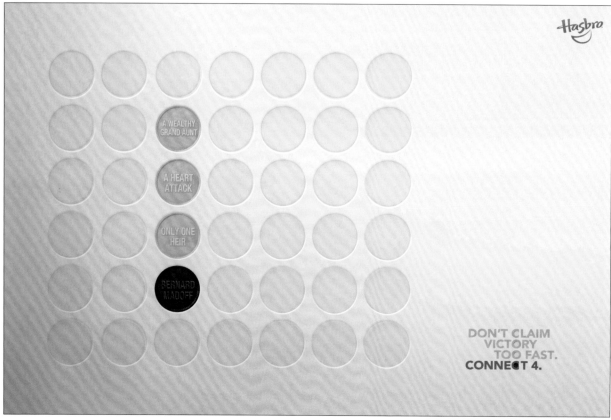

Agency	DDB, Paris
Creative Director	Alexandre Hervé
Copywriter	Jean-François Bouchet
Art Directors	Jessica Gerard-Durel
	Anaïs Bauser
Advertiser	Connect 4

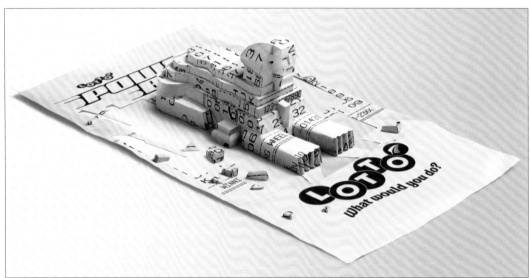

Agency	DDB Group, Auckland
Executive CDs	Andy Fackrell
	Toby Talbot
Creative Director	Regan Grafton
Copywriter	Simone Louis
Art Directors	Brett Colliver
	Scott Maddox
	Toby Morris
Photographer	Steve Boniface
Producer	Andy Robilliard
Retouching	Gordon Moir
Designer	Philip Fickling
Advertiser	Lotto, "Ticket to Dream"

186   **Recreation & Leisure**

Agency	TBWA\España, Madrid
Creative Directors	Juan Sánchez
	Guillermo Ginés
	Vicente Rodríguez
Copywriter	Vicente Rodríguez
Art Director	Fran López
Photographer	Jesús Alonso
Graphic Design	Digital Art Studio
Advertiser	Sony PlayStation

Agency	DDB Group, Hong Kong		**Agency**	DDB, Paris
Creative Directors	Jeffry Gamble		**Executive CD**	Alexandre Hervé
	Ong Shi Ping		**Copywriter**	Pierre-Antoine Dupin
	Paul Chan		**Art Director**	Frédéric Lahache
	Asawin Phanichwatana		**Photographer**	Roberto Badin
Copywriters	Jeffry Gamble		**Illustrator**	Alexis Taieb
	Paul Chan			Tyrsa, Paris
Art Directors	Asawin Phanichwatana		**Typographer**	Alexis Taieb
	Ciff Luk			Tyrsa, Paris
Illustrators	Surachai Puthikulangkura		**Advertiser**	Playskool,
	Supachai U-Rairat			"60 Years Couple"
Producer	Annie Tong			
Advertiser	Westone, "Tunnel"			

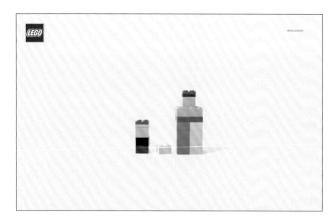

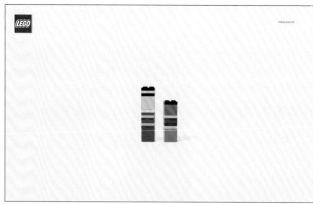

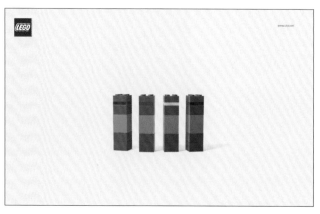

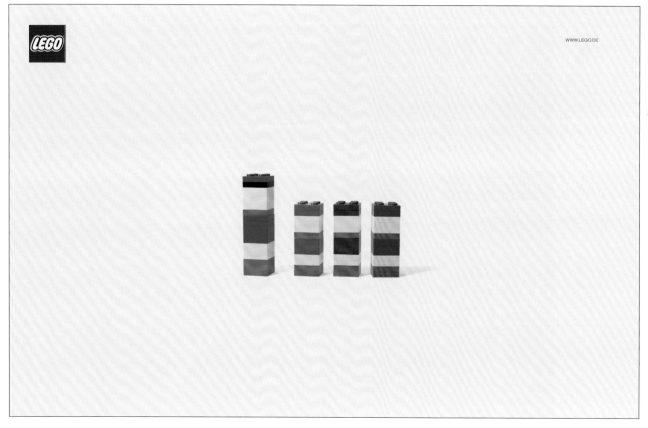

188   **Recreation & Leisure**

Agency	Jung von Matt, Hamburg	**Digital Artwork**	Matthias Christen
			Florian von Behr
CCO	Deneke von Weltzien		Faruk Heplevent
Creative Director	Karsten Ruddigkeit		The Scope Digital Studio
Copywriters	Johannes Milhoffer	**Producers**	Christian Will
	Corinna Ernst		Thomas Thiessen
Art Director	Reza Ramezani	**Account Mgr.**	Marc-Olaf Duncker
Graphic Design	Julian Lebel	**Client**	Katharina Sutch
	Daniel Zier	**Advertiser**	Lego

Agency	Grey, Paris
Creative Directors	Stephen Eynard
	Thierry Astier
Copywriters	Jean-Francois Le Marec
	Dimitri Hekimian
Art Directors	Laetitia Chretien
	Quentin Deronzier
Photographer	Franck Malthiery
Art Buying	Catherine Jarno
Advertiser	Lego, "Creativity
	Forgives Everything"

Agency	Havas Worldwide, Paris	On a blackboard, animated chalk words recount the most important events of 2011. They include Tunisia ablaze, Egypt collapsing, Fukushima fracturing, bombs falling on Libya, William and Kate's wedding, sainthood for Pope John Paul II, death for Bin Laden, shootings in Oslo, riots in the UK, the arrest of Dominique Strauss-Khan, the shattered Greek economy and the passing of Steve Jobs. "Fortunately, at the end it's always the same. Happy New Year 2012." The film is Euro RSCG's virtual greetings card, before the agency became Havas Worldwide.
Creative Director	Christophe Coffre	
Copywriter	Guillaume Blanc	
Art Director	Florian Roussel	
Production	Wizz, Paris	
Director	No Brushing	
Producers	François Brun	
	Isabelle Darroman	
Music	Sy Davis	
	Matthieu Sibony	
	Ultra Schmooze	
Advertiser	Euro RSCG C&O,	
	"Best Wishes 2012"	

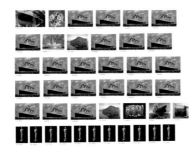

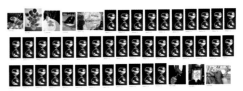

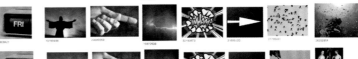

Agency	Ogilvy, Frankfurt	**Art Buying**	Valerie Opitz
CCO	Stephan Vogel	**Account Team**	Yves Rosengart
Creative Directors	Helmut Meyer		Eva Hoffmann
	Nico Ammann		Nadine Ries
Copywriter	Stephan Vogel	**Clients**	Edith Stier-Thompson
Art Director	Helmut Meyer		Gunilla Graudins
Photography	Picture Alliance	**Advertiser**	Picture Alliance,
Graphic Design	Joachim Becker		"All You Need
			to Tell the Story"
			Campaign

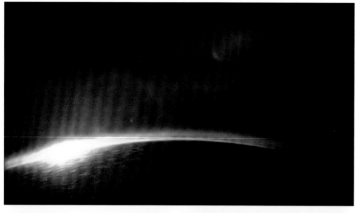

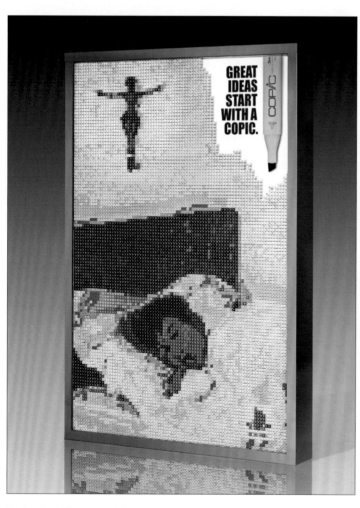

192   **Professional Products & Services**

Agency	BETC, London	The surface of a dark planet. A bright orange light suffuses the horizon. But this is no sunrise – as dramatic music swells, we see jets of flame exploding from the planet's surface. Soon it is entirely ablaze, consumed by fire. The camera pulls back and we realise we've been fooled: the "planet" is the head of a match being struck, magnified many times. Movies make everything look extraordinary, says cinema advertising sales house Pearl & Dean.
Creative Director	Neil Dawson	
Copywriter	Clive Pickering	
Art Director	Neil Dawson	
Production	MJZ, London	
Director	Stephen Johnson	
Producer	Debbie Turner	
Advertiser	Pearl & Dean, "Doomed Planet"	

Agencies	BBDO Proximity, Hamburg & Düsseldorf	**Producers**	Bernhard Burg
CCO	Wolfgang Schneider		Tobias Brockamp
Executive CDs	Volker Waesch		Tim Tibor
	Carsten Bolk	**Post Production**	NHB Video, Hamburg
Creative Directors	Detlef Rump	**Account Team**	Eva Sieweke
	Christian Mommertz		Kian Ghanai
Copywriter	Daniel Hoffmann	**Advertiser**	Copic Marker,
Art Directors	Christian Weigel		"Great Ideas
	Caner Ergel		Start With a Copic"

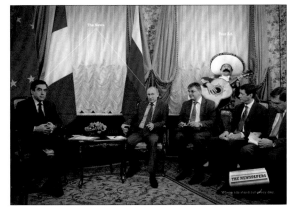

Professional Products & Services   193

Agency	Ogilvy, Frankfurt
CCO	Stephan Vogel
Creative Director	Helmut Meyer
Copywriter	Lothar Mueller
Art Director	Till Schaffarczyk
Photographer	Norman Konrad
Graphic Design	Peter Belz
	Christian Kuzman
Art Buying	Magdalena Ignatowski
Retouching	Paul Schaefer
Account Mgt.	Michael Fucks
Client	Joachim Donnerstag
Advertiser	ZMG, "Eyecatcher" Campaign

194	**Professional Products & Services**

Agency	Spillmann/Felser/
	Leo Burnett, Zurich
Creative Directors	Peter Brönnimann
	Johannes Raggio
	Pablo Schencke
Copywriters	Johannes Raggio
	Diana Rossi
Art Director	Pablo Schencke
Production	Cobblestone, Hamburg
Director	Axel Laubscher
Producer	Suzana Kovacevic
Advertiser	Migros Klubschule,
	"600 Courses"

Since the Migros Klubschule offers more than 600 part time courses, you can learn almost anything. This can come in handy in unlikely situations. For instance, a woman cashier being held at gunpoint at the bank calls on her "project management" and "Excel" skills to check how much money is available. Then she advises the robber to "relax – inhale…exhale" (Hatha Yoga). She tells her terrified colleagues: "Try to think of something pleasant." (Autogenic Training.) Finally, she compliments the robber on his balaclava: "Alpaca?" (Knitting.)

Agency	Alma DDB, Miami
Creative Directors	Luis Miguel Messianu
	Diego Yurkievich
	Hernan Cerdeiro
Copywriter	Julián Milanesi
Art Director	Hernan Pettinaroli
Photographer	Michael Bailey
Advertiser	Rosetta Stone
	Language School,
	"It's Time to
	Think in English"

Professional Products & Services **195**

Agency	Wire Advertising, Hamburg
Creative Directors	Horst Maus
	Peter Jooss
Copywriter	Philippe Struebbe
Art Director	Till Fischer
Photographer	Marius Wolfram
Digital Artwork	Pedro Rodriguez
Client Service	Annette Verbeek
Advertiser	Der Spiegel, "Placements that Work"

196 **Professional Products & Services**

Agency	Volt, Stockholm	Agency	Instinct, Moscow
Copywriter	Petter Nylind	Creative Directors	Roman Firainer
Art Directors	Karl Andersson		Yaroslav Orlov
	Stefan Lindros	Copywriter	Maksim Artemenko
Photographer	Sven Prim	Art Director	Artem Kostenko
Digital Artwork	Sven Prim	Production	Salamagica Studio
Final Art	Tina Andblad	Account Director	Irina Gornova
Account Team	Nils Odelius	Client	Alexei Kurakin
	Rebecca Sellei	Advertiser	Job.ru,
Advertiser	Scania Trucks,		"Clerk" & "Chéf"
	"The Evolution		
	of Mining"		

From scratch to masterpiece. **shutterst⊙ck**

From scratch to masterpiece. **shutterst⊙ck**

We look forward to developing permanently clean surfaces for you.

We can protect ships' hulls from biofouling, and much more besides. We are the creative surface specialists for industrial coatings, architectural coatings, printing inks and automotive needs. Which problem would you like us to solve for you?

Evonik. Power to create.

⊙ EVONIK
INDUSTRIES

Agency	Plan.Net, Paris	Agency	KNSK, Hamburg
Creative Director	Peter De Meurichy	Creative Directors	Vera Hampe
Copywriter	Nicolas Richard		Olaf Hörning
Art Director	Evelyne Erviti	Copywriter	Dirk Junski
Agency Director	Olivier Bronner	Art Directors	Martin Augner
Post Production	Poisson Rouge		Caroline Labitzke
Photography	Shutterstock	Photographer	Günther Philipp
Graphic Design	Evelyne Erviti	Account Team	Verena Gillwald
Account Director	Livia Posteuca		Hanna Petersen
Client	Sébastien Beysson	Advertiser	Evonik Plastics &
Advertiser	Shutterstock,		Coatings
	"From Scratch		
	to Masterpiece"		

Overactive Bladder.
Are the side-effects
as disagreeable as
the condition?

Constipation can be a disagreeable
anticholinergic side-effect.

Kentera patches have a 3.9% incidence
of constipation. What's more, they are
as effective as the first-line overactive
bladder (OAB) treatment.

KENTERA®
oxybutynin transdermal patch
Patient-friendly OAB control

managingOAB.co.uk

Overactive Bladder.
Are the side-effects
as intolerable as
the condition?

Dry mouth can be an intolerable
anticholinergic side-effect.

Kentera patches have an 8.6%
incidence of dry mouth. What's more,
they are as effective as the first-line
overactive bladder (OAB) treatment.

KENTERA®
oxybutynin transdermal patch
Patient-friendly OAB control

managingOAB.co.uk

198   **Prescription Products & Services**

Agency	Langland, Windsor
Creative Director	Andrew Spurgeon
Copywriter	Sue Blitz
Art Director	Andrew Morley
Photographer	Alex Telfer
Advertiser	Kentera, "Unwanted Side-Effects"

Prescription Products & Services   **199**

Agency	Spillmann/Felser/
	Leo Burnett, Zurich
Creative Director	Peter Brönnimann
Copywriter	Reto Vogler
Art Director	Roland Buob
Digital Artwork	Felix Schregenberger
Advertiser	Sanello, "Expertise"

200   **Prescription Products & Services**

Agency	Rocky Advertising, Helsinki		Agency	inVentiv Health Communications, London
Copywriters	Vesa Hyypiä Heikki Kärkkäinen		CCO Europe	Peter Comber
			CD/Copywriter	Richard Rayment
Art Directors	Jarkko Toijonen Aslak Bredenberg		Art Directors	Stavros Panayi John Timney
Photographer	Marko Rantanen		Illustration	Empereous
Illustrator	Fake Graphics, Helsinki		Typographer	Stavros Panayi
			Studio Team	Andy Haughton Louise Davies
Advertiser	Norspan,"Tattoo"		Advertiser	Listerine Advanced Defence Sensitive, "Cement Mixers"

It pays to trust – we turn your pharmaceutical problems into solutions.

Real problems, real answers. We at Evonik are better equipped to meet the pharmaceutical challenges you face because we understand them better than anyone else. If you'd like to know more good reasons why your problems are in excellent hands with us, go to **www.evonik.com/pharma**.

Evonik. Power to create.

EVONIK
INDUSTRIES

We make sure your active ingredient gets into the tablet.

Real problems, real answers. When it comes to taking care of the little things that make a big difference, such as formulating liquid APIs into tablets without gumming up the press, we've got just the right touch. If you'd like to know more good reasons for a solution partnership with us, go to **www.evonik.com/pharma**.

Evonik. Power to create.

EVONIK
INDUSTRIES

Prescription Products & Services   **201**

Agency	KNSK, Hamburg
Creative Directors	Vera Hampe
	Olaf Hörning
Copywriter	Dirk Junski
Art Directors	Martin Augner
	Caroline Labitzke
Photographer	Arthur Mebius
Account Team	Verena Gillwald
	Hanna Petersen
Advertiser	Evonik Pharma

202 **Corporate Image**

Agencies	Marcel, Paris	
	Publicis Conseil, Paris	
	Wam, Paris	
Production	Quad Productions,	
	Clichy	
Director	Bruno Aveillan	
Producer	Martin Coulais	
DOP	Patrick Duroux	
Soundtrack	Pierre Adenot	
Post Production	Digital District	
Advertiser	Cartier,	
	"Cartier Odyssey"	

Cartier launched this spectacular film to celebrate its 165th anniversary. Swooping into the luxury brand's Paris flagship store, we see its emblem – a jewelled panther – springing to life. In a series of magical vignettes, the panther travels around the world, visiting places where the brand is admired. First to an icy Russia, then across mountains to the Great Wall of China – where he is greeted by a gold dragon – and on to India, where he hitches a ride on an elephant. Next he leaps onto a vintage flying machine which whisks him back to Paris.

Volkswagen.
Surrounded by safety.

Das Auto.

Volkswagen.
Surrounded by safety.

Das Auto.

Corporate Image   **203**

Agency	Try/Apt, Oslo
Copywriter	Petter Bryde
Art Director	Thorbjørn Ruud
Photographer	Sigve Asplund
Designer	Thomas Bråten
Account Team	Morten Polmar
	Cathrine Wennersten
Advertiser	Volkswagen,
	"Safety Innovation"

Agency	TBWA\Stockholm
Creative Director	Kalle Widgren
Copywriter	Kalle Håkanson
Art Director	Arvid Wennel
Production	Bacon, Copenhagen
Director	Martin Werner
Producer	Mette Jermiin
Planner	Håkan Engler
Account Team	Robert Schelin
	Ulrika Sörensen
Advertiser	Svensk Fjärrvärme
	District Heating,
	"The Robot"

District Heating turns recycled waste into heat. The idea is illustrated by this charming tale about a little girl who spots an old plastic robot in an antique store. "Space attack," he bleats, weakly. The girl feels sorry for him, but her mother pulls her away. Soon the robot is thrown into the trash, even as the little girl wistfully draws a picture of him. One night she notices the plastic knob of her radiator winking at her with glowing green eyes. "Space attack?" she asks. Nothing goes to waste.

204   Corporate Image

Agency	Leo Burnett, London
Creative Director	Justin Tindall
Copywriters & ADs	Mark Franklin
	Rob Tenconi
Production	Moxie Pictures, London
Directors	Neil Gorringe
	Luke Franklin
Producers	Pheobe Matheson
	Graeme Light
Advertiser	McDonald's,
	"We All Make
	the Games"

Olympics sponsor McDonald's pays homage to the people who make the Games a success. Most of them are not athletes, but normal folk who watch or contribute in some way. So we meet "the journeyers, the jostlers, the anticipators… the cheerful greeters". Not to mention "the wiggler, the waver and the 'what's this all abouter?'". The poetic script adds emotion to real-life crowd scenes shot during the Games. We all make the Games.

Production	Edithouse Film Works,
	Gothenburg
Advertiser	Volvo Group,
	"Shaping Another Future"

"Business without caring is business without a future," observes the narrator, as we see budding leaves, soaring birds and undersea scenes, all rendered in cut out paper. In each scene, a Volvo transport solution is present. A Volvo bus takes kids to school, construction vehicles build the city of tomorrow, trucks deliver food and products to far-off places. The film establishes Volvo's position as a world leader in sustainable transport. "Together, we can move the world."

Some stars show you the way.
Muhammad Ali and a rising star. Phoenix, Arizona.

Follow him on louisvuittonjourneys.com/thegreatest

LOUIS VUITTON

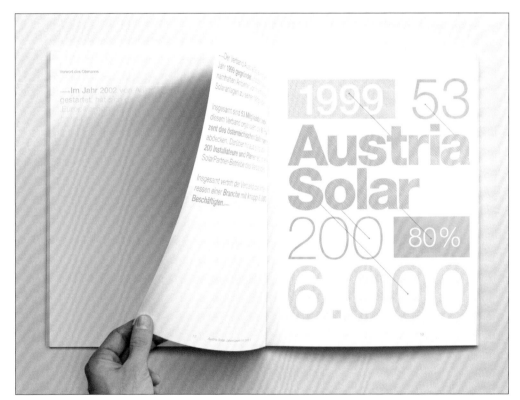

Agency	Ogilvy France, Paris	**Agency**	Serviceplan, Munich	Austria Solar is an association of companies that provide solar heating. So what better way of presenting its annual report than as a document that reacts to sunlight? The pages remain blank until they're exposed to the sun, at which point the text slowly appears. After two to three minutes without sunlight, the words fade again. The report was sent to association members, potential clients, journalists and opinion leaders. With an instruction: "Best read outside in daylight."
CCO	Chris Garbutt	**CCO**	Alexander Schill	
Creative Directors	Grant Parker	**Creative Directors**	Christoph Everke	
	Christian Reuilly		Cosimo Moeller	
Copywriters	Pierre Clavaud		Alexander Nagel	
	Andrew Jolliffe	**Copywriter**	Moritz Dornig	
Art Director	Grant Parker	**Art Director**	Matthaeus Frost	
Photographer	Annie Lebovitz	**Graphic Design**	Mathias Noesel	
Art Buying	Laurence Nahmias	**Producer**	Melanie Dienemann	
Account Mgr.	Samuel Giblin	**Printshop**	Mory & Meier, Munich	
Advertiser	Louis Vuitton, "Ali"	**Bookbinder**	Buchbinderei Ruffert	
		Advertiser	Verband Austria Solar,	
			"The Solar Annual Report"	

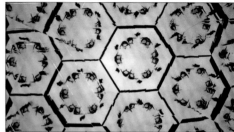

Many years ago, a truck fell off this road...

Knowing this can be a little scary

YOU'RE IN.
YA ESTÁS PREPARADO.

Agency	We Are Pi, Amsterdam	The TEDx Summit in Doha was a
Creative Directors	Rick Chant	week-long event combining a TED Talks
	Barney Hobson	opening night and meetings between 700
Production	Big Production, Paris	TED organisers from 120 countries. For
Producers	Jamie Nami Kim,	this promotional online film the agency
	Raphaël Carassic	created an eight meter high mirrored
Photographer	Koerner Union	structure suspended over a multi-colour-
DOP	Laurent Tangy	ed moving floor. Perfectly choreographed
Editor	Matthilde Carlier	dancers were added to create a kaleido-
Post Production	Mikros Image	scope of arabesque patterns with an X
Music	Yasmine Hamdan	shape at its core. Arabic singer Yasmine
Sound Design	Wave, Amsterdam	Hamdan contributed the soundtrack.
Advertiser	TEDx "Human Arabesque"	TED to the power of X.

Agency	Crispin Porter + Bogusky,	A vertiginous road snakes across a moun-
	Gothenburg	tainside. A large truck crawls along the
CCO	Rob Reilly	narrow, crumbling surface, its rear wheels
Executive CDs	Gustav Martner	often hanging over the sheer drop at the
	Bjorn Hoglund	edge. Leading truck builder Scania hosts
Creative Director	Mattias Berg	an annual competition to find the world's
Copywriter	Jim Connolly	most skilled truck drivers. To promote the
Art Director	Mattias Berg	event, it shot this man's journey along the
Post Production	Jorgen Bengtsson	perilous Balsas road in Peru. The driver
Producer	Cecilia Svard	explains to us that extreme concentration
DOP	Paul Blomgren	is needed here, not to mention "cojones".
Editor	Erika Gonzales	A sign at the side of the road tells him that
Advertiser	Scania, "Driver Competitions"	he qualifies for the contest: "You're in."

Brother,
I am the keeper
of a thousand trees
in every direction. Pray
do not try to pass through
here. Because if you do, I shall
ply this stick to your skull with such
flair that your head will sing for a week
with the clamour of consonants. Do not start
the car, brother. Okay, fine. You may pass but do
not dare presume to peek at my ladyfolk.

Child,
I've been watching with curiosity for
hours as you slowly crept towards me.
I now see that which you plan. Let me
dissuade you from this foolhardiness.
I'm not some dirt mound that you may
trifle with. I was born when the mighty
lips of continents sighed and slobbered
over each other. I have seen stars being
rubbed out of existence. You and your
contraption shall go no further. Damn
your insolence, child. That tickles.

Sir,
You are most sincerely mistaken.
There will be no crossing here. My bank
will offer no path and my bed no purchase.
I plan to sweep you away and drown you, sir.
Your flimsy hopes will be dashed against the
jagged teeth of my rocks. You shall ooze, sir.
Small fish will feed on your body's secrets.
Turn back in that vehicle of yours and
go around me. How preposterous!
Sir, I can feel you dancing
on my spine.

Corporate Image 207

Agency	Y&R, Dubai	**Digital Artwork**	Shahir Zag
Creative Directors	Shahir Zag		Kalpesh Patankar
	Kalpesh Patankar	**Production**	Amin Soltani
Copywriter	Shahir Zag	**Account Directors**	Sarah Locke
Art Director	Kalpesh Patankar		Pierre Farra
Illustrator	Gitten Tom	**Client**	Jean Atik
Graphic Design	Shahir Zag	**Advertiser**	Land Rover,
	Kalpesh Patankar		"Monologues"
Typographers	Shahir Zag		
	Kalpesh Patankar		

Corporate Image

Agency	Selmore, Amsterdam
Copywriter	Niels Westra
Art Director	Jakko Achterberg
Designer	Raphael Bartels
Advertiser	Selmore, "Thank You for Visiting Selmore" Bags

Amsterdam creative agency Selmore is actually named after a small American town in the state of Missouri. To thank its clients for "shopping" at Selmore, the agency created a series of cheeky shopping bags to take work home in and promote the agency at the same time.

Agency	Hypermedia, Warsaw
Creative Director	Maciej Nowicki
Copywriter	Jan Cieślar
Art Director	Krzysztof Jagiełо
Advertiser	PolskieRadio.pl, "Touch the Sound"

3D printing can turn the sound wave patterns generated by human speech into a sculpture. This proved an ideal way of promoting Polski-eRadio.pl, an online portal with a huge archive of radio recordings. From the Polish Second World War poem "We Demand Ammunition" to Martin Luther King's "I had a dream", famous speeches were transformed into sound wave sculptures and put on display in a temporary exhibit. An interactive banner and a Facebook app that let people vote on their favourite re-cordings from the 20th century.

The evidence for intelligent life on earth. [edit]

Wikipedia for world heritage!
Sign the petition on wikipedia.de/wke 🖉

Knowledge is power to the people. [edit]

Wikipedia for world heritage!
Sign the petition on wikipedia.de/wke 🖉

5.500 answers per second. Any questions? [edit]

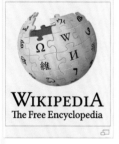

Wikipedia for world heritage!
Sign the petition on wikipedia.de/wke 🖉

Free knowledge to all. Media couldn't be more social. [edit]

Wikipedia for world heritage!
Sign the petition on wikipedia.de/wke 🖉

Agency   Leo Burnett, Frankfurt
CCO   Andreas Pauli
Creative Directors   Axel Tischer
   Hans-Juergen Kaemmerer
Copywriter   Axel Tischer
Art Director   Marcel Guenthel
Advertiser   Wikipedia, "Knowledge"

210 **Corporate Image**

Agency	Heimat, Berlin	**Producers**	Jessica Valin	At the Berlin Marathon in 2012, Adidas
Creative Directors	Ove Gley		Flo Hoffmann	built five 3D posters at different stages of
	Ole Vinck	**Clients**	Martin Schindler	the event. Cut-out silhouettes of marathon
Copywriter	Dominik Maass		Daniela Tomac	runners contained an artistic interpretation of
Art Director	Patrick Düver	**Advertiser**	Adidas,	participants' feelings at key points along the
Photographer	Olaf Heine		"The Five Stages	route: excitement (km 3), with a ticker tape
Illustrator	Klub 7		of a Marathon"	send-off; flow (km 12), with the sounds of a
Graphic Design	Lucas Schneider			DJ pumped through multi-coloured amplifi-
	Franziska Kriehn			ers; euphoria (km 22) with a vivid abstract

At the Berlin Marathon in 2012, Adidas built five 3D posters at different stages of the event. Cut-out silhouettes of marathon runners contained an artistic interpretation of participants' feelings at key points along the route: excitement (km 3), with a ticker tape send-off; flow (km 12), with the sounds of a DJ pumped through multi-coloured amplifiers; euphoria (km 22) with a vivid abstract artwork; pain (km 38), with sparks flying from circular saws; and finally celebration (km 42), which took the form of live drumming and dancing on a stage within the poster.

Agency	JVD/Jacobson Vellinga Design, Stockholm	**Account Mgr.**	Johan Johansson Xlent Strategy, Stockholm	Revent makes ovens for professional bakers. Not very sexy, you might think. But think again. Revent and its agency created the concept "In bread we trust" to demonstrate its passion for baking and for bread. Featuring hip and, yes, sexy young bakers, the campaign trans-formed well known proverbs to pay homage to the beauty of bread: "Blood, sweat and baguettes"; "Make ciabatta, not war", and so on. Revent has even launched the world's first bread finding app, BreadSeeker, which tells you the location of the nearest bakery, café or pastry shop, anywhere in the world!	
Creative Directors	John Jacobson Johan Johansson Olle Nordell	**Final Art** **Production**	Annica Vellinga Five Star Day, Malmö Wigardt Media, Stockholm Dohrns, Stockholm		
Copywriter	Olle Nordell				
Art Director	John Jacobson	**Advertiser**	Revent Baking Equipment, "In Bread We Trust"		
Photographer	Stefan Frank Jensen				

SFX of door being opened. Man starts getting euphoric:
She's coming! Oh! Oh! Oh! Oh!

Woman:
Brian, honey, I'm home...

Man, very excited:
OOOOOhhhh... Hi! Hello, Honey!! Hello, hello!!
It's so good to see you! So good!!
Here, put down your bag, put down your keys!
Now gime a hug! Gimme a hug! Gimme a Hug!

Woman, surprised by his reaction:
Ok, Calm down, honey, here's a hug.

Man continues in a very excited way:
I missed you so much!! So much!! I couldn't wait for you to get home!
I've been thinking about it all day, I've been waiting here,
I couldn't wait for you to get home, but now you're here!!
Hug me! Hug me! Hug me! Quick! Wait right here, I have to pee!

ANNCR:
No one loves you that much. Except your dog...

Man, still excited:
Gimme a hug!!!!

ANNCR:
Purina. Return the love.

A little girl says to her mum:
Mum, can we go to the park?

The mum starts getting euphoric.
That park nearby? That we can walk to?

Girl:
Yep...

Mother speaks in a very excited and fast way:
Ohh! You're the best, you're the best! I just love that park!
Love it! Love it! It's got trees! It's got grass! It's got a drinking fountain!
I can't believe it! I can't believe you wanna go like, like now, right?
You wanna go now, right? Say yes!

Girl:
Humm yes

Mother, almost screaming with happiness:
Thank you!!!! Big hug!

SFX: The mother gives her a tight hug.

Girl:
You're squashing me...

Mother keeps talking in a very excited way:
Let me get my bag. Ohh! Let me get my coat, I'll meet you by the door!
I'm over here by the door, can you see me? I was by the door and you
weren't there! I can't belive we are going to the
park! Thank you, thank you, thank you!

ANNCR:
No one loves you that much. Except your dog...

Mother, still excited:
We're going to the park!

ANNCR:
Purina. Return the love.

Agency	Publicis Brasil, Sao Paulo
Worldwide CD	Erik Vervroegen
Creative Director	Hugo Rodrigues
Copywriter	Luis Felipe Figueiredo
Art Director	Antonio Correa
Production	Bar1, New York
Director	Joe Barone
Audio Engineer	Tim Leitner
Advertiser	Purina, "Only a Dog" Campaign

MVO:
In Season 2 of HBO's Eastbound & Down, Kenny Powers lives like an outlaw in Mexico. You could buy the show, or you could try to experience it for yourself by driving to Mexico and trying to become an outlaw.

First you have to prove you're tough. Prison yard rules say find the biggest guy and drop him.

You find the grittiest cantina, walk in and relieve yourself on the bar.

Now, who wants to dance?

SFX: the man is punched and hits the floor.

It feels like you were only out for a second, but now you are wearing a studded dog collar and fishnets.

You are handcuffed to a chain linked fence on La Calma Avenue. They charge tourists two pesos to take photos with you... One peso for locals. And tonight, La Calma is unusually busy.

Why not leave kicking ass to Kenny, and buy HBO's Eastbound & Down Season 2 on DVD, Blu-ray or digital download.

MVO:
In Season 2 of HBO's Eastbound & Down, Kenny Powers goes to Mexico and becomes a cock fighter. You could buy the show, or you could go to Mexico and try and experience being a cock fighter yourself.

First order of business, find a fight. There, you put everything down on one bet. It's out of character for you, but you're being like Kenny, remember?

You pop open a malt beverage and scream with adulation like the other fans. Andale. Kill him. Andale.

Within minutes, the fight is busted up by federales.

All your money is on the blue-green cock, Señor Panchos, so you have no cash to bribe the corrupt cops.

Faster than you can say, "I shouldn't have bet everything on Señor Panchos," you've landed in Mexican prison.

The only difference between American prison and Mexican prison, is when they do horrible things to you, they speak Spanish.

No, it's better you watch Kenny do it from a safe distance. Buy HBO's Eastbound & Down Season 2 on DVD, Blu-ray, or digital download.

ANNCR:
Francis Lee is 75 years old today 75 years ago he was...

Young mom:
Francis, my dearest baby boy!

ANNCR:
60 years ago he became...

School head:
Mr. Francis Lee, Class Valedictorian!

ANNCR:
50 years ago he became...

Law firm boss:
Attorney Francis Lee, gentlemen, our new partner.

ANNCR:
45 years ago he became...

Wife:
Frankie, Honey, I vow to love you forever.

ANNCR:
40 years ago he became...

Son:
Daddy! I've got a star in math!

ANNCR:
10 years ago he became...

Grandchild:
Grandpa, we'll visit next week!

ANNCR:
5 years ago he became...

Nursing home staff:
Stupid old man in ward 4! Peed in his bed again!

ANNCR:
The elderly lose more than their youth.
They lose their dignity.
Let us remember to honour them and help ensure that they live the rest of their lives with dignity.
Because one day, we will all grow old too.

Reach out to the elderly.
Visit www.apex.org.sg

Agency	BBDO, New York
CCO	David Lubars
Executive CDs	Greg Hahn
	Mike Smith
Creative Director	Chris Beresford-Hill
Copywriter	Chris Beresford-Hill
Production	Bar1, New York
Producer	Chris Cassar
Sound Engineer	Tim Leitner
Advertiser	HBO, "Eastbound & Down"

Agency	Leo Burnett Group, Singapore
Creative Director	Chris Chiu
Copywriters	Sheila Dela Cuesta
	Mike Dela Cuesta
Art Director	Mike Dela Cuesta
Production	The Gunnery, Singapore
Advertiser	APEX Clubs of Singapore, "Somebody RC60s"

We hear a man talking fast, without any pauses and without breathing. He talks with an extremely high voice and keeps the same tone throughout:

Hello hello can anybody hear me of course you can because I'm ringing in your ear my name is Tinnitus but my friends just call me Tinny at least they would if I had any but it's hard to have friends when you're an annoying hearing condition like a tiny little torture I just get inside your head and then I talk and talk and talk and talk and talk and talk and talk until you want to pull your ears off and throw them out a window but don't try that because it actually won't help in fact a much better thing to do would be to go online to earringing.de and check out Akustika Spezial in Frankfurt because they're your best bet to find a way to shut – me – up.

After about two seconds of silence we hear a VO in a normal and calm voice:
To hear silence again, visit www.earringing.de

Agency	Leo Burnett, Frankfurt
CCO	Andreas Pauli
Creative Directors	Andreas Stalder
	Ulf Henniger von Wallersbrunn
	John Wilson
Copywriter	Mark-Marcel Mueller
Production	A.R.T. Studios, Frankfurt
Account Director	Carolin Boettcher
Advertiser	Akustika Spezial, "Tini"

MVO:
Welcome to the first official application procedure of the University of Music Hanover. We are searching for students with an absolute pitch. If you can hear that this

(Piano SFX: the note A)

is an A, and this

(Piano SFX: the note C)

is a C, then we are looking forward to receiving an email from you. Just send it to

(Piano SFX: the notes C-H-E-F)

at hmtm-hannover dot

(Piano SFX: the notes D-E).

Once again, so you can write it down:

(Piano SFX: the notes C-H-E-F)

 at hmtm-hannover dot

(Piano SFX: the notes D-E).

SFX: telephone ring-back tone

Nils Gugl:
Gugl! *(a common Austrian name, sounds like 'Google')*

Caller: Yes, I'd need a route please. Prison Stein to Vienna airport, international terminal. Quickest route please.

Nils Gugl: From where?

Caller: Stein, correctional facility. I'm in a hurry.

Nils Gugl, mumbling and typing: Who am I talking to please?

Caller: I can't tell you. I'll tell you in a minute.

Nils Gugl: Why can't you tell me?

Caller: For your own good. I don't want to drag you into this.

Nils Gugl: Pardon?

Caller: Nothing just really quickly, the basic instructions. Where do I start?

Nils Gugl: But, but I can't tell you the whole route.

Caller: Just quickly, how many kilometres? Quick!

Nils Gugl: 106 km.

Caller: 106 kilometres! I'll need a car for that! Please look up 'steal car' 'hotwire'.

SFX: Hanging up, busy tone

Off: Google on your mobile?

Agency	Ogilvy, Frankfurt
CCO	Stephan Vogel
Creative Director	Matthias Storath
Copywriter	Manuel Rentz
Production	Studio Funk, Berlin
Producers	Stephan Moritz
	Andy Schlegel
Account Team	Michael Fucks
	Sophie Gudat
Client	Melanie Bertram
Advertiser	HMTM Hannover,
	"The Absolute Pitch"

In German the musical scale goes C, D, E, F, G, A & H. So this encoded message spells out: chef@hmtm-hannover.de (with "chef" meaning "boss").

Agency	Demner, Merlicek &
	Bergmann, Vienna
Creative Directors	Francesco Bestagno
	Alexander Hofmann
Copywriters	Alexander Hofmann
	Isabelle Stadler
	Werner Buehringer
Sound Studio	Tic Music
Producer	Evelyn Berghold
Account Team	Christin Herrnberger
	Christian Ertl
	Tuende Kiss
Advertiser	A1 Telekom, "Google"

SFX: The music for a Renault ad begins

Female voice:
The Renault Clio with interior styling…

SFX: music for a Dacia ad

Male voice:
The Dacia Duster, a 4x4 that…

Woman:
Excuse me, but I was here first.

Man:
Yeah? Whatever, I reserved this spot before you sweetheart.

Woman:
And they say chivalry is dead.

Man:
I think it killed itself when it saw you coming.

Woman:
Funny.

Man:
Women selling cars *(He imitates her)* Renault Cliooo…

Woman:
 I do not sound like that!

Man:
Let me show you how it's done sugar *(then begins to read his script again)*
The Dacia Duster, a 4x4 that…

Woman:
The Dacia Duster, blah blah blah.

Man:
Grow up!

Woman:
You grow up!

Man:
Go bleach your mustache!

Woman:
At least I have one.

Man:
I've got one!

MVO (calm):
Remember, March 22nd is Road Courtesy Day.
Supported by the Renault group.

Woman:
Why don't you ask for directions because this isn't your commercial!

SFX: The music for a Renault ad begins

Female voice:
The Renault Clio, with interior styling's…

SFX: music for a Dacia ad

Male voice:
The Dacia Duster, a 4x4 with the power…

Woman:
Oh, hello.

Man:
I'm sorry, did I cut you off?

Woman:
No, that's all right please go ahead.

Man:
No, you were here before me.

Woman:
Now, I clearly side swiped you.

Man:
Nope, ladies first…

Woman:
No, I insist.

Man:
All right.

Both together:
The Renault Clio/ The Dacia Duster.

Man:
We just can't seem to get this thing right.

Woman:
Go ahead, there's only a couple seconds left.

They start again at the same time

Woman:
Renault Clio…

Man:
The Dacia Dust…

Laughter

MVO: Today is Road Courtesy Day, supported by the Renault group.

Man:
You have the right of way.

Agency	Publicis, Brussels
Worldwide CD	Erik Vervroegen
Associate CDs	Tom Berth
	Geert De Rocker
Creative Directors	Paul Servaes
	Alain Janssens
Copywriters	Wim Corremans
	Alex Gabriëls
Production	Bar1, New York
Producer	Katie Kelly
Sound Engineer	Joe Barone
Advertiser	Renault/Dacia,
	"Courtesy Day"

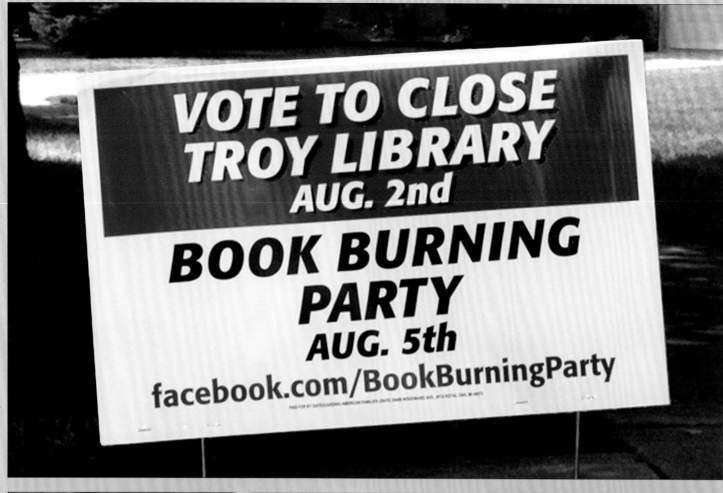

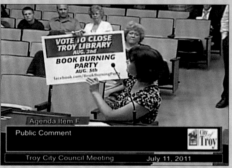

Agency	Leo Burnett, Detroit
Creative Directors	Peter McHugh
	Glen Hilzinger
	Bob Veasey
Copywriters	Glen Hilzinger
	Rob Thiemann
	Mike Davis
Art Directors	Bob Veasey
	Derek Tent
Producer	Jennie Hochthanner
Advertiser	Troy Public Library,
	"Book Burning Party"

When the town of Troy, Michigan proposed a small tax increase to save its local library, Tea Party campaigners turned the issue into an anti-tax crusade. The library needed to hit back. So it posted signs around town advertising a book burning party after the library's closure. These led to a Facebook page containing images of burning books and the news that a band had already been booked for the big day. Souvenir T-shirts and even a book bag were also on offer.

When the shock and outrage reached a peak, the library revealed its true intentions: "A vote against the library is like a vote to burn books." On voting day, the turnout was massive and the library was saved.

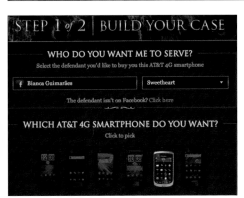

Consumer Direct   **217**

Agency	BBDO, New York
CCO	David Lubars
Executive CDs	Greg Hahn
	Mathias Appelblad
Creative Directors	Arturo Aranda
	George Ernst
Copywriters	Rick Williams
	Mark Anderson
Art Directors	Marcel Yunes
	Danny Adrain
Production	Caviar Content, LA
Exec. Producer	Julian Katz
Advertiser	AT&T, "You've Got a Case"

AT&T wanted to help young people convince their parents that they deserved a 4G smartphone. So it created super-smooth Facebook attorney Kent Wesley. Users could request Kent's help via a Facebook app. The app then automatically personalised a film of Kent's highly convincing plea to the jury by incorporating images of the user, their friends and other elements from their Facebook profile. The finished film could then be posted on the parents' timelines, allowing them to "settle out of court" by buying their kid the phone.

Consumer Direct

Agency	Leo Burnett, Moscow
Creative Directors	Grigory Sorokin
	Mikhail Kudashkin
Copywriters	Andrey Donov
	Alexander Ovsyankin
Art Directors	Grisha Sorokin
	Mikhail Yarovikov
	Andrey Klemenkov
	Alexander Pokhvalin
Illustrator	Fiodor Sumkin
Production	Kijjaa! Digital Miracles,
	Moscow
Advertiser	S7 Airlines

S7 is a cool Russian airline. But too many potential visitors associate Russia with out-dated clichés. To put this right, the agency created a print ad using ink that reacts to cold. Initially the image shows some standard Russian stereotypes: bears, heavy drinking, Lenin, Russian dolls and the nuclear threat. But after the image has been placed in the freezer for a while, a new picture appears: skiing, parties, hip bars and a warm welcome. To discover the real Russia, you need real Russian frost.

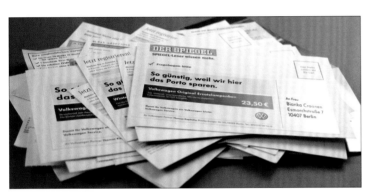

Agency	BBDO Proximity, Berlin	
CCO	Wolfgang Schneider	
MD	Jan Harbeck	
Creative Directors	Ton Hollander	
	Rens Ringena	
Copywriters	Lukas Liske	
	Fredric Antonsson	
Art Directors	Daniel Schweinzer	
	Thomas Tulinius	
	Sebastian Forsman	
Producers	Silke Rochow	
	Julia Diehl	
Advertiser	Smart Fortwo ED, "EBall"	

A quirky test drive event at the Frankfurt Motor Show was designed to showcase the Smart Fortwo Electric Drive's powerful acceleration and fun handling. Smart E-Ball turned two electric cars into virtual tennis rackets. The result resembled the classic video game Pong, with a radical difference: here the game was played by driving the car quickly forwards and backwards in order to hit the "ball". Each driver could experience the car's surprising acceleration and driving enjoyment.

Agency	DDB Tribal, Berlin
CCO	Eric Schoeffler
Creative Directors	Marc Isken
	Nils Haseborg
	Johannes Hicks
	Till Eckel
Copywriter	Lennart Frank
Art Director	Michael Janke
Graphic Design	Aylin Özkarakas
Producer	Peter Stumpe
Advertiser	Volkswagen, "Parasite Mailing"

Volkswagen wanted to prove that it saves every penny to make the lowest possible offers to its customers. So it developed the first "parasite mailing". Postage paid response cards and envelopes from existing direct mail promotions by other companies were highjacked – then a sticker was slapped on them showing new recipient addresses. The accompanying message announced, "So cheap, because we're saving the postage" and went on to describe Volkswagen's low-priced service offers.

Agency	BBDO, New York
CCO	David Lubars
Executive CDs	Greg Hahn
	Mike Smith
Creative Director	Rasmus Blaesbjerg
Copywriter	Jessica Coulter
Art Director	Matt Sorrell
Production Head	Niklas Lindstrom
Producers	Douglas Stivers
	Katrina Cass
Advertiser	HBO True Blood,
	"Glamour App"

In the HBO vampire series "True Blood", the bloodsuckers sometimes manipulate their victims by "glamouring" them with a hypnotic stare. To promote the release of the series on DVD, an app allowed users to "glamour" their Friends. The app allowed you to upload your own image, give it vampire-like traits and add a spooky vampire accent. The resulting film could be then posted on friends' and relatives' timelines, "glamouring" them as you compelled them to buy you the DVD.

Agency	Serviceplan, Munich
CCO	Alexander Schill
Creative Directors	Till Diestel
	Marc Vosshall
Copywriter	Andreas Schriewer
Production	German Wahnsinn
Producers	Philipp Feit
	Eduardo Garcia
	Florian Panier
Account Team	Kristian von Elm
	Ines Herbold
Advertiser	Johanniter-Unfall-Hilfe,
	"Radio Ghosts"

One out of eleven traffic accident fatalities in Germany is related to alcohol. To raise awareness of this, the agency created radio spots with actors playing the deceased victims and describing the accident that had killed them: radio ghosts. Spookier still, radio transmitters broadcasting the stories were placed within wooden crosses marking the sites of alcohol-related road deaths across Hamburg. Whenever a car stopped nearby, its radio was overridden by the eerie voice of the ghost, forcing the driver to listen.

Agency	Leo Burnett, Mumbai
Creative Directors	K V Sridhar
	Nitesh Tiwari
	Vikram Pandey
Art Director	Amit Thakur
Photographers	Kevin Periera
	Mugdha Gudhe
Production	Bhaarat Godbole
Advertiser	Door Step School, "Ink Pad"

Door Step School is an Indian NGO running literacy and other programmes in underprivileged communities. When it comes to signing documents, many illiterate adults use a thumbprint. But the agency turned the symbol of illiteracy – the thumbprint – in to a tool to write. Cut-outs of the Hindi alphabet were placed on top of a regular ink pad. Users could press their thumbs onto the letters that made up their names and transfer these to documents. In other words, the ink pad allowed users to print their names using their thumbs.

OUT OF OFFICE POETRY

Verstuur Chat Bijlage Adres Lettertypen Bewaar als

Van: jonas.verheyen@vnz.be

Kopie:

Onderwerp: OUT OF OFFICE POETRY

Dearly bemoaned,

Do not be afraid, I am not complete
in my absence, my body is likely
drifting in the air
gulping time, not thinking of
how cruel it must be
to work between [date departure] and [date return]
as you do, over there.

Oh, how I'd wish for you to be elsewhere in the light
of this long day, somewhere anywhere
a man is not needed, but allowed,
such as not here, me,

your absent, Jonas.

Stijn Vranken

===
26 January is POETRY DAY 2012
Support Poetry Day and use OUT OF OFFICE POETRY by Dutch and
Flemish poets such as Joke van Leeuwen, Stijn Vranken, Lies Van Gasse,
Ester Naomi Perquin and Joe Roxy.
Go to www.gedichtendag.com and choose your Out Of Office Poem
===

Agency	Leo Burnett, Brussels	The Reading Foundation in Belgium runs
Creative Directors	Tom Loockx	National Poetry Day as part of its mission
	Jorrit Hermans	to promote the joy of reading. But how to
Copywriters	Joke Van Leeuwen	spread the word on a limited budget – and
	Stijn Vranken	make poetry cool? Famous Dutch and
	Lies Van Gasse	Flemish poets such as Joke van Leeuwen,
	Ester Naomi Perquin	Stijn Vranken, Lies Van Gasse, Ester Naomi
Producers	Veronique Allard	Perquin and Joe Roxy were invited to write an
Graphic Design	Benoît Germeau	exclusive poem for an unexpected purpose –
Advertiser	The Reading	the out of office reply. Anyone could copy a
	Foundation,	poem from the Foundation's website and set
	"Out Of Office Poetry"	it as their own out of office reply. In this way,
		poetry became part of everyday lives.

Agency	McCann Erickson,	Rom chocolate bar is a symbol of Romanian pride,
	Bucharest	but since its last ad campaign sales were declining.
Creative Directors	Adrian Botan	The brief was to create a campaign for Romania's
	Catalin Dobre	National Day on December 1. The idea was based on
	Dinu Panescu	the alarming discovery that if one typed "Romanians
Copywriters	Sebastian Olar	are…" into Google, it came back with "stupid",
	Alexandru Vicol	"thieves" and similar terms. So Rom created roma-
Art Directors	Arpad Rezi	niansaresmart.com, where people could change this
	Laurentiu Stere	tendency by adding positive searches. The country's
Advertiser	Rom,	top bloggers were recruited to help and key opinion
	"Romanians	leaders urged people to join in via a viral campaign.
	are Smart"	TV news also took up the cause. The result: now
		everyone knows that "Romanians are Smart".

Agency	Publicis Conseil, Paris	At night on the streets, a young homeless woman is harassed by two guys. As the situation escalates it's clear they mean to rape her. She breaks free and runs to the nearest homeless shelter, where she hammers on the door. What happens next? The interactive film lets viewers decide. If they vote to save the only women's emergency shelter in Paris from closure, by clicking to share the film, the door is opened and the would-be rapists leave. If not, the door remains shut and she is dragged away...The campaign by French homeless charity Samusocial succeeded in saving the shelter.
CD/Copywriter	Veronique Sels	
Art Director	Bastien Grisolet	
Producers	Pierre Marcus	
	Timothe Rosenberg	
Digital Planner	Guillaume Sabbagh	
Director	Frederic Schoendoerffer	
Producer	Martin Coulais	
Editor	Stephane Couturier	
Account Team	Patrick Lara	
	Emmanuelle Henry	
	Debora Guarachi	
Advertiser	Samusocial	

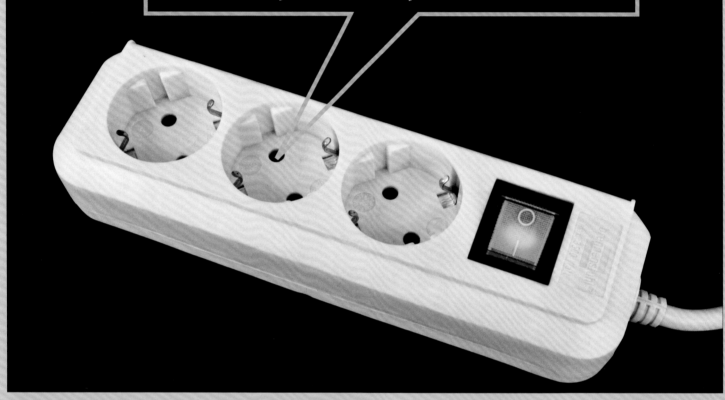

Agency	Wien Nord, Vienna
Creative Directors	Eduard Böhler
	Edmund Hochleitner
	Bernd Wilfinger
Art Directors	Andreas Lierzer
	Stefan Kopinits
Account Manager	Markus Mazuran
Advertiser	Opel Ampera,
	"The Most Credible
	Testimonial in the World"

Motoring journalists got an electric shock last year – but not in the traditional way. It was as a result of a direct mailing for the launch of the Opel Ampera, an electric car that could be recharged from any household plug socket. To express this idea, Opel and its agency recruited electricity itself as their spokesman. A power socket was mailed to motoring journalists, who were asked to plug it in. When they did, it began to speak. "Hello...this is electric power speaking...with me, you can finally drive a car."

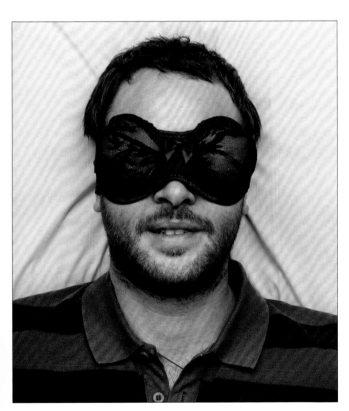

Agency	Leo Burnett, Melbourne
Creative Director	Jason Williams
Copywriter	Sarah McGregor
Art Director	Matt Portch
Advertiser	Arts Centre Melbourne The Famous Spiegeltent, "Box of Curiosities"

Every year, The Famous Spiegeltent, a vintage mixture of circus, cabaret and stand-up, comes to Melbourne. But it was in need of sponsors. To get the attention of CEOs, the agency subverted the classic corporate hamper by filling it with bizarre goodies: lady beard soap, petrified toenail clippings and an edible toupee, to name a few. The products looked like genuine artifacts from a mysterious emporium. Within a week, the "season of curiosities" had found a major sponsor: Singapore Airlines.

Agencies	Interone, Munich, Hamburg & Düsseldorf
Executive CDs	Marco Mehrwald Thomas Pakull
Creative Directors	Marco Mehrwald Thomas Pakull Gunnar Immisch Stefan Wurster
Copywriter	Tobias Schwarz
Art Director	Christopher Grouls
Producer	Jens Pastyrik
Advertiser	Beate Uhse, "Face Bra"

Beate Uhse is the European market leader in sex toys, lingerie and erotic clothing. This mailing was an invitation for selected clients to the international lingerie salon in Paris. Since most of the invitees would be travelling by train and plane, Beate Uhse's top-selling lingerie product – the lace bra – was turned into a "face bra" to help them sleep during the journey. Erotic dreams guaranteed.

226   **Business to Business Direct**

Agency	Kolle Rebbe, Hamburg	**Production**	Pasta Prima	Gerstenberg Publishing House is a small company specialising in culinary and art books – a crowded market. In order to stand out, it launched The Real Cookbook: the first book that readers can actually cook and eat. Its pages are made of 100% fresh pasta. The book was sent to business partners and the media to generate buzz. With a little sauce between the pages and a sprinkle of cheese on top, The Real Cookbook becomes a lasagne that can be baked in the oven at 200 °C. Food for thought.
Executive CDs	Sascha Hanke		Buchbinderei Zwang	
	Antje Hedde	**Producer**	Martin Lühe	
Creative Directors	Antje Hedde	**Graphic Design**	Christine Knies	
	Katrin Oeding	**Typography**	Christine Knies	
Copywriter	Gereon Klug		Reginald Wagner	
Art Directors	Reginald Wagner	**Account Team**	Gereon Klug	
	Antje Hedde		Inga Eickholt	
Photographers	Jan Burwick	**Advertiser**	Gerstenberg	
	Christoph Himmel		Publishing House,	
			"The Real Cookbook"	

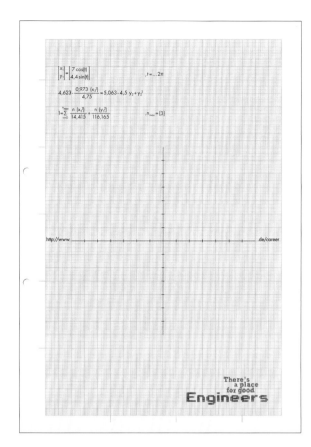

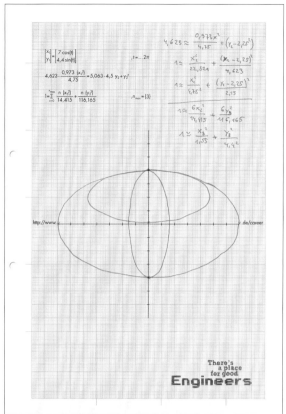

Agency	Saatchi & Saatchi, Düsseldorf	Toyota wanted to recruit more engineers – but only the best would do. So it created an unbranded ad showing a mathematical equation and placed it in the magazines of Germany's technical universities. This ad challenged young and talented engineering students to come up with the solution to the equation. Those that did would unveil Toyota as the advertiser and find a web address with a link to an application form. Of more than 400 applications, three engineers were hired.
Creative Directors	Alexander Reiss Marco Obermann	
Copywriters	Marko Werth Schakir Islamow	
Art Directors	Jean-Pierre Gregor Ingmar Krannich	
Producer	Alexandra Beck	
Graphic Design	Thomas Demeter Dörte Leismann Fabian Haumann	
Advertiser	Toyota Recruitment	

Agency	Scholz & Friends, Berlin	Alfa-Telefon is a German organisation fighting illiteracy. To attract potential sponsors, it asked them a question: how does it feel to be illiterate? The answer came in the form of a book that couldn't be opened because it had two sealed spines. The "unbook" shows how written content remains unaccessible to those who are illiterate. A short text on the back of the book explains the thinking behind the mailing. The cover letter is in the form of a bookmark.
Creative Directors	Martin Pross Matthias Spaetgens Mathias Rebmann Florian Schwalme	
Copywriters	Felix Heine Ulrike Keitel	
Art Director	Johannes Stoll	
Producer	Franziska Ibe	
Account Team	Christina Ritzenhoff Michaela Zischek	
Advertiser	Alfa-Telefon, "The Hidden World"	

228   **Business to Business Direct**

Agency	Red Urban, Munich	From the Occupy protests to demonstrations over austerity cuts in Europe, this is the age of movements. Using the motto "Now or never – start your own movement", Getty Images reflected this zeitgeist in an amusing way. It allowed people to adapt film from its archives to start their own movements – often quirky and quite harmless – and share them via social networks. It was a smart way of promoting Getty's film archive, when the image library is mostly known for its photographs.
Creative Director	Andreas Klemp	
Copywriter	Uwe Schatz	
Art Directors	Adrian Pavic	
	Malte Schleemilch	
Advertiser	Getty Images, "Start Your Own Movement"	

Agency	Scholz & Friends, Berlin
Creative Directors	Martin Pross
	Matthias Spaetgens
	Mathias Rebmann
	Florian Schwalme
Copywriters	Felix Heine
	Mateo Sacchetti
Art Director	Johannes Stoll
Production	MPR Werbefactory
Advertiser	Stihl TS 500i, "Champagne Mailing"

The new TS500i from Stihl is one hell of a cutting machine: a power saw with electronically controlled fuel injection. But how to convince top dealers to test its powers? They were sent a block of concrete with a bottle of champagne embedded in it. When they called Stihl, a sales rep came around with the saw. After some awesome cutting action, the champagne was released and glasses were raised to the new saw.

Agency	Boomtown Strategic Brand Agency, Port Elizabeth
Creative Director	Andrew MacKenzie
Copywriter	Gary Welsh
Art Director	Senzo Xulu
Designers	Louw Sevenster
	Tarryn Rennie
Advertiser	Aggreko Power Generators, "Always On"

London-based Aggreko is a global provider of power generators, but it had a low profile in South Africa, where it wanted to attract clients in the mining and manufacturing industries – which are plagued by the country's frequent power outages. The mailing took the form of a box with a large switch turned to the "on" position. When recipients switched it off, it immediately switched itself on again. Aggreko – for power that's always on.

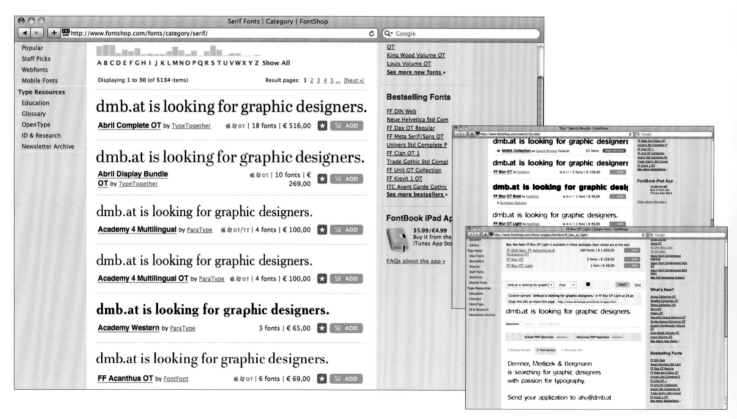

Agency	Havas Worldwide, Zurich	The agency wanted to recruit a new web developer, so a flyer was handed out in technical universities. It featured an unfinished QR code and ten technical questions. Each answer was linked to a square on the code. The applicants had to find the right answer and then either fill in the black square or leave it white. It they made the right decisions, the finished QR code led to a page where the developer could apply for the job. The result: Katie, the company's new web developer.
Creative Directors	Axel Eckstein Alexander Holtz Frank Bodin	
Copywriter	Nicolas Baechtold	
Advertiser	Havas Worldwide Recruitment, "Finding Katie"	

Agency	Demner, Merlicek & Bergmann, Vienna	Austrian agency Demner, Merlicek and Bergmann needed a graphic designer. The trouble is, such creative types rarely scan the job pages or reply to classic recruitment ads. However, graphic designers do spend a great deal of time browsing online font platforms. In cooperation with Austria's leading font platform, fontshop. com, the agency replaced the regular sample text with a job offer: dmb.at is looking for graphic designers. A click on the font provided more details.
Creative Directors	Alistair Thompson Rene Pichler	
Copywriters	Alistair Thompson Patrick Hein	
Producer	Cornelia Huber	
Graphic Design	Lukas Hueter Lilly Reich	
Account Mgt.	Lisa Benischek	
Advertiser	DMB Recruitment, "Look for a Font. Find a Job."	

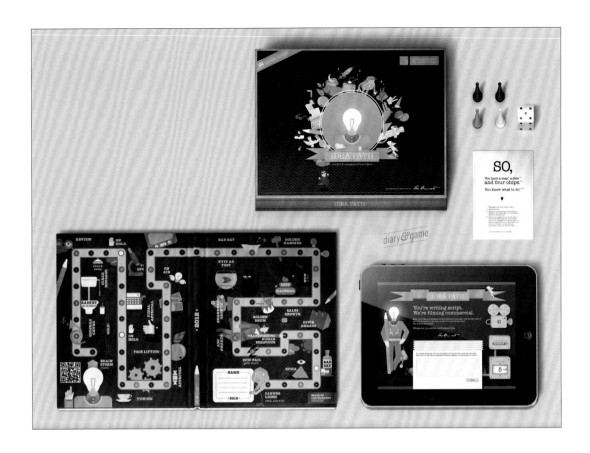

Agency	Leo Burnett, Kiev	**Agency**	Serviceplan, Munich
Creative Director	Tatiana Fedorenko	**CCO**	Alexander Schill
Copywriters	Eugeniy Gryaznov	**Executive CD**	Matthias Harbeck
	Tatiana Fedorenko	**Creative Director**	Oliver Palmer
Art Director	Vlad Kunets	**Copywriter**	Sebastian Wolf
Illustrator	Maxim Podolyanyuk	**Art Directors**	Michel Maurice Lueck
Producers	Katerina Duda		Sebastian Struppler
	Katerina Denisenko	**Production**	Demo Designmodellbau
	Allen Dis	**Programmer**	NFQ/Netzfrequenz
Advertiser	Leo Burnett,	**Online**	Ret Lauterbach
	"Idea Path Diary"	**Advertiser**	Thomas Cook Travel,
			"Temperatures Calendar"

Each year Leo Burnett makes a diary, which it sends to its clients as a gift. This year, the front and back covers of the diary opened up to make a board game demonstrating to clients how ideas are born, how they develop and how they struggle to survive. The goal of the game was to win a Cannes Lion. But clients could also link to a website via a QR code, where they could join in the process of writing a script for an ad campaign. The agency promised to produce the best ideas to emerge from this competition.

Travel agent Thomas Cook came up with a fiendish way of making potential customers dream of their next holiday destination. This designer calendar is also a temperature station and a mini travel agency. It displays the day's date in the form of temperatures at destinations around the world: on January 31, 2012 it was 31° in Rio, 1° in New York and 12° in Cairo. The calendar also displays flight availability and allows people to book a trip on the spot via a QR code. It was placed not only in travel agencies, but in cafés and hotels. A calendar for people who like to stay on the move.

Agency	Jung von Matt, Hamburg
CCOs	Dörte Spengler-Ahrens
	Jan Rexhausen
Creative Director	Felix Fenz
Copywriter	David Wegener
Art Directors	Alexander Norvilas
	Eric van den Hoonaard
Producer	Philipp Breidthardt
	Slaughterhouse, Hamburg
Account Director	Raphael Brinkert
Advertiser	Stolpersteine,
	"Online Holocaust
	Memorial"

The "Stumbling Stones" are brass stones commemorating people who were murdered during the Holocaust, embedded in the pavement outside the buildings they were deported from. There are 32,000 stones all over Europe. As research showed many young Germans were unaware of the Holocaust, something more had to be done. So the Stumbling Stones were added to Google Places.

Now when anyone visits Berlin via Google Street View, they will see not only the names of shops and restaurants, but also those of Julius Löwenstein, Simon Blumenthal and many other victims of the Nazis. A microsite provides further information; there is also an iPhone app that makes the Stumbling Stones an interactive experience.

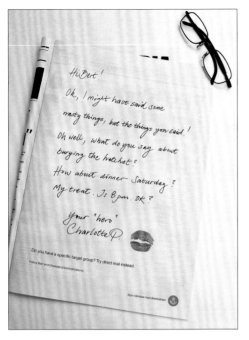

Agency	Åkestam Holst, Stockholm
Creative Director	Andreas Ullenius
Copywriter	Tor Lemhag
Art Director	Mats Gadestam
Planner	Lars Friberg
Account Team	Jacob Stjärne
	Anna Nolendorfs
Advertiser	The Swedish Post, "Celebrity Ceasefire"

Using mass media is foolish when you can send a targeted message more economically by post. To prove this, the Swedish Post Office persuaded two celebrities who had fallen out (singer Charlotte Perelli and her former producer Bert Karlsson) to get in touch, bury the hatchet and organize a reconciliation dinner, using only mass media. Through press ads, radio spots, TV, outdoor and even banner-towing aeroplanes, the pair eventually made up, but at the cost of €150,000. Had they used direct mail they could have achieved the same results by spending 50 cents on a stamp.

234   **Media Innovation - Traditional Media**

Agency	Razorfish, London
Creative Director	Sean Chambers
Copywriter	David Cadjy-Newby
Art Director	Damian Simor
Production	Sonny, London
Producer	Nicole Saganice
Account Director	Kerry Molloy
Media Agency	Mindshare Europe
Advertiser	Axe Anarchy/Lynx Attract, "Breaking News"

Axe is well known for its power to attract women. But what if it made a body spray for both men and women? The result: Anarchy! The launch took the form of fake news stories about the fragrance sparking a wave of uncontrolled lust between men and women, amidst rumours of the product selling on the black market. In another PR element, "flash snogs" were organized in the real world, as men and women dropped whatever they were doing and succumbed to the Axe effect.

Agency	Memac Ogilvy Label, Tunis
Creative Director	Nicolas Courant
Copywriters	Asma Kanzari
	Mehdi Lamloum
	Yosri Mimouna
Art Directors	Gerald Heraud
	Yassine Boughaba
Producers	Aziz M'Bazaia
	Bedis Benamor
	Moez Nemsi
Advertiser	Engagement Citoyen, "The Return of Dictator Ben Ali"

Tunisian pro-democracy charity Engagement Citoyen placed a giant poster of ousted dictator Ben Ali in the centre of La Goulette. When people tore down the picture in anger, they saw a message warning them to vote in the forthcoming free elections. The event was filmed and posted online, where it was massively shared. The stunt was aired on all Tunisian and Arabic news channels. Most importantly, there was an 88% turnout for the election, far higher than the expected 55%.

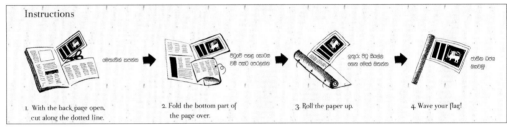

Instructions

1. With the back page open, cut along the dotted line.

2. Fold the bottom part of the page over.

3. Roll the paper up.

4. Wave your flag!

Agency	Leo Burnett Solutions, Colombo
CCO	Sachin Ambekar
Creative Director	Subhash Pinnapola
Copywriters	Eraj Wirasinha
	Ranjana Amaradeva
Art Director	Shayani Obeyesekere
Illustrator	Prasad Chaturanga
Producer	Mohamed Ikram
Media Team	Nilusha Wanasinghe
	Chandani Abeyratne
Production	Ranjith Perera
Advertiser	Mawbima, "Paper Flag"

Sri Lankan newspaper Mawbima wanted to strengthen its relationship with its readers on the country's Independence Day. Instead of simply creating content around the event, it also created a means of taking part in the celebrations. It printed the country's flag on both sides of the back page. By following a few simple instructions, anyone could turn their newspaper into the flag of Sri Lanka, for waving on Independence Day. Suddenly, a newspaper had become a way for people to express their love of their country.

Agency	New Moment, Tirana
Creative Director	Dusan Drakalski
Copywriter	Nikola Vojnov
Art Director	Nikola Vojnov
Production	New Moment, Tirana
Advertiser	Abissnet,
	"Buffering Live"

Waiting for an online film to load is a frustrating experience. To promote its super fast service, internet provider Abissnet recreated this annoyance on TV. It persuaded national broadcaster Vizion Plus to let it apply the "buffering effect" to a major talent show and a key football match. Astonished viewers waited for the live TV images to load, but relief and hopefully smiles came with the restoration of normal viewing and the words: "For faster internet switch to Abissnet."

Agency	Forsman & Bodenfors, Gothenburg	The Gothenburg Opera in Sweden struggles to attract young audiences. Meanwhile, Gothenburg has one of the highest rates of single people in Sweden, at around 50%. Factor in a new performance of West Side Story, a musical about love against the odds, and an inspired idea emerges: Mis-Match.com, a site encouraging you to "date your total opposite" with a night at the opera. The site was promoted across media and more than 5.000 mismatched couples joined in the fun. West Side Story was a huge hit, with 62% of the 15.000 tickets sold to young people.
Copywriters	Leo Magnusson	
	Elisabeth Christensson	
	Björn Engström	
Art Director	Pål Eneroth	
Designers	Marc Eastmond	
	Icka Samrin	
Producer	Malin Careborg	
Web Design	Sophia Lindholm	
Account Team	Greger Andersson	
	Åsa Pedersen	
Advertiser	Gothenburg Opera	

VYSAJE VŠETKO!
Ultrasilný S8 Uniq

Miele

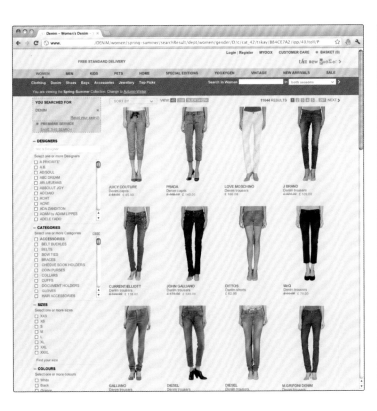

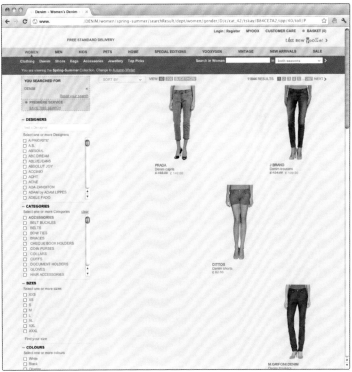

Agency	Mayer McCann Erickson, Bratislava	The Miele S8 vacuum cleaner has monster suction power and can "vacuum
Creative Directors	Boris Prexta Vlado Slivka	everything". To show this, the agency created a poster that didn't exist – and
Copywriter	Juraj Stehlík	an online film that did. Viewers shared the
Art Director	Peter Bruško	speeded-up video footage of vehicles being
Advertiser	Miele S8 UniQ Vacuum Cleaner, "Miele Tunnel"	"sucked" into a tunnel in Slovakia, debated whether or not the installation was real and created lively buzz around the product. All for zero media spend.

Agencies	Interone, Munich, Hamburg & Düsseldorf	EarthLink wanted to confront consumers with the issue of child labour and encourage them
Creative Directors	Marco Mehrwald Thomas Pakull Markus Boeger Ilker Aslan	to change their behaviour. So it created the aVOID Plugin. When a user visits an online shopping site, the app hides all products from companies associated with child labour,
Creative Dev.	Thomas Fink	replacing them with a "stop" hand symbol.
Copywriter	Tobias Schwarz	It uses data from the Active Against Child
Art Director	Gregor Myszor	Labour campaign. To further raise awareness,
Concept Design	Joerg Radehaus	aVOID tracks the number of avoided products
Account Director	Andrea Schurr	and feeds it into concerned blogs, websites
Advertiser	Earth Link, "Avoid Plugin"	and social networks. The number of avoided products quickly reached over a million.

Don't miss the christening tonight on TV4 10:03 PM. ④

TELE2
Born to be cheap

SFX: Rock music playing in the background

DJ: And to get things going, the song coming up next is a 90's hit, That is still making noise people! It's a song that I want to share with all of you listeners. It's a loud one! Just how we like it. Here it goes; I hope you like it.

VO INTEGRATION: Alfa Rock apologizes for the inconvenience. Fred Virella is not himself when he's hungry. When he finishes eating his Snickers, we will be back with our regular programming.

SFX: Salsa music playing in the background

DJ: A lot of flavor and spice is what I got for you guys here in SalSoul 98.5. Jay Pérez in "Turn It Up" with SalSoul. And now a real hit, I'm really going to enjoy this one because this song will really make me shake it! Here on "Turn It Up" with SalSoul.

VO INTEGRATION: Cadena SalSoul apologizes for the inconvenience. Jay Pérez is not himself when he's hungry. When he finishes eating his Snickers, we will be back with our regular programming.

SFX: Hip hop music playing in the background

DJ: This is dope right here! My peeps, I want to play one of my favorite songs, it has a lot of flow and it's really sick! I know this hit is gonna fire both you and I up. Here we go!

VO INTEGRATION: Reggaeton 94 apologizes for the inconvenience. El Coyote is not himself when he's hungry. When he finishes eating his Snickers, we will be back with our regular programming.

238 **Media Innovation - Traditional Media**

Agency	Forsman & Bodenfors, Gothenburg	
Copywriters	Martin Ringqvist	
	David Lundgren	
Art Directors	Lars Elfman	
	Kim Cramer	
Production	Acne, Stockholm	
Producer	Alexander Blidner	
Designers	Icka Samrin	
	Marc Eastmond	
Account Team	Jerk Zander	
	Erica Berghagen	
Advertiser	Tele2, "The Christening"	

On the same day as the christening of Sweden's new crown princess, Tele2's spokesperson Frank – the black sheep – stole the show by christening his own baby on prime time TV.

Agency	BBDO Puerto Rico, Guaynabo
Creative Director	José Antillón
Copywriter	Ilia Márquez
Production	Boomerang
Producers	Chede Caro
Editors	Christopher Díaz
	Ricky Gómez
Media Planner	Guillermo Rodríguez
Account Team	Hecmarilys Ortiz
	Glorycela Rosado
Advertiser	Snickers, "DJ's"

Hunger can affect your concentration, your mood – and your work. So what happens when a radio DJ is famished? Snickers persuaded the hosts of no less than 37 radio shows to simulate the effects of hunger by playing tracks that had no place on their station (opera on a rap station, salsa on a rock show). Afterwards, an apologetic message from the station: "Our DJ is hungry. When he finishes his Snickers, we'll be back with our normal programming." Snickers. You're not yourself when you're hungry.

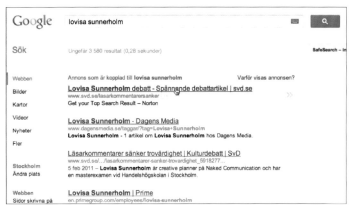

Agency	Naked Communications, Stockholm	When someone looks you up on Google, the results aren't always flattering: that ancient photo of you at a drunken fancy dress party, for example. The problem is that Google controls the search results. To prove that Norton cares about protecting your online reputation, it created the "Top Search Result" service. By buying the rights to your name as an adword on Google and giving it to you for free, it put the control of search results back in your hands – sometimes with quite legendary results.	
Creative Director	Christoffer Dymling		
Art Directors	Mårten Hedbom		
	Filip Tydén		
	Fredrik Preisler		
Production	Society 46, Stockholm		
Visualizer	August Zachrisson		
Account Team	Johan Falk		
	Lovisa Sunnerholm		
Advertiser	Norton, "Top Search Result"		

Agency	Frank, Oslo	The Walking Dead is a cult TV show about zombies, who have a notoriously hard time hanging on to their limbs. Hence this poster, which invited passersby to rip the limbs and other body parts from life-size zombies. Each limb included the URL for a site offering fans the chance to win the new iPhone. Without paying an arm and a leg.	
Creative Directors	Jason Kinsella		
	Erik Heisholt		
Copywriter	Erik Heisholt		
Art Director	Jason Kinsella		
Producer	Janniche Rassmusen		
Advertiser	Fox Crime Channel, "The Walking Dead Tear-Off Poster"		

Media Innovation - Traditional Media

Agencies	BBDO Proximity, Hamburg & Düsseldorf		Agency	LBi, London
CCO	Wolfgang Schneider		Director	Tom Harper
CDs/MDs	Detlef Rump Christian Mommertz		Advertiser	Sony Xperia Smartphone, "Xperia Studio -The Swarm"
Executive CDs	Volker Waesch Carsten Bolk			
Copywriter	Daniel Hoffmann			
Art Directors	Christian Weigel Caner Ergel			
Producers	Bernhard Burg Tobias Brockamp			
Advertiser	Copic Markers			

Marker pen Copic was celebrating its 25th anniversary. To underline its positioning as "the world's most creative marker", it went to the Cannes Lions Festival and recreated four of the most famous advertising campaigns in history, using only Copic pen caps – 44,000 of them in all. The 3D installations where placed directly in front of the Palais du Festival, where no creative type could miss them.

Sony's Xperia Studio teams the world's most creative people with Xperia smartphones and asks them to create something, document the result and share it socially. One Xperia Studio project was 'The Swarm', a science fiction film shot entirely on Xperia phones by British director Tom Harper. The director was inspired by the fact that these days natural disasters – hurricanes, meteor showers – are often captured by mobile phone footage. So what would happen during an alien invasion?

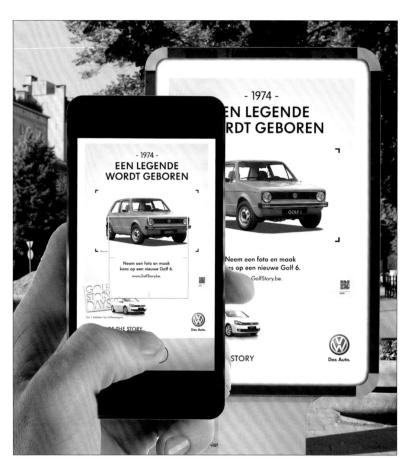

Agency	DDB, Brussels	The Golf Story Game app was developed
Creative Director	Peter Aerts	to allow gamers to go Golf spotting.
Creative Team	Massimo De Pascale	Different models earn different points and
	Danny Vissers	unlock badges you can share on Twitter
	François Massinon	and Facebook along with the pictures.
Head of Strategy	Dominique Poncin	The more points you earn the more
Account Director	Sylvie De Couvreur	chance of winning a Golf or one of the
RTV Producer	Brigitte Verduyckt	weekly prizes. Vintage or special models
Production	Caviar	earned you more points and badges. The
	Sonicville	game was promoted by a TV, radio and
	In The Pocket	poster campaign.
Advertiser	Volkswagen Golf,	
	"Golf Story Game"	

Agency	Havas Worldwide,	Leading Austrian insect repellent Vandal
	Vienna	wanted to demonstrate the effectiveness of
CCO	Frank Bodin	its adhesive strips. So it created a billboard
Copywriter	Christoph Pausz	featuring a chameleon whose tongue was
Art Directors	Marco Peis	made of one of the strips. Needless to say
	Christian Homann	the chameleon caught a lot of flies, proving
Graphic Design	Tobias Werkner	the claim "Vandal works phenomenally."
	Antonia Heyden-Linden	
	Tamara Osadcha	
Advertiser	Vandal,	
	"The World's First	
	Fly-Catching Billboard"	

Für die Umwelt unsichtbar.
F-CELL mit 0,0 Emissionen.

Mercedes-Benz

Agency	Jung von Matt, Hamburg	Producer	Martin Schoen	The Mercedes-Benz F-CELL is a hydrogen powered car, which means it has zero impact on the environment. To get this message across, an F-CELL was fitted with LED panels on one side and a camera on the other. The camera filmed the car's surroundings and projected them onto its surfaces, rendering it almost invisible. A car that fuses with its environment, leaving no visible impact.
Global CCO	Armin Jochum	Designer	Daniel Soares	
CCOs	Thimoteus Wagner	Director	Daniel Schmidt	
	Goetz Ulmer	DOP	Jakob Suess	
	Fabian Frese	Post Production	Tina Rentzsch	
Creative Directors	Michael Ohanian	Programmers	Bettina Ackermann	
	Jonas Keller		Christoph Schultz	
	Martin Strutz	Editor	Daniel Schmidt	
Copywriter	Michael Ohanian	Advertiser	Mercedes-Benz	
Art Directors	Jonas Keller		B-Class F-CELL,	
	Andreas Wagner		"The Invisible Drive"	
Production	Markenfilm-Crossing, Hamburg			

Agency	TBWA\Paris	French rail company the SNCF wanted to
Creative Directors	Eric Holden	discourage uncivil behaviour in its trains
	Rémi Noël	and stations. So alongside a conventional
	Philippe Simonet	print campaign, these two giant sculptures
	Franck Botbol	were placed at a major railway station: a
Copywriter	Stephane Kaczorowski	giant cigarette and an equally large ball of
Art Director	Sebastien Skrzypczak	discarded chewing gum. The message:
Production	Napoleon Events	there's no such thing as a small incivility.
	Double FX	
	Caporal Films	
Advertiser	SNCF	
	(French Railways),	
	"Incivility"	

Agency	Try/Apt, Oslo	DNB's telephone banking service is an
Creative Directors	Petter Bryde	automated voice that had never been used
	Thorbjorn Ruud	as a creative medium. At Christmas, DNB
Copywriters	Janne Brenda Lyso	wanted to remind its customers that it
	Petter Bryde	sponsored the Norwegian Boys' Choir. So
Art Directors	Stian Johansen	the choir was recruited to sing the service's
	Thorbjørn Ruud	automated menu. In addition, Norwe-
Production	Bade	gians get a bigger pay check in December
Director	Petter Jahre	because of a 50% tax reduction. So the
Advertiser	DNB Bank,	choir would be adding to their mood of
	"Merry Paycheck"	seasonal joy. Merry pay check!

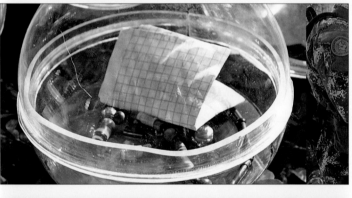

Media Innovation - Alternative Media

Agency	Lowe/SSP3, Bogotá	PAHD is an organization promoting "humanitarian demobilisation". In short – peace. To persuade FARC guerrillas to lay down their weapons for Christmas, it executed an operation with military precision. Friends and relatives of the guerrillas, as well as people from war-torn areas, were encouraged to send messages, letters and gifts inviting the guerrillas to come back home for the festive season. These messages were sealed in airtight illuminated capsules which lit up the rivers near the guerrilla camps – and the route to freedom.
Creative Directors	José Miguel Sokoloff	
	Jaime Duque	
	Gustavo Marioni	
Copywriters	Sergio León	
	Mario Lagos	
Art Director	Carlos Andrés	
	Rodríguez	
Photographer	Tonka	
Producer	José Vicente Altamar	
Account Director	Juan Pablo García	
Advertiser	PAHD,	
	"Rivers Of Light"	

Agency	Lukas Lindemann Rosinski, Hamburg
Creative Directors	Arno Lindemann
	Bernhard Lukas
	Marcus Kremer
	Thomas Heyen
Production	Markenfilm Crossing
Producers	Jascha Oevermann
	Gero Quast
	Oliver Hack
	Martin Schön
DOP	Fabian Hothan
Advertiser	Mercedes-Benz Viano

An interactive billboard at Berlin's Friedrichstrasse subway station came to life when onlookers clicked it with their remote car keys – no matter which brand of car. On the screen, the sliding door of a Mercedes Viano opened and different passengers stepped out: a samba dance troupe, female body-builders, or a robot, all illustrating the Viano's spaciousness. The luckiest participants triggered a clip showing a liveried chauffeur inviting them to take a ride in the Viano. On-site Mercedes-Benz staffers escorted the lucky winners to a Viano and they completed their journey in style.

Agency	Serviceplan, Munich
CCO	Alexander Schill
Executive CD	Matthias Harbeck
Creative Directors	Oliver Palmer
	Alexander Rehm
Copywriters	Nicolas Becker
	Lorenz Langgartner
Art Directors	Andreas Balog
	Marijo Sanje
Producer	Florian Panier
Graphic Design	Anna Tracy Wodera
Advertiser	Lego,
	"Builders of Sound"

To celebrate Lego's partnership with Star Wars for the release of Star Wars Episode 1 in 3D, the building block brand turned Lego bricks into a musical instrument. A giant barrel organ was made entirely from Lego Star Wars kits. More than 20,000 bricks were cunningly arranged so that they played the legendary Star Wars theme. The organ toured cinemas all over Germany and the featured kits could be ordered instantly via a QR Code. And thanks to an online campaign leading to a microsite, other fans could play the organ too.

246 **Media Innovation - Alternative Media**

Agency	Ogilvy, Frankfurt	Drilling holes is tricky and can leave permanent damage. So why not use a new super-strong adhesive instead? It can be removed and leaves no trace behind. To demonstrate this, fake screws – actually magnetically attached – were "drilled" into car doors in the parking lots of DIY stores. When the initially angry drivers discovered to their relief that they'd been tricked, they also found a product sample and a free towel hook.	
CCO	Michael Kutschinski		
Executive CD	Uwe Jakob		
Creative Director	Jens Steffen		
Copywriter & AD	Christian Urbanski		
Production	Red Works		
Producer	Bernhard Schmidt		
Art Buying	Martina Diederichs		
Account Mgr.	Larissa Pohl		
Clients	Martin Klasterka		
	Christiane Nadol		
Advertiser	Nie Wieder Bohren, "Driller Killer"		

Agency	Jung von Matt, Stuttgart	The Nike Vapor Flash Jacket keeps runners safe in the dark with its amazing reflective properties. For its launch, the people of Vienna and online participants were invited to "Catch the Flash" during an exciting nocturnal chase. They had to snap photos of 50 "Flash Runners" in Vapor Flash Jackets. Those who collected the most jacket numbers won a 10,000 euro platinum bar. The rest of the world took part in an online game by chasing the runners via GPS.	
Creative Directors	Kai Heuser		
	Joerg Jahn		
	Jacques Pense		
Copywriters	Gün Aydemir		
	Matthias Hess		
	Christoph Moll		
Art Director	Matias Müller		
Photographer	Mat Neidhardt		
Art Buying	Bianca Winter		
Advertiser	Nike Vapor Flash Jacket, "Catch the Flash"		

Agency	Ogilvy & Mather, Amsterdam
Creative Directors	Darre van Dijk
	Henk Nieuwenhuis
Copywriters	Henk Nieuwenhuis
	Joost van Nistelrooij
Art Directors	Darre van Dijk
	Oscar Flinterman
Producer	Brenda Bentz van den Berg
Strategy	Mariette Hamer
Account Mgr.	Zilla Smith
Advertiser	IBM, "Flashing Zebra Crossing"

IBM is striving for a "Smarter Planet". This starts with thinking creatively – like children do. So IBM launched a competition asking kids to submit smart ideas. The winning idea was to make pedestrians safer with zebra crossings that light up when you walk on them. IBM built one in the busiest street in Rotterdam and filmed the results. In combination with a billboard explaining the idea, it made people realise that anything can happen if you challenge the status quo. The billboard directed people to a website and more smart solutions from kids.

Agency	JWT, Kiev
Creative Director	Vladyslava Denys
Copywriter	Anna Geraskina
Art Director	Denys Savchenko
Photographer	Stas Bespolit
Illustrator	Denys Savchenko
Producer	Natalya Pavlova
Advertiser	Shell, "Pedestrian Ghost"

Ukraine has the highest rate of pedestrian-related accidents in Eastern Europe. Often they're caused by motorists who fail to slow for zebra crossings. As part of its social responsibility program, oil company Shell decided to draw attention to the problem. It hid an inflatable "ghost" inside a manhole cover on a crossing. When speeding drivers unwittingly triggered a radar, the ghost filled with helium and floated upward. The driver had no choice but to slow down. The experiment was filmed and posted online to drive debate.

248 **Media Innovation - Alternative Media**

Agency	Voskhod, Yekaterinburg
Creative Director	Andrey Gubaydullin
Copywriters	Evgeny Primachenko
	Egor Gavrilin
Art Directors	Vladislav Derevyannykh
	Dmitry Maslakov
Illustrator	Alex T
Production	Voskhod, Yekaterinburg
Advertiser	Ura.ru Information
	Agency, "Make the
	Politicians Work!"

Yekaterinburg was notorious for its badly maintained roads. City living site Ura.ru decided to remind local authorities that roads are their responsibility. One night, on three of the largest potholes in the city centre, it painted faces of the governor, the mayor and the vice-mayor. The next day municipal workers were duly dispatched – to cover up the portraits. This act was filmed. The campaigners came back and wrote next to the holes: "Painting it is not fixing it." The story became a viral sensation and the holes were soon filled.

Agency	Ogilvy, Frankfurt
CCO	Stephan Vogel
Creative Director	Peter Strauss
Copywriters	Sergej Chursyn
	Stephan Vogel
Art Directors	Sergej Chursyn
	Christian Leithner
Account Mgt.	Michael Fucks
Client	Birthe Hesebeck
Advertiser	OroVerde
	Rainforest Foundation,
	"The Donation Army"

OroVerde Germany is a small organization campaigning to stop the destruction of rainforests. It desperately needed new donation collectors. So who would tirelessly work to save trees? The trees themselves! An "army" of 600 trees in pedestrian areas, shopping streets and parks throughout Germany were equipped to resemble collectors – and get the message across.

Agency	Jung von Matt, Hamburg
CCOs	Dörte Spengler-Ahrens
	Jan Rexhausen
Creative Director	Felix Fenz
Copywriters	Andreas Hilbig
	Marc Freitag
	Christina Drescher
Art Director	Eric van der Hoonard
Production	Markenfilm Crossing
Producers	Martin Schön
	Laura Weber
Advertiser	German Red Cross,
	"Online Street Musicians"

Many of Germany's homeless scrape a living as street musicians. But these days passers-by are so busy looking at their mobile devices that they rarely pause to give money. So the German Red Cross took the musicians to a place where today's audiences might notice them: the internet. Instead of playing in front of bricks and mortar stores, they played in front of online shops – as interactive banners. With one click people could donate money to the Red Cross and comment or tweet about the project.

Agency	Abbott Mead Vickers
	BBDO, London
Creative Directors	Alex Grieve
	Adrian Rossi
Copywriter	Tim Riley
Art Director	Tim Riley
Production	Nomadic Films
Advertiser	Snickers,
	"Twitter Campaign"

"You're not you when you're hungry", is the slogan of Snickers chocolate bar. To illustrate the claim, it took over the Twitter feeds of several UK celebrities. For example, model Katie Price tweeted about macro-economics, attracting praise from experts. And England soccer star Rio Ferdinand tweeted about his new hobby: knitting. The media buzz was considerable. Katie, Rio and their colleagues have since resumed tweeting as usual. Presumably after a hunger-busting Snickers.

Media Innovation - Alternative Media

Agency	Leo Burnett, Shanghai
Creative Directors	Amanda Yang
	Gordon Hughes
	Forest Young
Copywriter	Jason Su
Art Directors	Xiao Kun
	Chocolate Huang
Photographer	Sean Naesrimu
Illustrator	Colin Lu
Advertiser	A.O. Smith - Solar
	Powered Water
	Heater, "Sun Bathing"

Chinese water heater manufacturer A.O. Smith launched a solar powered water heater. To promote this, it constructed a "sun bathing" experience in the heart of Shanghai. This consisted of a dark shower room with a nozzle fitted into the ceiling. It looked just like any other bathroom, except the shower nozzle sprinkled sunlight over users rather than water. But thanks to A.O. Smith, you really can shower using the sun.

Agency	Leo Burnett, Frankfurt
CCO	Andreas Pauli
Creative Director	Hans-Juergen Kaemmerer
Copywriter	Benjamin Merkel
Art Director	Helge Kniess
Producers	Netti Weber
	Gabi Sanchez-Palacio
Account Director	Carolin Boettcher
Advertiser	Sea Life Aquarium,
	"Flying Sharks"

Shoppers in Frankfurt were amazed when they faced being attacked by sharks – on dry land. Fortunately, the flying predators were perfectly harmless. The remote controlled fish were designed to make waves about the city's new Sealife aquarium. And they succeeded, taking big bites of press coverage and generating a frenzy of enthusiasm for the new attraction. As a result, the aquarium's opening went swimmingly.

Media Innovation - Alternative Media   251

Agency	BBDO Guerrero, Manila	The phrase "Pepsi Light" took on a whole new meaning in the Philippines, where the soft drinks giant joined forces with local charity MyShelter Foundation to turn old plastic bottles into low-cost, carbon-free lights. They work by refracting sunlight into a 55W light source. Pepsi established a centre to train the local community on how to install the lights. The word was spread online and at the time of writing, the project had brightened more than 46,000 lives.	**Agency**	BBDO, Toronto	The new Mercedes-Benz C-Class Coupe has racy lines. So one of the cars was parked in front of an artificially blurred wall and sidewalk, with a billboard that read: "Looks fast. Even in park." To complete the illusion, 3D models of a blurred fire hydrant, parking sign and mailbox were installed as part of the street scene.

Agency   BBDO Guerrero, Manila
Creative Director   Dale Lopez
Copywriters   Rachel Teotico
   Raymund Sison
   David Guerrero
Art Directors   Dennis Nierra
   Tim Villela
   Ley Mababangloob
Producers   Al Salvador
   Jing Abellera
   Ino Magno
Advertiser   Pepsi, "Bottle Light"

The phrase "Pepsi Light" took on a whole new meaning in the Philippines, where the soft drinks giant joined forces with local charity MyShelter Foundation to turn old plastic bottles into low-cost, carbon-free lights. They work by refracting sunlight into a 55W light source. Pepsi established a centre to train the local community on how to install the lights. The word was spread online and at the time of writing, the project had brightened more than 46,000 lives.

Agency   BBDO, Toronto
Creative Directors   Peter Ignazi
   Carlos Moreno
Copywriter   Frank Macera
Art Director   Jonathan Guy
Photographer   Philip Rostron
Production   Instil Productions
Producer   Kathie Hintsa
Event Company   Newad
Advertiser   Mercedes-Benz C-Class Coupe, "Blur"

The new Mercedes-Benz C-Class Coupe has racy lines. So one of the cars was parked in front of an artificially blurred wall and sidewalk, with a billboard that read: "Looks fast. Even in park." To complete the illusion, 3D models of a blurred fire hydrant, parking sign and mailbox were installed as part of the street scene.

Agency	Y&R, Dubai
Creative Directors	Shahir Zag
	Joseph Bihag
Copywriter	William Mathovani
Art Director	Joseph Bihag
Photographers	Mojtaba Komeili
	Arturo D. Smith
Illustrator	Joseph Bihag
Production Head	Amin Soltani
Advertiser	Gulf News,
	"The Headline News
	Cup Sleeve"

Gulf News, the UAE's leading English daily newspaper, wanted to reach more readers and convert them into subscribers. Since fresh news goes well with fresh coffee, it converted coffee cup "sleeves" at café chain Tim Hortons into a new medium: the headline news sleeve. When Tim Hortons customers bought a cup of coffee, they also got the latest news, thanks to a printer that typed out tweets from the Gulf News Twitter account. The URL and QR codes on the sleeve then directed them to the Gulf News website where they could read the full story.

Agency	Serviceplan, Munich
CCO	Alexander Schill
Executive CDs	Maik Kaehler
	Christoph Nann
Production	Inch-Design Service,
	Hamburg
Producers	Florian Panier
	Bianca Schreck
	Reinhold Kathoefer
Account Team	Florian Klietz
	Kristian von Elm
Advertiser	BMW, "EfficientDynamics
	Sculpture"

Every BMW is equipped with Efficient Dynamics technology, which combines reduced consumption with high performance. At the BMW Welt exhibition space in Munich, this melding of seemingly contradictory ideas was captured in an eight metre long sculpture. Seen from one side, it reads "EFFICIENT". But change your point of view and you see "DYNAMICS".

Agency	DDB, Stockholm	**Digital Design**	Susanna Averpil	
Creative Directors	Magnus Jakobsson	**Digital Production**	Jojo Brännström	
	Fredrik Simonsson	**Technical Director**	Andreas Fabbe	
Copywriter	Olle Langseth	**Print Production**	Anna Hellenberg	
Art Director	Tove Langseth	**Retouch Artist**	Christian Björnerhag	
Design	Elin Skogqvist	**Motion Graphics**	Eskil Lundberg	
	Anders Lövgren	**Business Director**	Maria Lundvall	
Planner	Karl Wikström	**Account Manager**	Tina Munck	
Web Developers	Sebastian Ross	**Advertiser**	Stockholm Royal Opera,	
	Alexander Ekman		"Opera Soap"	
	Rickard Berggren			

Even people who rarely go to the opera sometimes belt out a classic in the shower. (Don't deny it: we heard you warbling Nessun Dorma this morning.) To attract more visitors, the Royal Opera in Stockholm created Opera Soap, a range of soaps for use in the shower. On the bottles, three different arias were displayed to inspire amateur singers. The bottles were also tickets to the Royal Opera, so purchasers could compare their sudsy performance to the real thing.

Agency	Sapient, Guragon
Worldwide CCO	Gaston Legorburu
Creative Director	Suchitar Gahlot
Copywriter	Sunil Vallu
Producer	Ashish Nagpal
	BeatFactory, Guragon
Film Production	Jamun Films
Sound Design	Antara Aneja
Sound Production	Amit Yadav
Executive Director	Sohini Pani
Account Director	Ruchika Khanna
Advertiser	Absolut Vodka,
	"Absolut India"

Sound can provide a window into a culture. Absolut India was a sound installation that made its debut at the India Art Fair in New Delhi. Ten Absolut bottles contained "bottled up" Indian sounds, each one labelled according to the noises inside. When visitors approached a bottle, hidden sensors triggered the pre-recorded sound clips and delivered an aural distillation of pure India.

Agency	Hasan & Partners, Helsinki
CCO	Ami Hasan
Executive CDs	Eka Ruola
	Tony Hogqvist
Creative Directors	Eka Ruola
	Magnus Ericsson
Art Director	Martin Samuelson
Production	Perfect Fools, Helsinki
Producers	Sivi Uitto
	Tämer Mohsen
	Carlos Naude
Advertiser	World Design
	Capital Helsinki 2012

Design is all around us, but few people notice or think about it. World Design Capital Helsinki 2012 wanted to change that. Introducing Kauko: a "moving" café with design features that anyone can control in real-time on the web. Chairs, tables and other fittings move at the nudge of a mouse, demonstrating the impact of poor design. Users were then invited to share their own design ideas. The café was promoted via a print, outdoor and banner campaign.

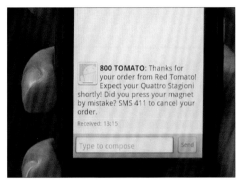

Agency	TBWA\RAAD, Dubai	
Creative Director	Rafael Guida	
Head of Digital	Preethi Mariappan	
Head of Content	Melanie Clancy	
Producer	Kishore Ramachandran	
Motion Designer	Juan Behrens	
User Interface	Jerome Conde	
Technical Lead	Navin Chauhan	
Account Team	Mohammad Khan	
	Weam Elhila	
Advertiser	Red Tomato Pizza,	
	"VIP Fridge Magnet"	

Dubai pizzeria Red Tomato realized that in a city of over 200 nationalities, telephone orders can be messed up by language problems. The solution: Red Tomato delivered very special fridge magnets to regular customers. In fact, the magnets were pizza emergency buttons. After linking the device to their mobile phones, pizza addicts could order anytime at the touch of a button. And if their topping preference changed, they could edit their preferences online.

Agency	Grey Worldwide, Düsseldorf
CCO	Roland Vanoni
Creative Directors	Mark Hendy
	Neil Elliot
Copywriters	Thomas Voelker
	Dominik Janning
Art Directors	Alphons Conzen
	Frederico Gasparian
Production	Parasol Island, Düsseldorf
Advertiser	Viacom International Media
	Networks Northern Europe,
	"Comedy Central"

To promote Comedy Central's new TV show "Happy Endings", TV itself wasn't the solution – a bus stop was. While people waited at the bus stop, Comedy Central scriptwriters concealed nearby wrote rapid-fire jokes and commentary about them, which instantly appeared as speech or thought bubbles on a screen above their heads. Online, people could write their own jokes and send them in real time to the Comedy Central Facebook page.

Agency	TBWA\Istanbul
Creative Directors	Ilkay Gurpinar
	Evren Dograr
Copywriter	Sanli Kayabolen
Art Director	Mustafa Gulsen
Photographer	Firat Kilic
Producer	Ovunc Hitay
Advertiser	42 Maslak,
	"Artful Construction
	Vehicles"

42 Maslak in Istanbul was a construction project that would result in a jewel of "artful living": arty apartments, offices, shops and art galleries for seekers of good taste. But how to promote the site before a single brick had been laid? By creating "artful" construction vehicles. The usually dull yellow vehicles were transformed by local artists into colourful design objects that were visible from the sales office overlooking the site. Print ads and a TV commercial showcased the decorative diggers, creating buzz across traditional and digital media.

Agency	Red Urban, Toronto	
Creative Director	Christina Yu	
Copywriter	Dave Barber	
Art Director	Joel Pylypiw	
Production	Untitled Films, Toronto	
Producer	Andrea Hull	
Account Director	Sonia Ruckemann	
Advertiser	Volkswagen Jetta GLI,	
	"Art Heist"	

Anyone would love to get their hands on the new VW Jetta GLI. But some would have to content themselves with a piece of related artwork. Long-exposure light paintings created by the Jetta during the filming of its launch ad were displayed at pop-up galleries in unusual locations all over Canada. Each limited edition print was hand-numbered and framed...and up for grabs. Viewers just had to possess the chutzpah to nick the picture. Many did.

Agency	Exxtra Kommunikation, Zurich
Creative Directors	Markus Gut
	Dominik Oberwiler
	Martin Stulz
Art Director	Oliver Glutz von Blotzheim
Typographer	Sarah Paul
MD	Susan Baumgartner
Account Manager	Rémy Müller
Advertiser	Audi,
	"Night Vision Assist"

Wild animals cause around 20,000 motor accidents in Switzerland every year. That's why Audi developed its infrared Night Vision Assistant, which can make out animals – and people – even in pitch darkness. To demonstrate this, life-sized, luminous wild animal silhouettes were installed beside busy streets with no lighting. The explanation followed on a luminous billboard.

bloemen.nl
don't forget

Agency	Publicis, Amsterdam	
Creative Directors	Marcel Hartog	
	Jeroen van ZWam	
Copywriters	Marcel Hartog	
	Vanessa Burgmans	
Art Directors	Jeroen van Zwam	
	Billy Witbraad	
Editor	Francisco Rodriguez	
	Bouzas	
Advertiser	Bloemen.nl Flowers,	
	"Is this Spam"	

Marketing people are stalking you online. But sometimes that's a good thing. Take flower delivery service Bloemen.nl. Online, its agency found numerous wedding pictures, including lots of flowers, along with dates and names. A bit of extra research turned up the grooms' email addresses.

So on their wedding anniversary they were sent a postcard showing their own wedding photo, along with a suggestion that they buy a bouquet for their wives – in the nick of time. Is that spam? Is that scary? Well, orders went up and nobody complained. And imagine what would have happened if they'd forgotten…

Agency	Kids Love Jetlag, Paris	To launch its new claim "Luck is an attitude", Martini cast the stars of its next commercial through social networks. Beyond a promise of worldwide fame and $150,000 payday, the prizes appealed to basic human urges: for men, an opportunity to kiss 10 models; for women, 12 pairs of designer shoes. The casting call was rolled out on TV, Internet and print, all leading to the Martini Facebook page. People from all over the world participated, supported their favourites and spread the word.
Creative Directors	Fred & Farid	
Advertiser	Martini Royale, "Martini Royale Casting"	

Agency	DDB Tribal, Berlin	The goal was to alert female drivers to the dangers of applying makeup while driving. So Volkswagen and its agency cooperated with one of the best known makeup artists on YouTube: Nikkie. Her Haul channel has over 190,000 subscribers and her videos of makeup tips and tricks have been viewed more than 30 million times. The film begins like one of Nikkie's regular videos, as she chats away while applying sequins to her face. But suddenly she's hurled towards the screen as if she's in a car smash. Sequins everywhere. The real thing would be much worse.
Creative Directors	Marc Isken	
	Nils Haseborg	
Copywriter	Valerie von Meiss	
Art Director	Lilli Langenheim	
Production	Mr. Bob Films	
Director	Milo	
Producers	Susi Schneider	
	Ben Foehr	
Editor	Sebastian Gross	
	Pirates'n Paradise	
Advertiser	Volkswagen, "Don't Make-Up and Drive"	

Agency	Forsman & Bodenfors, Gothenburg
Copywriter	Johan Olivero
Art Director	Jeremy Phang
Production	F&B Factory
Producer	Helena Wård
Media	Annki Bryhn-Jansson
PR	Lina Thomsgård
Account Team	Hans Andersson
	Helena Lignell
Client	Per Bergkrantz
Advertiser	UR-Educational TV & Radio

UR, the Swedish Educational Broadcasting Company, wanted to tell everyone its TV programmes were now available free on its website. So it recruited 7,369 new Programme Directors, one for each show on the site. To be made Programme Director, all you had to do was find a show you really liked and share it with your friends. In return, you got a status update or tweet announcing your cool new job. And an opportunity to promote a subject you cared about, from wildlife to artificial intelligence.

Agencies	Proximity China
	Goodstein & Partners, Beijing
Executive CD	Georg Warga
Creative Directors	Daryl Villanueva
	Felipe Ferreira
	Flavio Vidigal
Copywriters	Jojo Zhang
	Vivian Liu
	Derek Lui
Art Directors	Andy Li
	Zoro Cui
Advertiser	VW, "Hover Car"

The future of driving is here. Volkswagen asked the people of China to submit new ideas for cars. The Peoples' Car Project attracted 141,000 ideas over the course of a year. Wang Jia (or user Dark520), a young lady from Chengdu, submitted the winning idea: a hover car, which VW turned into a virtual prototype. It announced the news by inviting Wang Jia and her friends to a private movie premiere, where a film showed her parents at the wheel of the futuristic concept car. The story quickly spread to local and international press.

THE CHECK-IN THIEF

IGOR PAVIC

Paris Hilton @ParisHilton
At @SnoopDogg's party with... house party. Snoop is spinni... #Legend. ☺♫♡

Kiefer Sutherland @RealKiefer · 12 Apr
"There's a little Captain in all of us." shooting #Touch on Santa Monica Pier. Kind of cool! pic.twitter.com/gtGsYWue

Justin Bieber @justinbi...
good night in the studio

Rihanna @rihanna · 8 Apr
Happy Easter all the way from Sydney instagr.am/p/JI3E33BM9O/
View photo

Busy night. Happy to be here... on the red carpet at #GoldenGlobes bit.ly/xjhqvC

Hugh Hefner
I'll be spending S...
the girls, playing...

Victoria Beckham @victoriabeckham · 3m
On route to China!!!! Excited!!!! X vb

Paris Hilton @ParisHilton · 7h
At @SnoopDogg's party with @DJAfrojack & @CamRaFace. Fun lil house party. Snoop is spinning on the decks. Love him, such a #Legend. ☺♫♡

Hugh Hefner @hughhefner · 11h
I'll be spending Sunday afternoon in the Game House with Shera & the girls, playing a little backgammon with Joel Berliner.

Victoria Beckham @victoriabeckham · 17h
Cabin crew prepare for landing! Welcome to Beijing!! X vb
pic.twitter.com/L1o0rjsAK
View photo

Social Networks 261

Agency	Serviceplan, Munich	
CCO	Alexander Schill	
Creative Directors	Till Diestel	
	Marc Vosshall	
Digital Director	Friedrich von Zitzewitz	
Producer	Florian Panier	
Advertiser	Santec Video Security, "The Check-In Thief""	

A lot of people use social networks to share their whereabouts. Even famous people. But they're effectively telling the world that they're not at home. Security firm Santec took this idea a step further with its own "check-in thief", Igor Pavic. When celebrities announced on Twitter or Facebook that they were out and about, Igor sent them a polite "thank you" note and a link to his own site, where he posted a cheeky picture of himself in front of their home. Oops. The payoff: with Santec Security Cameras your home is safe, even when you're not there.

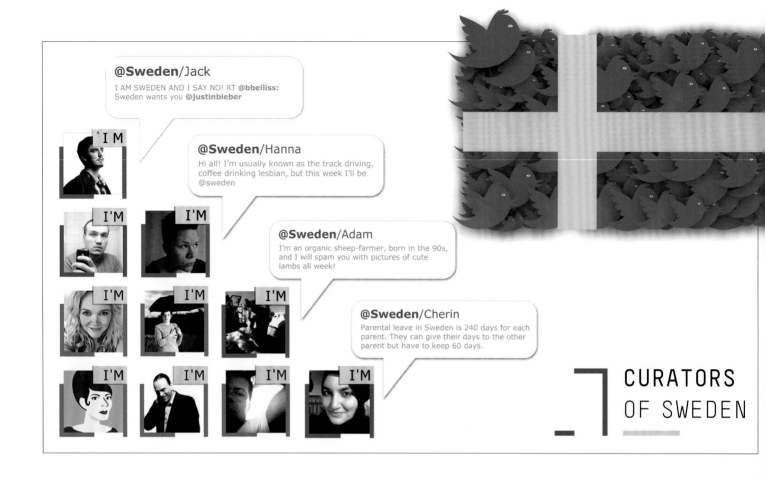

CURATORS
OF SWEDEN

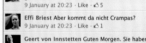

Agency	Volontaire, Stockholm
Creative Team	Volontaire
Advertisers	Swedish Institute & VisitSweden, "Curators of Sweden"

For those who don't know it, Sweden can seem a cold and remote country. But actually it's open and innovative. So Sweden became the first country in the world to hand over its official communication channel to its citizens. Every week, someone in Sweden became @Sweden: sole owner of the world's most democratic Twitter account. For seven days, they shared their everyday life (a shepherd promised to bombard us with pictures of lambs), private opinions and general thoughts. The results built into a new image of Sweden, free of all clichés.

Agency	Jung von Matt, Berlin
Executive CDs	Mathias Stiller
	Till Eckel
Creative Directors	Christian Kroll
	Peter Gocht
Copywriter	Patrick Klebba
Art Director	Christian Kies
Production	Tony Petersen Film
Director	Fabian Bernhard
Producer	Julia Cramer
Head of IT	Alexander Hensel
Advertiser	Maxim Gorki Theatre, "Effi Briest 2.0"

Most young people would rather go online than to the theatre. So one week prior to the premiere of the play "Effi Briest" at Berlin's Maxim Gorki Theatre, the cast went live on Facebook. All the characters got their own Facebook profile. And they used Facebook options tell the story: comments, likes, photos, films, shared links and so on. Online visitors could interact with the play by collaborating on a love letter or choosing the main character's wedding dress. Press coverage was huge and soon the real theatre performances were sold out.

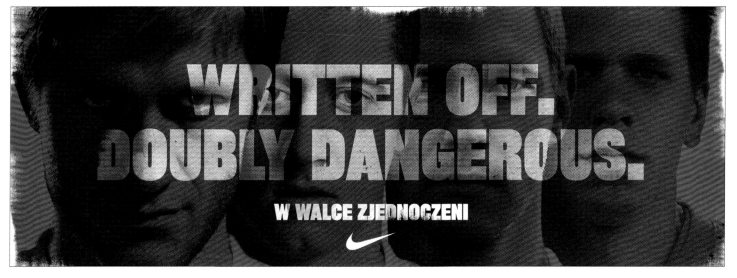

Agency	AKQA, London	
Executive CD	Duan Evans	
Creative Directors	Phil Haworth	
	Davor Krvavac	
Producer	Charlotte Davies	
Planning Director	Dan Hill	
Designers	Ali Freeman	
	Eva Wong	
Account Mgr.	Stephen Strong	
Advertiser	Nike Poland,	
	"United We Fight"	

In 2011 Poland was preparing to co-host the upcoming European Football Championship, but the national team was in free-fall, the nation was cynical and morale was at a low ebb. Hence the "United We Fight" campaign from Nike; to bond together the young team and its fans and to re-establish Polish football on a global stage. It gave the team a new iconic identity, celebrated their defiance, let fans into the inner sanctum and inspired it to new heights.

First, a new logo was created, along with a stunning new kit. Outdoor ads proclaimed: "Written off. Doubly dangerous." A Facebook app allowed fans to send messages of support to the team, which were posted on its locker room walls. This content was also screened on billboards during the inaugural match. The result: united Poles, signing the national anthem together and an honourable performance from their team (2 draws and 1 loss).

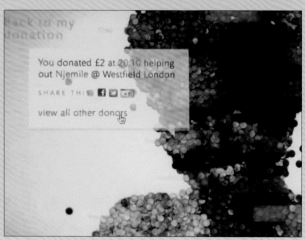

Mobile Communications

Agency	DLKW Lowe, London	Production	Absolute Post Production	
Executive CDs	Richard Denney		Rogue	
	Dave Henderson		Grand Visual	
Creative Director	Greg Delaney	Directors	The Tubby Brothers	
Copywriter	Richard J Warren	Project Mgr.	Gidon Z Cohen	
Art Director	Paul Hancock	Acct. Director	Gabrielle Gribbin	
Photographer	Oli Kellett	Planner	Venetia Sturdy	
Producer	Ally Dean	Advertiser	The MicroLoan Foundation,	
Web Design	Jamie Craven		"Pennies for Life"	
	Nick Smith			

The MicroLoan Foundation is a charity that helps women in Africa set up their own small businesses. On a digital poster site, unfinished portraits of African women were made of virtual pennies. Onlookers were invited to complete each picture by texting a donation. As soon as it arrived, the money dropped into place on the screen in the form of additional pennies. Donors got a personal "thank you" on the poster, and a credit on the charity's microsite. From one poster site, in its first weekend, 21 women who had nothing received enough funds to start their own small businesses.

Agency	Crispin Porter + Bogusky, Gothenburg	
CCO	Rob Reilly	
Executive CDs	Gustav Martner	
	Bjorn Hoglund	
CD & AD	Mattias Berg	
Copywriter	Jim Connolly	
Production	Adore You	
Tech. Director	Per Rundgren	
Interactive Head	Marcus Åslund	
Producer	Mikael Lindqvist	
Advertiser	Ubisoft-Just Dance 3, "Autodance"	

Just Dance is a dance video game series that anyone can pick up and play. The audience had been limited to teenage girls, but for the launch of Just Dance 3 the aim was to expand the audience. Hence the Autodance app. Record your friends doing…well, anything, really…and the app syncs their movements to a dance track from the video game. The hilarious video can then be shared online. And of course each user-generated video acts as an ad for Just Dance 3, featuring the tagline "Anyone can Just Dance".

Agency	plan.net/Serviceplan, Munich
CCO	Alexander Schill
Creative Directors	Markus Maczey
	Cornelia Blasy-Steiner
Copywriter	Christian Aussem
Art Director	Tobias Pechstein
Photographer	Michael Leiss
Producer	Katharina Hofmann
	Neverest, Munich
Digital Officer	Friedrich von Zitzewitz
Programmer	Stefan Schrader
Advertiser	BFF "Beating Facts"

This horribly effective iPad ad was created for the Federal German Association of Women Against Violence on a national day to raise awareness of the issue. It was inserted in the iPad edition of German Vogue. As users "swiped" through the edition they passed three harmless images – but on the fourth they appeared to slap the model in the face. It demonstrated that every fourth woman in Germany is a victim of violence.

Agency	Red Urban, Toronto	The latest incarnation of the legendary VW
Creative Director	Christina Yu	Beetle is more punchy than its predeces-
Copywriters	Matt Syberg-Olsen	sors. So the campaign juiced up the Beetle
	Jon Taylor	by using augmented reality. After download-
Art Directors	Liam Johnstone	ing an app, users in various locations could
	Damian Simev	use their phones to see the Beetle bursting
Producers	Andrea Hull	through a transit shelter after streaking down
	Sam Benson	a long tunnel; punching holes through bill-
App Developer	Bully! Entertainment	boards; or performing aerial stunts on a
Acct. Director	Nicole Milette	giant half-pipe sticking out of a building.
Advertiser	Volkswagen Beetle,	Consumers were also driven to YouTube,
	"The Beetle Juiced Up"	where they could experience the juiced up
		Beetle in the comfort of their own homes.

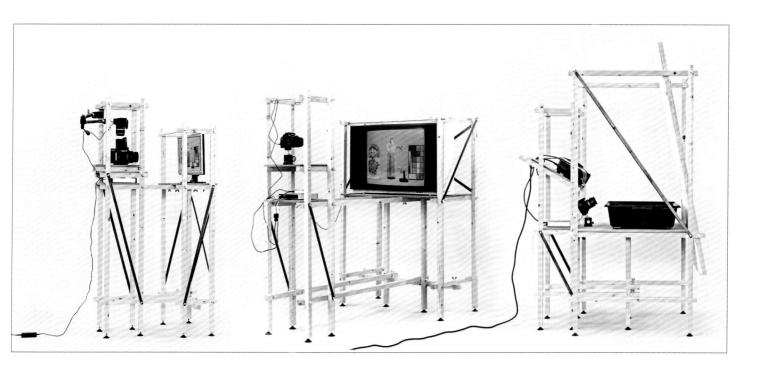

Agency	Naked Communications, Stockholm	People love photography apps like Instagram, which add cool filters to pictures. Grolsch Photo Machines did the same, but different. They were real analogue photo filters, not digital gizmos. For example, images sent via the app were displayed on a real vintage TV, photographed and sent back to users. Or filtered through a real medium format camera. And for a short period only, live illustrators hand drew copies of the image and sent them back to delighted users. "Choose interesting", says Grolsch.	
Creative Director	Fredrik Preisler		
Copywriter	Filip Tydén		
Art Directors	August Zachrisson		
	Erik Nordenankar		
Photographers	August Zachrisson		
	Noah Beyene		
Production	Society 46, Stockholm		
Producers	Anna Wallin		
	Sofia Beme		
	Gabriella Wollo		
Advertiser	Grolsch, "Photo Machines"		

Agency	Work Club, London	Ballantine's positions itself as "the whisky for people who leave an impression". That's why it has invented a T-shirt that can display a status update. In fact, it's the world's first wearable, shareable status update made of 100% cotton. Fully programmable by an app and boasting a full colour screen, accelerometer, headphone jack and megapixel camera, the garment can do "whatever you can think of". Which is more than you can say of most clothing.	
Creative Partners	Andy Sandoz		
	Ben Mooge		
Creative Lead	Joe Corcoran		
Creative Director	Julie Barnes		
Design Lead	Dan Scott		
Strategist	Niccolo Rigo		
Production	MediaMonks, Hilversum		
Project Director	Joris Pol		
Producers	Xander Amo		
	Tom Gardner		
Advertiser	Ballantine's, "T-shirt OS"		

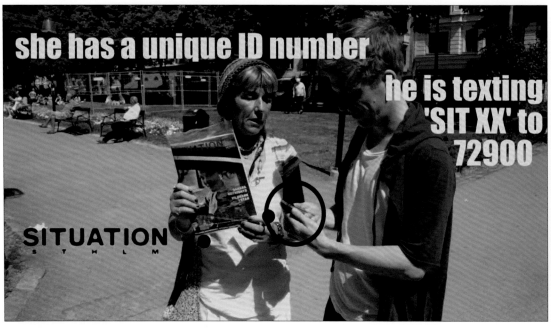

Mobile Communications

Agencies	Publicis Conseil, Paris		**Agency**	Mobiento, Stockholm
	Marcel, Paris		**Lead Developer**	Per Eriksson
Creative Directors	Steve O'Leary		**Acct. Director**	Nikolaj Alepliotis
	Julien Benmoussa		**Advertiser**	Situation Sthlm
Copywriters	Antonin Jacquot			Magazine, "SMS is King!"

Agencies Publicis Conseil, Paris
Marcel, Paris
Creative Directors Steve O'Leary
Julien Benmoussa
Copywriters Antonin Jacquot
Nicolas Martinez
Laurent Nicourt
Art Directors Philippe d'Orgeville
Samantha de Biasi
Photographer Achim Lippoth
Production La Pac, Paris
Director David Shane
Advertiser Guigoz, "Speak Baby"

Babies are cute, but often you can't understand what they're saying. A TV ad suggested that the babies sometimes play on this to tease us in secret. But now an app is at hand to translate baby talk. Film your little one and the app automatically translates his babbling. Well, sort of...

Agency Mobiento, Stockholm
Lead Developer Per Eriksson
Acct. Director Nikolaj Alepliotis
Advertiser Situation Sthlm
Magazine, "SMS is King!"

Situation Sthlm is a monthly local magazine sold by the city's homeless. All proceeds go to the vendors. Unfortunately, these days more people carry cards than loose change, so sales of the magazine were waning. The vendors couldn't carry credit card readers. But since 90% of people never leave home without their mobile, the answer was at hand. Buyers simply send an SMS with the seller's unique ID to a short number. A reporting tool tracks the sales of each vendor, so on arriving at the magazine's HQ they can pick up their earnings.

Scan cover

See weight in wood

Free a tree

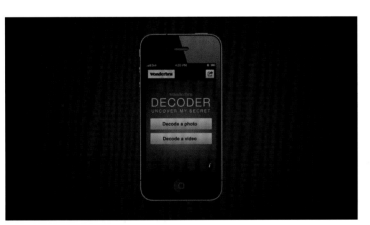

Agency	Leo Burnett, Moscow
Creative Director	Grigory Sorokin
Art Directors	Grigory Sorokin
	Mikhail Derkach
Producer	Alexey Kolokolnikov
Designer	Andrey Sergeev
Advertiser	Google Technology,
	"Free a Tree"

Free-a-tree is an app developed with the support of Google and the WWF. Every time you see a book you'd like to buy, scan it with the app. Free-a-tree will search for its electronic version in online bookstores. The app will also count the book's pages, determine density and the format of the paper, and then show how much wood it took to produce the book. After the online purchase, the percentage of wood you saved is added to a "growing" virtual tree on the app. Part of the purchase price is donated to the WWF by partner bookstores.

Agency	Digitas, Paris
CCO	Bridget Jung
Creative Director	Patrick Dacquin
Creative Techs.	Julien Terraz
	Stéphane Maguet
Art Directors	Jérôme Meunier
	Frederic Roux
Project Mgr.	Julie Tinetti
Planning	Jean-Philippe Martzel
Deputy MD	Vincent Druguet
Advertiser	Wonderbra,
	"Wonderbra Decoder"

The brief was to demonstrate that the Wonderbra comes in a range of designs. The result was the Wonderbra "decoder". Download the app, hold your phone over the print ads and a magical x-ray effect takes place. The model's clothes instantly vanish, leaving her in the undies and thus unveiling each particular design. The app also synchronises with a YouTube video where you can undress Adriana Cernanova, the brand's new star. The app was aimed at female consumers. Honest.

270   **Mobile Communications**

Agency	Ogilvy, Beijing
Creative Directors	Doug Schiff
	Kama Yu
	Paul Ho
Copywriters	Song Lei
	Doug Schiff
Art Directors	Yang Ge
	Zhang Minsheng
	Kirk Zheng
Producers	Morris Ku
	Rita Yang
Advertiser	Volkswagen,
	"Electric Cafe"

At the unveiling of the new electric VW Golf in Hong Kong, the brand used the launch venue's café to its advantage. While waiting to get behind the wheel, attendees could use a special app to see how far the car could run on the electricity used by various appliances in the café. They could also download the app for use on their own phones.

Agency	Jung von Matt, Hamburg
Creative Directors	Armin Jochum
	Wolf Heumann
	Andreas Ottensmeier
Copywriters	Christian Kutscheid
	Torben Otten
	Georg Baur
Art Directors	Hendrik Frey
	Hans-Peter Sporer
	Tilman Gossner
Producers	Danilo Kloefer
	Guido Wolff
Advertiser	Noah, "Code:Noah"

Noah is a German animal protection society fighting against animal experiments. It replaced the QR codes on outdoor cosmetics ads with its own QR codes, which led to gruesome video clips of animal experiments. Consumers could also print out the codes and continue the fight by sticking them on other cosmetics ads. The beauty industry eventually got the campaign shut down – which caused even more media buzz.

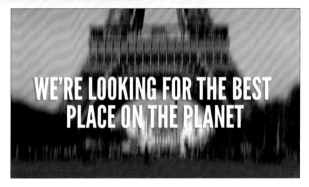

Agency	Ester, Stockholm	Over the summer hordes of young people head off on vacation and many of them have unprotected sex along the way. Aids prevention campaigners LAFA wanted to get their attention. So it created an online travel guide – to the best places on the planet to get laid. A guide where visitors could upload tips on the most beautiful and exciting locations to…well, you know.	They included everything from a five star hotel to the back seat of a car. But crucially, the site offered free condoms that could be delivered direct to their door. The condom packaging took the form of postcards. The guide was also available as a mobile app.
Creative Director	Roger Kempe		
Copywriter	Emma Zetterholm		
Art Director	Marcelo Melo		
Production	Rebenga		
Producer	Anna Wennerström		
Advertiser	LAFA, "Where's the Best Get-Laid-Place in the World"		

THE BEAUTY OF A **SECOND**
the shortest short-film challenge, ever.

272   **Branded Entertainment**

Agency	Leo Burnett, Milan	Montblanc is famous for its beautiful pens.	People were challenged to capture beauty
Executive CDs	Paolo Dematteis	But it also makes luxury timepieces, including	in one-second films, which were posted
	Riccardo Robiglio	a new chronograph named after the man	to a Montblanc micro site as well as on
Web CD	Paolo Boccardi	who invented the device 190 years ago:	Vimeo. The challenge generated news and
Copywriters	Francesco Simonetti	Nicolas Rieussec. How to raise awareness	blog reports, not to mention thousands of
	Markus Johansson	of the Rieussec watch, the anniversary of his	shares across social media. Edited com-
Art Director	Andrè Gidoin	invention and Montblanc as a watch-maker?	pilations began to appear on YouTube;
Advertiser	Montblanc	Since Rieussec was the first to measure time	and by popular demand the site's official
	Nicolas Rieussec	to within one-fifth of a second, Montblanc	soundtrack was released on iTunes.
	Chronograph,	teamed up with filmmaker Wim Wenders	
	"The Beauty	to celebrate "The Beauty of a Second".	
	of a Second"		

Agency	Ogilvy France, Paris
CCO	Chris Garbutt
Creative Director	Thierry Chiumino
Copywriter	Benjamin Dessagne
Art Director	Stéphane Santana
Production	Moonwalk Films, Paris
Producer	Antoine Bagot
Designers	Jeremie Bouchet
	Kevin O'Connor
Director	Clement Beauvais
Planner	Hadi Zabad
Advertiser	Ford, "Pin Ball Park"

The French are famous for their unconventional approach to parking. If a space is too small, some bumping and shunting will always make it bigger. So Paris was the perfect place for Ford to showcase its "Active Park Assist" technology. A giant pinball machine was positioned over a free parking space hemmed in with cars that reacted like pinball bumpers. Hidden cameras captured the brutal parking techniques. The worst driver won a chance to try a Ford equipped with Active Park Assist. But the most effective promotion was a YouTube film attracting thousands of views.

Agency	Ogilvy France, Paris
CCO	Chris Garbutt
Creative Director	Kurt Novack
Copywriter	Amandine Fabian
Art Director	Adrien Havet
Production	Steam Films
Producers	Annette Hallum
	Paul Mathews
Directors	Stuart McIntyre
	Talla Seck
Project Mgrs.	Adrien Leygues
	Claude-Yves Duchatel
Advertiser	Louis Vuitton

Louis Vuitton paid homage to legendary boxer Muhammad Ali as part of its ongoing Journeys campaign. But Vuitton's online film depicts his skills in an unusual way. Ali was known for his rhyming poetry, used to taunt his opponents or to talk about his vision of a better world. To pay tribute to Muhammed Ali's life journey, Vuitton invited rapper Mos Def to reinterpret four of Ali's poems inside a boxing ring. At the same time calligrapher Niels 'Shoe' Meulman transcribed one word from each poem onto the canvas.

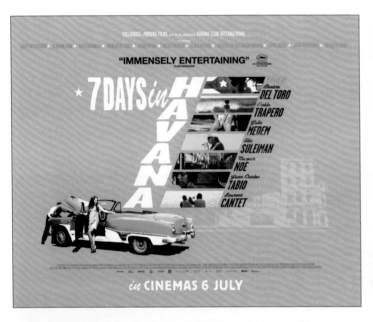

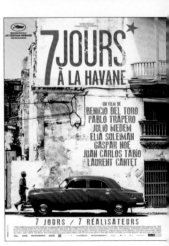

274   **Branded Entertainment**

Agency	fischerAppelt, Stuttgart
Creative Directors	Mirco Völker
	Michael Pickart
Copywriter	Björn Fischer
Production	fischerAppelt
Advertiser	Mercedes-Benz,
	"Stories About True
	Commitment: the Blind
	Motor Mechanic
	Bart Hickey"

To underline the authenticity of the Mercedes brand and the commitment of its fans, the automotive legend created a series of online films featuring remarkable people and their cars. This particular film centres on the craft of blind motor mechanic Bart Hickey, who's been working with Mercedes engines all his life. Even though he can't see them, he knows a great car when he feels it. The film features the admiring testimonies of Hickey's friends and customers.

Agency	M&C Saatchi.GAD,
	Paris
Creative Directors	Daniel Fohr
	Antoine Barthuel
Production	Wild Bunch, Paris
	Full House, Paris
	Morena Films, Madrid
Advertiser	Havana Club,
	"7 Days In Havana"

A feature film distributed in cinemas as well as online may be the ultimate in branded entertainment. And that's exactly what this is: a movie depicting the magical city of Havana through the eyes of seven different movie directors: Julio Médem, Laurent Cantet, Juan Carlos Tabío, Benicio del Toro, Gaspar Noé, Pablo Trapero and Elia Suleiman, with a screenplay by the Cuban novelist Leonardo Padura Fuentes. The full-length movie was a joint production between Spain's Morena Films, France's Full House – and iconic Cuban rum Havana Club.

Agency	Heye & Partner, Munich	
Creative Directors	Peter Prislin	
	Andreas Forberger	
Copywriters	Peter Prislin	
	Andreas Forberger	
Art Director	Andrew Schofield	
Production	Carmen Schumacher	
	Filmproduktion	
Producer	Denise Kaiser	
Idea	Amir Kassaei	
Advertiser	McDonald's,	
	"The Gourmet	
	Experiment"	

Some people don't believe in – or are too snobby to appreciate – the quality of Mc-Donald's. The burger chain attempted to change their minds with an event. Without revealing its true identity, it invited foodies and gastronomy critics to "The Gourmet Event of the Year", hosted by hot young chef Bernd Arold at a chic restaurant in Munich. The diners sampled a beautifully presented gourmet meal and applauded the chef. And then the big reveal: the meal had been entirely created from McDonald's products, freshly bought around the corner.

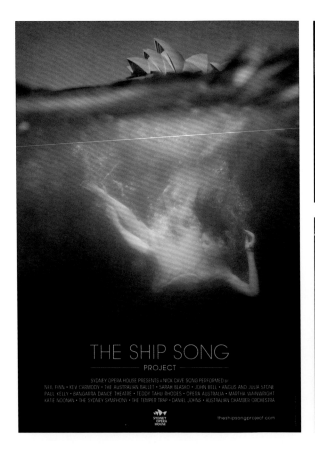

THE SHIP SONG
PROJECT

276 **Branded Entertainment**

Agency	The Monkeys, Sydney	This project aimed to show a different and more accessible side to the Sydney Opera House by inviting the world inside the iconic building. The video features a new version of Nick Cave's ballad "The Ship Song", interpreted by 100 pre-eminent artists - filmed over a 12 month period in total secrecy - while the camera weaves through the opera house, exploring stages, wings and behind the scenes. Finally, it comes to rest on a street musician outside. The uplifting film was seeded via social media sites to wide acclaim.
Executive CD	Justin Drape	
Creative Director	Noah Regan	
Copywriters	Noah Regan	
	Justin Drape	
	Simone Loius	
Art Director	Noah Regan	
Production	Exit Films	
Director	Paul Goldman	
Producer	Thea Carone	
Advertiser	Sydney Opera House, "The Ship Song Project"	

Agency	C-The Branded Content Agency, Ramat-Gan	As a worldwide partner of the Olympic Games, P&G decided to show its support for the women behind the athletes. The name of the campaign says it all: "Proud Sponsor of Moms". The MOMumentaries Project was a series of films telling the stories of Olympians through their mothers' eyes. Tales of sacrifice and devotion, hope and guidance – and unconditional love regardless of success or failure.
Creative Director	Erez Bergbaum	
Production	Kuperman Prods, Tel-Aviv	
Director	Sarit Haymian	
VP Clients	Gil Lederer	
Content Mgr.	Adi Hendler	
Producers	Ilanit Bauman	
	Oren Kestenbaum	
	Enav Shenhar	
Advertiser	Procter & Gamble	

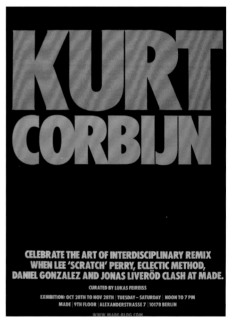

Agency	TBWA\Berlin	Producer	Katrin Dettmann	Media Agency	Lioneye	
Creative Directors	Philip Borchardt	Graphic Design	Andrew Morgan	Account Team	Alexis Mardon	
	Nico Zeh		Ricardo Mueller		Luise Biesalski	
	Tadi Rock		Kim Mueller		Philip Gaedicke	
	Dirk Henkelmann		Moni Eckey		Linn Kuhlmann	
Copywriters	Andrew Morgan	Editor/Director	Sammy Metwalli		Lukas Freireiss	
	Philip Borchardt	Sound Design	Eclectic Method		Ilja Bentscheff	
	Nico Zeh	Content Architect	Erik Scholz		Alexis Dornier	
Art Directors	Andrew Morgan	Planner	Judith Schmalzhaf	Advertiser	Absolut Vodka,	
	Philipp Migeod	Artists	Lee "Scratch" Perry		"MADE Scratch'n'Cut"	
	Stefano de Luccia		Jonas Liveroed			
Photographers	Niels Krueger		Daniel Gonzales			
	Robert Wunsch		Eclectic Method			

MADE is Absolut's art gallery and events space in Berlin. Absolut is renowned for its commitment to culture and MADE provides an ideal platform to explore unusual creative partnerships to arrive at unique experiences and artworks. To capture the spirit of creative collaboration, this campaign used wordplay to "mash up" icons from different cultural spheres, resulting in chimeras such as Tyra Banksy (model graffiti artist) and Muhammad Dali (boxing surrealist). The "scratch'n'cut" campaign included a range of limited editon T-shirts – we're told Tyra Banks even bought one.

278   **Branded Entertainment**

Agency	Havas Worldwide, London
Executive CD	Mick Mahoney
Copywriter	Russell Schaller
Art Director	Ben Clapp
Producer	Jodie Potts
Advertiser	Durex, "Durex Vinyl Facebook Game"

Durex Intense is a new condom aimed at couples; it speeds her up and slows him down, because often men and women just aren't in sync when it comes to sex. The new product was launched with a film featuring two turntables playing at different speeds. Finally they're brought into harmony, allowing Marvin Gaye to sing "Let's Get It On". The Facebook version of the commercial allowed couples to "get it on" live by testing how in sync they were. They were challenged to speed up or slow down well-known songs on the turntables in order to hear them correctly. The most in-sync couples were then invited to a VIP party to celebrate.

Agencies	Leg, Paris
	AKQA, London & Paris
Executive CD	Duan Evans
Creative Directors	Gabriel Gaultier
	Peter Lund
Associate CD	Nicolai Smith
Copywriters	Dimitri Lucas
	Nat Cantor
Art Director	Gregory Ferembach
Production	Carnibird, Paris
	Stink Digital, London
Director	Scott Corbett
Advertiser	Nike, "Barber Shop"

What makes footballers different from other blokes? Their haircuts, of course! To launch its new European soccer kit and celebrate the European cup among fans and a wider audience, Nike created the Nike Barbershop. A film launched on YouTube featured Italian footballer Mario Balotelli. The barber suggests different hairstyles associated with football legends of the past before Mario settles for his own individual look. It invited fans to imitate their idols by getting similarly cool haircuts. They could do this either virtually on Facebook or in real life in one of the seven pop up Nike Barbershops around the world.

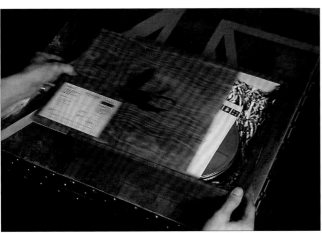

Agency	Abbott Mead Vickers BBDO, London	**Post Production**	Digital Domain	
Copywriters	Paul Knott	**Digital Prod'n**	Unit 9	
	Tim Vance		Weapon7	
Art Directors	Tim Vance		AMV Lab	
	Paul Knott	**Music**	11:59	
Production	RSA, London	**Sound Design**	Factory	
Director	Carl Erik Rinsch	**Mobile Prod'n**	Blippar	
Producers	Margo Mars	**Advertiser**	Mercedes-Benz,	
	Emmalou Johnson		"Escape the Map"	
	Esther Cunliffe			

How to get a younger audience interested in Mercedes? Create a multimedia game featuring a young woman in need of help. Via a YouTube trailer, players were challenged to guide a girl trapped in Streetview to safety for a chance to win a C-Class Coupé. They could trigger a plea for help from the trapped girl, Marie, by holding their phones over ads or posters. She even sent instructions by e-mail. They also received "real" phone calls from her. And Marie's own Twitter feed further blurred the borders between the virtual and the real.

Branded Entertainment

Agency	DDB Tribal Group, Düsseldorf	Steinway and Sons created a grand piano in honour of John Lennon: the Imagine Series Limited Edition. The company felt that everyone should be able to experience this instrument for themselves. So on the anniversary of Lennon's famous Bed-In peace protest, Steinway installed the piano in the same room at the same hotel – The Amsterdam Hilton – and made the keyboard virtually accessible to everyone. Users could contribute a song for peace to the microsite using their computer keyboards. Then the songs were magically played by the piano thanks to animatronics and streamed live online.
CCO	Eric Schoeffler	
Executive CD	Dennis May	
Creative Directors	Holger Scheuermann	
	Jan Propach	
Copywriters	Michael Schilling	
	Tobias Hecking	
Art Directors	Christian Bültmann	
	Fabian Jung	
	Nadim Habib	
Production	Markenfilm Crossing	
Advertiser	Steinway & Sons	

Agency	Ogilvy France, Paris	This stunt for the fresh-tasting mint featured the first ever fainting flash mob. In a square in the French town of Rouen, a man stops a passerby to ask for directions. The pedestrian opens his mouth to respond but his bad breath causes the questioner to faint. And then everyone in the square. And then everyone in town. Finally the person who was the first to faint recovers enough to offer the bemused victim of the stunt a Tic Tac. The brilliantly choreographed fun was clearly designed to amuse YouTube viewers.
CCO	Chris Garbutt	
Creative Directors	Baptiste Clinet	
	Nicolas Lautier	
	Florian Bodet	
Copywriter	Charles-Henry Joyaut	
Art Director	Salome Jestin	
Digital Head	Frédéric Levron	
Production	Fighting Fish	
Director	François Nemeta	
Producer	Hugo Diaz	
Advertiser	Tic Tac, "The Worst Breath in the World"	

Agency	AKQA, London	Web Developers	Owain Llewellyn	
Executive CD	Duan Evans		Maz Porta	
Creative Director	Masaya Nakade		Robert Wakeford	
Copywriter	Guy Bingley	QA Analyst	John Owen	
Art Director	Nick Bastian	Production	Onformative	
Development CD	Andy Hood	Generative AD	Cedric Keifer	
Creative Developer	Harald Krefting	Sound Designer	Jens C. Fischer,	
Programme Director	Daniela Michelon	Software Developer	Enrico Viola	
Technical Director	Gareth Scrivens	Account Team	Gareth Nettleton	
Project Manager	Luke Ellis		Sarah Meynell	
Tech. Delivery Mgr.	Jakes Lamprecht	Advertiser	Nike+ Fuelband,	
Software Engineer	Robin Weston		"Nike Fuel Station"	

The Nike+ FuelBand tracks your physical activity and turns burning energy into a game. But launching the FuelBand in the UK was a challenge as the product wasn't yet available to buy, so consumers couldn't touch it or experience it. And retail stores can be passive and sedentary. The solution was to turn the retail experience into a sports event. It was based on the Microsoft Kinect motion sensor, which mirrors physical movements on screen.

Users could see a 3D particle silhouette of their bodies. As they burned energy, their bodies turned from red to green. They could record this effect and share the film though an iPad app. The installation was the centrepiece of London's new Nike Fuel Station, where the futures of retail and sport intersect.

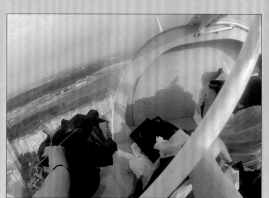

Public Relations

Agency	Studio Total, Malmö		
Creative Directors	Tomas Mazetti		
	Hannah Lina Frey		
	Per Cromwell		
	Linda Karlsson		
Producer	Linda Karlsson		
Advertiser	Belarus Human Rights, "Bears Over Belarus"		

The human rights situation in Belarus is so bad that an activist who dotted Minsk with cuddly toys holding signs demanding freedom of speech was arrested. The agency was asked by a human rights group to draw attention to what was happening in Belarus, so it decided to show its support for the jailed man by airdropping 800 protesting teddy bears into Minsk.

But no pilot was brave enough to risk being shot down by Belarus air defence – so the agency staffers bought a plane, learned to fly and completed the mission themselves. The event drew worldwide media coverage. As a result of the operation, the Belarus dictator Alexander Lukashenko dismissed his foreign minister, fired his heads of air force and border defence, expelled all the Swedish diplomats from Minsk and closed his embassy in Stockholm. All of which resulted in even more media coverage!

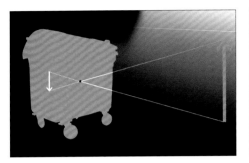

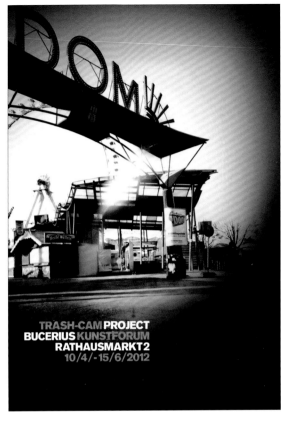

TRASH-CAM PROJECT
BUCERIUS KUNSTFORUM
RATHAUSMARKT 2
10/4/-15/6/2012

Agency	Scholz & Friends, Berlin		**Agency**	Mark BBDO,

Agency — Scholz & Friends, Berlin
Creative Directors — Martin Pross
Matthias Spaetgens
Mirko Derpmann
Christoph Blaschke
Copywriter — Mirko Derpmann
Art Directors — Christoph Keller
Sebastian Frese
Producers — Sandro Buschke
Benito Schumacher
Post Production — Fabian Behrendt
Advertiser — City Cleaning Hamburg,
"Trashcam Hamburg"

Hamburg is a clean, beautiful and cultural city. But who spares a second thought for its refuse collectors? To put the dustbin men in the public eye, they were turned into artists. They were asked to photograph their favourite places in the city – using their bins. These were transformed into giant pinhole cameras by drilling a hole in the front and placing a giant piece of photographic paper in the back. The resulting pictures were exhibited at the Bucerius Art Forum, a respected contemporary art space. The story and the photographs delighted the press in Germany and beyond.

Agency — Mark BBDO, Prague
Creative Directors — Andrej Stuk
Leon Sverdlin
Copywriters — Jenda Holecek
Tomas Novotny
Iva Macku
Art Directors — Lubos Vacke
Ales Kolaja
Producers — Jan Šoupa
Zuzka Hajasova
Advertiser — Pepsi,
"Pepsi Epopée"

Pepsi is on a mission to "Refresh your world". In this project, 20 young Czech artists "refreshed" the famous "Slavic Epopée" by Alfons Mucha: the story of the Slavs in 20 paintings. The artists interpreted the 1910 originals to reflect the attitudes of young people today. For example, a painting in which troops gather on a mountaintop before a battle is replaced with an deserted peak and the word "nobody", reflecting modern disgust with war. In another new interpretation, a DJ takes the place of spiritual leader Jan Hus. The images were displayed during a major design expo.

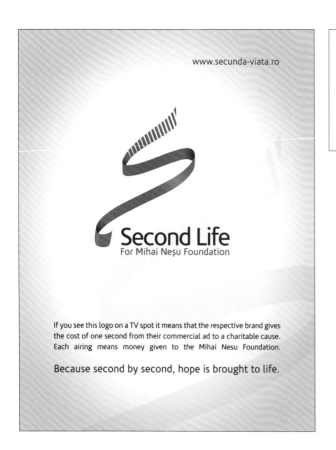

www.secunda-viata.ro

Second Life
For Mihai Neşu Foundation

If you see this logo on a TV spot it means that the respective brand gives the cost of one second from their commercial ad to a charitable cause. Each airing means money given to the Mihai Nesu Foundation.

Because second by second, hope is brought to life.

30" TV SPOT vs 29" TV SPOT = 3,33% LESS MEDIA COST

Frankfurt baut das neue Städel

Frankfurt baut das neue Städel

284   **Public Relations**

Agency	Leo Burnett & Target, Bucharest
Creative Directors	Carmen Tiderle, Victor Stroe, Tudor Cuciuc
Copywriter	Irina Becher
Art Directors	Liviu Toader, Florina Moisi, Zoltan Fulop
Brand Com. Mgr.	Diana Alexa
Advertiser	Gazeta Sporturilor, "Second Life"

Romanian sports journal Gazeta Sporturilor wanted to help wheelchair-bound former soccer star Mihai Nesu raise money for his charity supporting kids with mobility problems. The Second Life campaign persuaded advertisers to cut one second from all their TV spots and donate the savings to Nesu's cause. In return, they earned the right to show the Second Life logo at the end of their commercials. A pro bono TV and print campaign explained the meaning of this logo - so consumers could appreciate the generosity of participating advertisers.

Agency	Ogilvy & Mather, Frankfurt
Creative Directors	Stephan Vogel, Helmut Meyer
Copywriter	Stephan Vogel
Art Director	Helmut Meyer
Planner	Anna Hoehn
Account Mgr.	Sabina Pal
Client	Kerstin Schultheis
Advertiser	Städel Museum, "Frankfurt is Building the New Städel"

The Frankfurt Städel Museum needed more space to showcase the treasures in its archives. But it also had to convince Frankfurt citizens to donate the five million euros required for a new building. So it launched the campaign "Frankfurt is building the new Städel" and adopted yellow builder's boots as a visual trigger. Whenever the boots appeared in the press, no matter how unlikely the person wearing it – from city officials to local celebrities and even the entire local football team – the bright boots reminded viewers about the museum project and suggested that everyone in Frankfurt was pulling their weight to get it built.

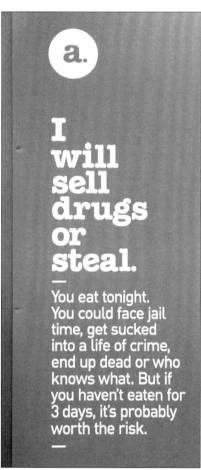

a.

I will sell drugs or steal.
—
You eat tonight. You could face jail time, get sucked into a life of crime, end up dead or who knows what. But if you haven't eaten for 3 days, it's probably worth the risk.
—

Agency	Leo Burnett, Toronto
CCO	Judy John
Creative Directors	Judy John
	Lisa Greenberg
Copywriter	Steve Persico
Art Director	Anthony Chelvanathan
Producer	Kim Burchiel
Account Team	Natasha Dagenais
	Jeremy Farncomb
Advertiser	Raising the Roof,
	"The Street House"

Toronto hosts an annual festival called Doors Open, during which the owners of the city's most beautiful and interesting homes open their doors to the public. But some of the city's residents don't even have a home. To draw attention to the issue, the Raising the Roof charity erected The Street House – a structure dedicated to those without a home. Inside, the "cardboard" home, sculptures, panels and installations explored and undermined stereotypical views of the homeless: that they're lazy, addicted to drugs or prepared to prostitute themselves. A tour of the home was a tour of a homeless person's harsh world.

I see a great winter coming.

They tell me how the winter will be.

....we're gonna have a bloody great winter.

An ant from the Netherlands!

Come see us...we won't bite!

Book your winter holidays now
MySwitzerland.com

Switzerland.
get natural.

MySwitzerland.com

THE GREAT PAPER AIRPLANE PROJECT

WHERE KIDS FOLD PLANES
AND SOAR INTO HISTORY.

SATURDAY, JANUARY 14
PIMA AIR & SPACE MUSEUM

JOIN THE FLY-OFF

NO PURCHASE NECESSARY.
ENDS 1/14/12. FOR OFFICIAL RULES,
VISIT WWW.GREATPAPERPLANE.ORG

FLY YOUR PLANE. SOAR INTO HISTORY.

THE GREAT PAPER AIRPLANE PROJECT

Win our Fly-Off at the Pima Air & Space Museum and have your design inspire one
of the world's largest paper airplane launches.

FLY-OFF: JANUARY 14, 2012 | HISTORIC LAUNCH: FEBRUARY 2012

PIMA AIR & SPACE MUSEUM

RVSP at: GreatPaperAirplane.org

286   Public Relations

Agency	Spillmann/Felser/ Leo Burnett, Zurich	Everyone loved Switzerland Tourism's ad featuring eccentric "weather prophet" Martin Horat, who could predict the weather by observing ants. Well, maybe not everyone: animal rights campaigners contacted the Federal Office for the Environment and insisted that the tourist office stop using the spot in case it "encouraged other people to sit on anthills". When the press heard about the ban, it went into overdrive. Thousands of Martin's fans protested and soon the film was back online – and more popular than ever.
Creative Directors	Martin Spillmann Peter Brönnimann	
Copywriters	Martin Spillmann Peter Brönnimann	
Production	Plan B, Zurich	
Advertiser	Switzerland Tourism, "Horat-the Weather Prophet"	

Agency	BBDO, San Francisco	The Pima Air & Space Museum in Tucson, Arizona, wanted to talk to kids about the science of flight and attract more visitors. So its agency came up with a big idea: the world's biggest paper plane. First, kids were invited to test their own designs in a "fly-off". The lucky 12-year-old boy who won got to join the project team and watch his design be transformed into a 45-foot long prototype. Finally the big day came – and the plane soared into aviation history, flying almost one mile over the Arizona desert! Today, the giant paper plane is on permanent display at the museum.
Creative Directors	Mike McKay Bryan Houlette	
Copywriters	Jack Harding Dan Hofstadter	
Art Director	Sara Nicely	
Production	BeCore, Los Angeles Region-C, Austin	
Producers	Louise Doherty Lindsey Wood Sam Barrett Jan O'Malley	
Advertiser	Pima Space Museum	

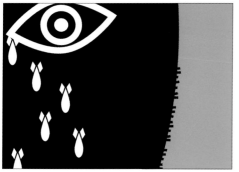

MAKE LOVE NOT SHOPPING!

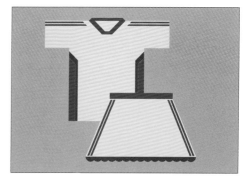

The Unfinished

The expedition that finished a piece of musical history.

1912

2012

A MUSIC EXPEDITION

The Unfinished

1912 ★ 2012
41° 44' N, 49° 57' W

KONZERTHAUS DORTMUND

Agency	cohnandjansen JWT, Bucharest	In a pro bono gesture of social engagement, the agency decided to give an outdoor site in
Creative Director	Andrei Cohn	the centre of Bucharest a controversial voice.
Copywriter	Andrei Ignat	The poster in Arthur Verona street was used
Art Directors	Andrei Cohn	to express funny or trenchant views on hot
	Evelin Bundur	Romanian topics: the elections, the national
	Alexandru Stanciu	soccer team, celebrities, movies, special
Advertiser	The Arthur Verona	occasions, floods.. People were also invited

Agency cohnandjansen JWT, Bucharest
Creative Director Andrei Cohn
Copywriter Andrei Ignat
Art Directors Andrei Cohn
Evelin Bundur
Alexandru Stanciu
Advertiser The Arthur Verona Billboard, "Saving the Soul of a Billboard"

In a pro bono gesture of social engagement, the agency decided to give an outdoor site in the centre of Bucharest a controversial voice. The poster in Arthur Verona street was used to express funny or trenchant views on hot Romanian topics: the elections, the national soccer team, celebrities, movies, special occasions, floods.. People were also invited to make their own contributions online. The free speech billboard changed the character of the entire street, attracting graffiti artists to the surrounding wall and even an outdoor arts and crafts festival.

Agency Jung von Matt, Hamburg
Creative Directors Tobias Grimm
Jens Pfau
Production Markenfilm, Wedel
Copywriters Alexandra Stock
Julia Radlwimmer
Art Directors Samuel Huber
Katrin Stanek
Thimon Machatzke
Post Production Infected Postproduction
Advertiser Konzerthaus Dortmund, "The Unfinished"

The task was to raise awareness of the Konzerthaus Dortmund classical music venue and attract the best international talent. Eight musicians from the Konzerthaus were sent with the Titanic memorial cruise ship on a commemorative journey to the resting place of the fated liner. Floating above the ship's watery grave, they finished – exactly one hundred years later – the last piece played by the Titanic's courageous orchestra. Thanks to the media aboard the memorial vessel, the pictures of the orchestra played a key role in the Titanic commemorations.

The... The pictures are kind of weird!

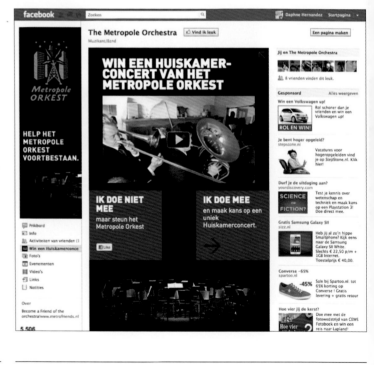

Agency	Cake Paris, Puteaux
Creative Director	Alban Penicaut
Copywriter	Constantin de La Borde
Art Director	Vincent Boursaud
Photographer	Michael Vojinovic
Production	Emmanuelle, Paris
Advertiser	Canal+ Borgia Series, "Discover What You Should Not Have"

French TV channel Canal+ was launching "Borgia", a new show about the infamous pope's family and the sex, violence and corruption that swirled around them and the Vatican in the late 15th century. To get bloggers chatting about the new show, they were chauffeured to a secret party in specially hired taxis. On the back seat, they found "mislaid" cameras containing amateur-style shots of what looked like orgiastic religious scenes, featuring priests and nubile young ladies. The bloggers were shocked and amused – and it was only when they arrived at the party that the stunt was revealed.

Agency	Havas Worldwide, Amsterdam
Creative Directors	Peter Hamelinck
	Thijs de Boer
Copywriters	Thijs de Boer
	Huibert-Jan van der Fange
Art Directors	Peter Hamelinck
	Demy Sapthu
Strategy	Remko Herremans
Account Mgr.	Budi Gonzalez de Chaves
Advertiser	The Metropole Orchestra, "Save an Orchestra"

The conservative Dutch government wanted to slash its funding of the Metropole Orchestra. The politicians now considered the combination of symphony orchestra, jazz and easy-listening as "left-wing hobbies", to quote one of them. To prove them wrong, the orchestra recorded a pop single. "Worldwide Orchestra" roared up the hit parade to number one. More publicity was garnered when a Facebook campaign offered fans the chance to win a concert in their own homes. The media response was huge and funding was soon renewed for 4 more years..

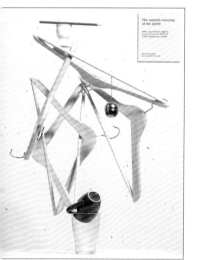

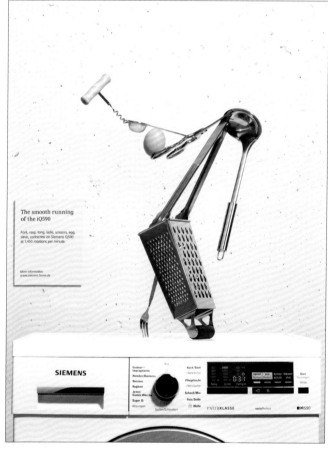

Agency	Scholz & Friends, Berlin	**Photographer**	Szymon Plewa	
Creative Directors	Martin Pross	**Production**	Partizan	
	Matthias Spaetgens	**Producers**	Nele Siegl	
	Robert Krause		Franziska Ibe	
	Florian Schwalme	**Sculptures**	Szymon Plewa	
	Mathias Rebmann	**Graphics**	Susan Wesarg	
	Markus Daubenbuechel		Philipp Bertisch	
Copywriter	Stefan Sohlau	**Account Team**	Kerstin Seidel	
Art Directors	Bjoern Kernspeckt		Mehibe Tuncel	
	René Gebhardt	**Advertiser**	Siemens	
	Sebastian Kamp		Washing Machines,	
			"The Laundry Gallery"	

Siemens washing machines with anti-vibration technology run so smoothly that they never shake, even on fast spin. To demonstrate this, a local artist created fragile sculptures from normal household items and balanced them precariously on the machines. Then the spin cycle was switched on and the balance sculptures remained intact. Eight of the sculptures were shown in a pop-up art gallery in the center of Berlin – the "Laundry Gallery". Posters, an online film and advertisements in local magazines attracted a curious crowd to the opening. And the spin doctors proved their point.

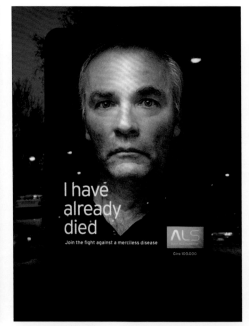
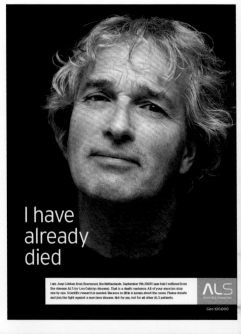

290 | **Public Relations**

Agency	Forsman & Bodenfors, Gothenburg	Ikea launched Uppleva, a new product integrating a TV into a stylish piece of furniture. Although the product was only available in five European cities, Ikea wanted worldwide attention. So it used YouTube to tell homeowners they could say goodbye to messy wires and cables. But Ikea really struck gold when US talk show host Conan O'Brien spoofed the film by suggesting customers would have to build the TV from scratch, in true Ikea style, using thousands of tiny electronic components and an instruction manual – in Swedish.
Art Directors	Agnes Stenberg-Schentz Jeremy Phang Silla Levin	
Production	Acne, Stockholm	
Director	Marcus Svanberg	
Producers	Alexander Blidner Pål Åsberg Christian Rehnfors	
Designer	Ellinor Bjarnolf	
Advertiser	Ikea, "Uppleva"	

Agencies	Publicis, Amsterdam Starcom, Amsterdam	ALS (also known as Lou Gehrig's disease) is an incurable and deadly disease of the nervous system. On average patients die within three years of being diagnosed. To raise awareness of the disease and encourage donations to the ALS Foundation, a confrontational strategy was adopted. ALS sufferers explained the disease and asked for donations – but not for themselves, because their statements were aired after they had died. The campaign was launched on the national news and became a talking point across media.
Creative Directors	Marcel Hartog Jeroen van Zwam	
Photographer	Lukas Göbel	
Production	In Case of Fire	
Director	Olaf van Gerwen	
Producers	Marja Borkus Ron Townsend	
Designer	Dave Fransen	
Post Production	Jan Hibma	
Advertiser	ALS Foundation, "I Have Already Died"	

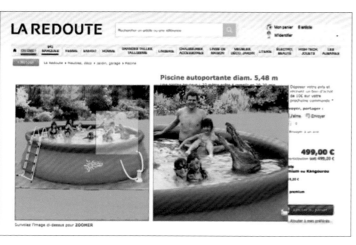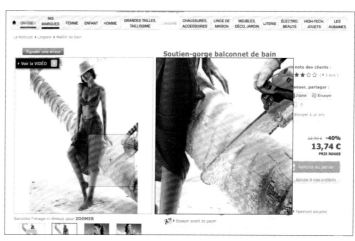

		An honest mistake became a media sensation when the image of a naked male bather was spotted in the background of a photo for children's clothing on French retailer La Redoute's website. The retailer removed the picture straight away, but it was too late – La Redoute was already a laughing stock and the subject of the second most tweeted story in the world, with their naked man cropping up in images across the internet.	So what did they do? Sit tight and wait for the fuss to die down? Instead, on the advice of its agency, the retailer turned the massive mistake to its advantage with a funny online competition. It planted 14 fake "fails" among the 33,600 images on its website and challenged people to find them via an amusing online video. In less than 48 hours, all the pictures were found and thousands of articles had praised La Redoute for regaining control of its e-reputation.
Agency	CLM BBDO, Paris		
Creative Directors	Matthieu Elkaim		
	Benjamin Marchal		
	Olivier Lefebvre		
Art Director	Ronan Coursin		
Production	CLM BBDO		
Head of Digital	Nicolas Carlotti		
Comm. Director	Amelie Poisson		
Account Team	Audrey Bedoucha		
	Anne-Lise Sellier		
Advertiser	La Redoute,		
	"The Naked Man"		

Alexey Fadeev, Depot WPF, CD, Moscow, Russia

Isabella Bernardi, Y&R, Vice CD, Milan, Italy

Gideon Amichay, Shalmor Avnon Amichay/Y&R Interactive, Former CCO, Tel Aviv, Israel

Jeff Goodby, Goodby, Silverstein & Partners, Co-founder, Co-chairman, San Francisco, USA

Agustin Acosta, Lowe Ginkgo, Art Director, Montevideo, Uruguay

Adriano Alarcon, Giovanni+DraftFCB, Senior Art Director, São Paulo, Brazil

Kazoo Sato, TBWA\Hakuhodo, ECD, Tokyo, Japan

Kenichiro Shigetomi, I&S BBDO, Art Director, Tokyo, Japan

Camilla Bjørnhaug, TRY, Copywriter, Oslo, Norway

Mariano Serkin, Del Campo Nazca Saatchi & Saatchi, ECD, Buenos Aires, Argentina

Weerachon Weeraworawit, Well Done Bangkok, Head of Creative, Founder, Thailand

Lulo Calió, DraftFCB, CD, Buenos Aires, Argentina

Aricio Fortes, Pereira & O'Dell, CD, San Francisco, USA

Guga Ketzer, Loducca, Partner, CCO, São Paulo, Brazil

Sergio Valente, DDB, CEO, President, São Paulo, Brazil

Ted Royer, Drogas, Partner, ECD, New York, USA

Tham Khai Meng, Ogilvy & Mather, Worldwide CCO, Chairman, New York, USA

Sir John Hegarty, BBH, Worldwide CD, Founder, London, UK

Lo Sheung Yan, JWT, ECD, Chairman North East Asia, Shanghai, China

Aaron Reynolds, Wave Studios, CD, London, UK

Matt Clack, Grow Interactive, Art Director, Norfolk, USA

Eduardo Marques, Ogilvy, Integrated CD, São Paulo, Brazil

Erik Ravelo, FABRICA, CD, Treviso, Italy

Jenny Glover, NETWORK BBDO, CD, Scriptwriter, Johannesburg, South Africa

Kaoru Sugano, Dentsu, CD, Tokyo, Japan

Markus Ivan Johansson, Leo Burnett, Copywriter, Milan, Italy

Jeff Benjamin, North America, CCO, Founder, Minneapolis, USA

Michael Canning, Leo Burnett, ECD, Senior V.President, New York, USA

Koichiro Tanaka, Projector, CD, Tokyo, Japan

Jaime Rosado, JWT, Vice President, Regional CD, San Juan, Puerto Rico

Luca Lorenzini, Saatchi&Saatchi, CD, Milan, Italy

Bob Greenberg, R/GA, Chairman, Founder, CEO, Global CCO, New York, USA

Chris Chiu, Ren Partnership, Founder, CCO, Singapore

Sir John Hegarty, BBH, Worldwide CD, Founder, London, UK

Sergio Valente, DDB, CEO, President, São Paulo, Brazil

Kazoo Sato, TBWA\Hakuhodo, ECD, Tokyo, Japan

Mariano Serkin, Del Campo Nazca Saatchi & Saatchi, ECD, Buenos Aires, Argentina

Chris Chiu, Ren Partnership, Founder, CCO, Singapore

Jeff Goodby, Goodby, Silverstein & Partners, Co-founder, Co-chairman, San Francisco, USA

Ted Royer, Drogas, Partner, ECD, New York, USA

Lulo Calió, DraftFCB, CD, Buenos Aires, Argentina

Markus Ivan Johansson, Leo Burnett, Copywriter, Milan, Italy

Eduardo Marques, Ogilvy, Integrated CD, São Paulo, Brazil

Luca Lorenzini, Saatchi&Saatchi, CD, Milan, Italy

Alexey Fadeev, Depot WPF, CD, Moscow, Russia

Matt Clack, Grow Interactive, Art Director, Norfolk, USA

Kenichiro Shigetomi, I&S BBDO, Art Director, Tokyo, Japan

Jenny Glover, NETWORK BBDO, CD, Scriptwriter, Johannesburg, South Africa

Weerachon Weeraworawit, Well Done Bangkok, Head of Creative, Founder, Thailand

Agustin Acosta, Lowe Ginkgo, Art Director, Montevideo, Uruguay

Isabella Bernardi, Y&R, Vice CD, Milan, Italy

Adriano Alarcon, Giovanni+DraftFCB, Senior Art Director, São Paulo, Brazil

Erik Ravelo, FABRICA, CD, Treviso, Italy

Kaoru Sugano, Dentsu, CD, Tokyo, Japan

Agency	Dmitry & Oleg, Moscow
Creative Directors	Dmitry Chigirin
	Oleg Izosimov
Copywriter	Dmitry Chigirin
Art Director	Oleg Izosimov
Photographers	Dmitry Chigirin
	Oleg Izosimov
Film Director	Hrant Abovyan
Editors	Hrant Abovyan
	Sergey Teryaev
Advertiser	Dmitry & Oleg, "The Best Recommendation Ever"

Young creative duo Dmitry & Oleg from Siberia set out to do for themselves what they'll do for their future clients – create an amazing promotion. They went to the Cannes Lions festival to meet the jurors and other creative luminaries. Every ad-land star they met was asked to write a single letter on a sheet of white paper and sign it.

The pair then used the letters to form recommendations for a video, posters and their website. "Oleg & Dmitry are the best"; they "smile like the Giaconda"; "speak can like Yoda"; "know MS Paint" and so on. Sir John Hegarty, Jeff Goodby were among the 33 creative gurus who signed letters. Industry media covered the project, Facebook and Twitter buzzed, the video got 10,000 views, the website attracted 1000 visitors a day. And Oleg & Dmitry got 18 job offers.

Agency	DDB Tribal, Vienna
CCO	Eric Schoeffler
Creative Directors	Sebastian Kainz
	Vera Steinhäuser
	Hannes Böker
Copywriter	Antonia Kiefhaber
Art Director	Marian Grabmayer
Digital Manager	Florian Grünwald
Digital Concept	Sebastian Schöndorfer
Programming	Liechtenecker
Client Service	Elisabeth Pelzer
Advertiser	Ikea, "Sofa Swap"

The Museumsquartier is one of the most beautiful places in Vienna, but the seats there aren't very comfy. So Ikea swapped them for 44 sofas, which visitors could lounge on day and night. What's more, by using an app on the Ikea Facebook page, they could upload pictures of themselves on their favourite couch. Those with the best photos won their sofa.

Agency	Åkestam Holst,
	Stockholm
Creative Director	Andreas Ullenius
Copywriter	Adam Reuterskiöld
Art Director	Fredrik Josefsson
Production	From Stockholm with
	Love, Stockholm
Digital Producer	Johan Eklund
Graphic Design	Oscar Gardö
Planner	Lars Friberg
Account Team	Magnus Hamberg
	Marie Höglin
Advertiser	Swebus

Every year, amazingly, the Swedish rail service virtually grinds to a halt when it snows. That means long delays for travellers. Swebus, on the other hand, claims to be the most reliable and punctual public transport system in the country. To prove this it challenged travellers to play "Swebus Jackpot". During the month of December, anyone could bet on which would be the most delayed trains over Christmas. Those who guessed the right trains and duration of delays won bus tickets worth €100. Almost 50,000 people played the game and 100 free trips were won.

USER-GENERATED CONTENT

Take a box. Have a Great Move. IKEA

MOVING BOX

Agency	Ogilvy & Mather, Kiev
Creative Directors	Alexandra Doroguntsova
	Will Rust
Copywriter	Evgeniya Dzyubenko
Art Directors	Taras Dzendrovskii
	Dima Lebedev
Production House	Umbrella
	Case
	FIX Digital
	Positive Pictures
Producer	Irina Pigal
Advertiser	Borjomi Water, "The World's Deepest Website"

Borjomi mineral water comes from a spring deep in the Georgian mountains. At 8,000 metres, the source is far deeper than most mineral waters, which typically come from 100 metres below ground. Visitors were challenged to scroll down the world's deepest website – an eight kilometre voyage that took an average of nine hours. Over 300,000 people attempted the journey during the first month and 1,000 made it to the bottom where they could check-in on Facebook and leave a commemorative plaque. Some users managed to reach the bottom faster – but they cheated by getting machines to scroll for them.

Agency	Leo Burnett, Toronto
CCO	Judy John
Group CDs	David Federico
	Morgan Kurchak
Creative Director	Lisa Greenberg
Copywriters	Andrew Caie
	Matthew Doran
Art Directors	Noel Fenn
	Sean Perkins
Producers	David Eades
	Thomas Degez
	Anne Peck
Advertiser	Ikea, "Moving Day"

Due to a law that requires rent agreements to end or be renewed on June 30, thousands of the citizens of Quebec move house over the July 1 weekend. The date is known as Moving Day. And what do you need when you move? That's right – boxes. So since 2011 Ikea has provided free boxes, with a difference. They're printed with packing tips, coupons for meals at Ikea and money-off vouchers for furniture. Others still become furniture themselves. And in 2012 Ikea introduced the Moving Box truck, which people could track via GPS and call up for a box delivery.

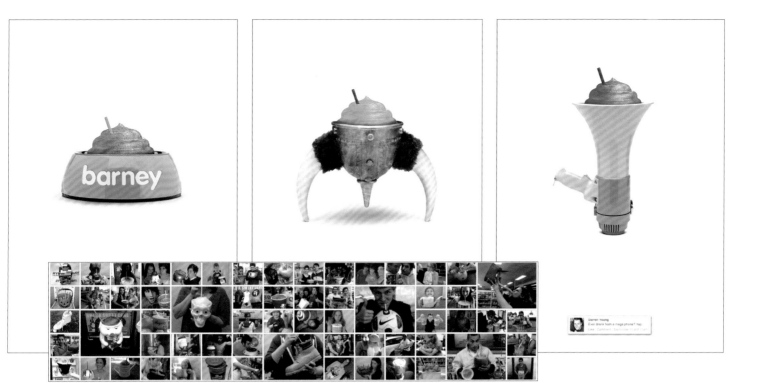

Agency	Leo Burnett, Melbourne	Slurpee faced a challenge as aggressive competitors entered the Australian frozen drink market. To remind drinkers why they loved Slurpee, it focused on a crucial part of the drinking experience – the cup. On "Bring Your Own Cup Day" people were invited to fill up any vessel they liked for the price of a medium Slurpee. The idea was seeded on Facebook by asking people to submit creative cup ideas. On the day itself, Australians responded by filling over 80,000 objects, from boots to goldfish bowls, with nearly half a million litres: the highest Slurpee sales in history.
Creative Director	Jason Williams	
Copywriters	Andrew Woodhead	
	Elle Bullen	
	Eamonn Dixon	
Art Director	James Orr	
Digital Build	Rodeo	
PR	Haystac	
Media	OMD	
Advertiser	Slurpee, "BYO Cup Day"	

Agency	Ogilvy & Mather, Prague	Not every charity fundraiser on the street is working for a real charity. To combat the rise of fundraising fraud in the Czech Republic, Darujspravne.cz was set up as an online portal allowing safe donations to approved charities. To promote the site, teams were sent out to ask pedestrians for a donation of 20 Czech crowns to an unnamed charity. If they did so, they received a gift: a box with 20 crowns in it and the message, "Here is your 20 crowns back, but next time be careful who you give your money to."
Creative Director	Jan Havlicek	
Copywriter	Radek Antl	
Art Director	Bernard Netopil	
Illustrator	Tomas Jursik	
Production	Avion	
	Postproduction	
Account Team	Michal Kroupa	
	Alan Ostarek	
	Tomas Jindrisek	
Advertiser	Daruj Správně, "Give it Back"	

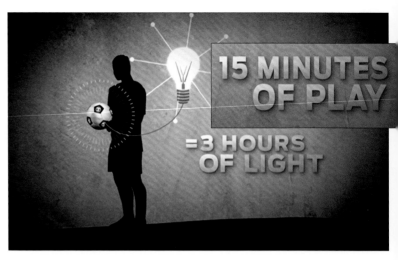

Agencies	Alma DDB, Miami
	TMA, Chicago
CCO	Luis Miguel Messianu
Executive CDs	Diego Yurkievich
	Hernan Cerdeiro
Creative Director	Juan Diego Guzman
Copywriter	Danilo Lauria
Art Director	Alex Ohannessian
Producers	Diego Colombo
	Alberto Farinas
	Francisco Sanchez
Digital Director	Luz Maria Velez
Advertiser	State Farm Insurance

State Farm collaborated with the inventors of the "soccket ball" to help poor Latin American communities that have no electricity. Play soccer with the ball for 15 minutes and it generates enough energy for three hours of light when an LED bulb is plugged in. The initiative was launched at the Gold Cup soccer tournament, sponsored by State Farm. Online, people got involved by playing a digital football game: the more virtual minutes of light they generated by playing with the ball, the more "soccket balls" were donated.

Agency	Leo Burnett, Toronto
CCO	Judy John
Group CDs	Anthony Chelvanathan
	Steve Persico
Creative Director	Lisa Greenberg
Copywriter	Steve Persico
Producers	Franca Piacente
	Gladys Bachand
	Kim Burchiel
Editor	David Nakata
Music	TA2 Sound & Music
Advertiser	James Ready,
	"Spelling Bee Lottery"

Beer brand James Ready is famous for printing funny messages under its bottle caps. This year the caps bore letters, numbers and punctuation. Every Tuesday and Friday at 5pm precisely, James Ready fans visited the brand's Facebook page, where a video revealed a "semi-awesome prize" (a horse head mask, for instance) and a quirky phrase, such as "magnificent moustache". The first person to post a picture of the phrase spelled out in JR bottle caps on the brand's Facebook page won the prize.

Agencies	Publicis & Publicis Dialog, Amsterdam
Creative Directors	Marcel Hartog
	Jeroen van Zwam
Associate CDs	Lynsey Schouten,
	Boudewijn Pompe
Illustrator	Erwin Kho
Event Manager	Mirjam Heffels
Designers	Janneke de Graaf-Koning
	Gaby Poel
Advertiser	Wagner Big Pizza, "Moto Cross Delivery"

The Dutch Black Motocross Festival is a three day jamboree of motorbikes, camping, music and beer that draws 150,000 visitors a year. They're the kind of people who love scoffing pizza – but tend to scoff at advertising. So event sponsor Wagner Big Pizza came up with a more direct approach: Moto Cross Pizza Delivery. The motocross fans could have their Wagner Big Pizza delivered anywhere on the camp site by 450cc Yamaha pro dirt bikes.

Agency	Wirz BBDO, Zurich
Creative Directors	Philipp Skrabal
	Thomas Kurzmeyer
	Markus Schärer
Copywriters	Andi Portmann
	Torsten Maas
	Winfried Schneider
Art Directors	Rob Hartmann
	Marco Zimmerli
	Rahel Nemitz
Graphic Design	Sarah Kahn
	Tanja Jablanovic
Advertiser	Ikea, "Rothenburg"

Ikea was opening its eighth store in Switzerland, in the town of Rothenburg. Not much of a story – so how to attract media attention? The retailer invented a fictitious problem: it had so many products that it was already running out of space in its new store, before it even opened. Through press ads and online, it asked if people would be willing to loan their private homes as Ikea showrooms. These were furnished with Ikea items and opened to the public for six weeks – in return the home-owners could keep the furnishings.

Stacja docelowa	Kategoria	Peron	Czas odjazdu	Opóźnienie	Zdążysz zjeść
Destination	Category	Platform	Scheduled	Delay	Enough time to eat
ŁÓDŹ KALISKA	TLK	4	12:15	40	
MIĘDZYLESIE	IR	4	12:22		
WIEN WESTBHF	EC	3	12:25		
PRZEMYŚL GŁÓWNY	IR	3	12:30		
WROCŁAW GŁÓWNY	TLK	4	12:42		
KRAKÓW GŁÓWNY	Ex	3	12:55		
LUBLIN	TLK	1	12:57		
BYDGOSZCZ GŁÓWNA	TLK	3	13:00		
KRAKÓW PŁASZÓW	TLK	3	13:05		
KOŁOBRZEG	TLK	2	13:15		

Agency	DDB, Warsaw
Creative Directors	Zuzanna Duchniewska-Sobczak Maciej Waligora
Copywriter	Mateusz Ksiazek
Art Director	Magdalena Drozdowska
Producer	Kasia Seyfried
Digital Prod'n	Robert Grabowski Marek Kozlowski Andrzej Krok,
Production Mgr.	Jacek Lukasik
Advertiser	McDonald's, "Hamburger Timetable"

Waiting at a railway station can be miserable, especially when your train has been delayed. But at Warsaw's central station, McDonald's and its agency turned waiting into an opportunity. The Hamburger Timetable displays real-time train information alongside images of the type of McDonald's meal you'll have time to eat before your train leaves. It even made adjustments according to delays. The longer you have to wait, the more menu items are shown on the screen. So why not go and wait at McDonald's?

Agency	Jung von Matt, Berlin
Executive CDs	Mathias Stiller Till Eckel
Creative Directors	Christian Kroll Peter Gocht
Copywriter	Bjoern Ingenleuf
Art Director	Javier Suarez Argueta
Art Buying	Marjorie Jorrot
Producer	Julia Cramer
Account Team	Stefanie Gombert Marie Braun
Advertiser	Mercedes-Benz, "Aidbag"

Every year a Mercedes-Benz invention saves thousands of lives: the airbag. To highlight this, genuine airbags from crashed Mercedes-Benz cars were recycled and turned into fashion items. Presenting the Aidbag: a must-have accessory. Each Aidbag was unique and came with its own story. All the bags had genuinely saved lives; now they carried on saving lives by being sold to raise money for Doctors Without Borders. The bags were launched at the Mercedes-Benz Fashion Week in Berlin before being made available through the marque's flagship showrooms worldwide.

Agency	DDB & Tribal, Amsterdam	Remember the flight when you were forced
Creative Directors	Olaf van der Geld	to sit next to an obnoxious guy who tried
	Sanne Braam	to sell you insurance? KLM's Meet & Seat
Copywriters	Paul Fraser	enables you to chose who you want to
	Sharon Cleary	sit next to by sharing and comparing your
Art Directors	Christopher Pugmire	social media profile with those of other
	Keith Kornson	passengers. To launch the concept, films
Photographer	Bert Teunissen	and print ads played on the idea of sitting
Production	MediaMonks, Hilversum	next to soccer star Ruud Gullit, fashion
	Caviar, Amsterdam	model Yfke Sturm or DJ Armin Van Buuren.
Producers	Steven Beukers	Visitors to the KLM site were invited to take
	Denise Wolterbeek	part in a virtual chat with one of six Dutch
Advertiser	KLM, "Be My Guest"	celebrities – and win a real flight with them.

Agency	Lemz, Amsterdam	Hardly anybody reads the safety labels
Creative Directors	Bram Tervoort	on household chemicals. Which is how
	Chester de Vries	thousands of people end up in hospital every
Copywriters	Daniel te Lindert	year. The Dutch Consumer Safety Associa-
	Chester de Vries	tion wanted to change this. So it sneaked
Art Directors	Bram Tervoort	a message into the labels of selected
	Luiz Risi	products: "Congratulations! By reading
Producers	Laura Bremerkamp	this label you've just won €1,000." Nobody
3D & Design	INDG, Amsterdam	noticed. The money stayed in the bank. Until
Advertiser	VeiligheidNL	a press release about the operation resulted
	Consumer Safety	in widespread media coverage. Suddenly,
	Association,	everyone started digging out old household
	"The Label Lottery"	cleaning products to read the labels.

Agency	Ubisoft, Montpellier
Production	Ubisoft Production International, Paris
Director	Andy's
Post Production	Unit Image, Paris
Advertiser	Ubisoft ZombiU, "ZombiU Game Trailer"

Ubisoft's ZombiU is a terrifying video game in which zombies take over the UK. In this equally scary trailer, we see still life tableaus of the living dead wreaking havoc across London. Terrified humans battle zombies on a red London bus, in the City, on Tower Bridge and even right outside Buckingham Palace, where we see a guardsman fighting for his life. All rendered in horribly beautiful 3D animation.

Agency	Publicis Conseil, Paris
Creative Director	Olivier Altmann
Copywriters	David McDonald
	Benjamin Sanial
Art Director	Andrea Leupold
Production	Wanda Productions, Paris
Director	The Glue Society
	Gary Freedman
Producers	Jérôme Denis
	Pierre Marcus
	Guillaume Delmas
Animation	Akama Studio
Advertiser	Orange, "Christmas"

A family open their Christmas presents in a snow-covered home. But then we see they're being watched by animated Christmas figures: an angel, a gnome, three wise men, a Santa Claus candle and even a snowman peering through the window. They all stare in amazement at the gifts unwrapped by the family, an analogy for the entertaining content available from Orange.

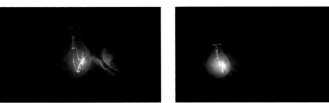

Agency	dirk&philip kommunikation, Berlin
Creative Directors	Dirk Henkelmann
	Philip Borchardt
Copywriters & ADs	Dirk Henkelmann
	Philip Borchardt
Production	Polynoid, Berlin
Producer	Johannes von Liebenstein
	Lovestone Films
Advertiser	Absolut Vodka-MADE Future Self Exhibition, "Moth"

A moth fluttering near a bulb creates an electric mirror image of itself as the filament bends, transforms and mimics its shape. The pair share a beautiful dance together. The film promoted the "Future Self" exhibition at Absolut's MADE gallery in Berlin. At the heart of the event was an installation that mirrored movement with light – just like the filament and the moth.

Agency	AMV BBDO, London
Creative Director	Paul Brazier
Copywriter	Diane Leaver
Art Director	Simon Rice
Production	Psyop
	Smuggler
Producers	Yvonne Chalkley
	Neysa Horsburgh
	Hillary Thomas
	Amanda Miller
	Mary Knockles
	Jenn Dewey
Advertiser	Twinings, "Sea"

A lone woman rows a tiny boat across a stormy sea. When a violent wave hits, she loses her oars. She looks in desperate peril, until the spray itself forms birds that bear the boat aloft and deposit it in calmer waters, which carry it gently ashore. Climbing from the boat, the woman meets an image of herself, calmly sipping a cup of tea. Powerful animation meets evocative storytelling to show that Twinings tea "brings you back to you".

302 **Animation**

Production	Dans Digital Technology, Shenzhen
Director	Deng Bohong
Animation	Wu Qinlin
	Xiang Hongming
	Fan Kai
Special Effects	Liu Hao
Composer	Li Yan
Editing	Duan Yuping
	Rong Yuxuan
Advertiser	Gemdale Group "Lake City-Art"

The camera appears to pan back from a serene lake to a nearby road, where a sports car glides past. Panning to the right, the camera finds a modern luxury apartment block, where a woman sips a glass of champagne on her balcony. The image pans back further still, to reveal that the apartment is the studio of a successful artist, who is admiring the view. The promotional film for the Lake City development in China used a combination of sketches, watercolours, oil painting and real life to create a seamless depiction of luxury living.

Agency	BBDO, New York
CCO	David Lubars
Senior CD	Linda Honan
Copywriters	Nick Sonderup
	Ginger Robinson
Art Director	Kim Haxton
Production	Elastic, Santa Monica
Director	Andy Hall
Producers	Jennifer Sofio Hall
	Heather Johann
	Jesse Brihn
Advertiser	American Red Cross, "Stuff"

In a white paper world, an animated clay man is preparing for Christmas: making lists of stuff, shopping for stuff, and bringing stuff home. He changes his mind about stuff, wraps stuff, mails and receives stuff – all helpfully labelled with the word "stuff" in big red letters. But when he decides to make a donation to the Red Cross, the word "stuff" transforms into "hope", "compassion" and "help". And his red Christmas parcel opens out into a red cross.

Agency	Agency V, Paris
Creative Director	Christian Vince
Copywriter	Jocelyn Devaux
Art Director	Sylvain Guyomard
Production	Wanda Productions, Paris
Director	Akama Studio
Producers	Claude Fayolle
	Corinne Persch
	Malika Hamladji
Animation	Akama Studio
Advertiser	Volkswagen Golf, "Hedgehogs"

Under the light of a full moon, hundreds of extraordinarily realistic hedgehogs scurry towards a mysterious destination: a cathedral-like space beneath a giant tree-trunk. The hedgehogs appear to be worshipping a key-chain with the Volkswagen logo on it. In flashback we find out why: not so long ago, a hedgehog was saved from certain death when a Golf's advanced technology allowed its driver to spot and avoid the little creature on the road.

Agency	BBDO, New York
CCO	David Lubars
Executive CDs	Greg Hahn
	Mike Smith
Senior CDs	Tom Kraemer
	Nick Klinkert
Creative Director	Chris Beresford-Hill
Production	Psyop
	Smuggler
Directors	Marco Spier
	Marie Hyon
Producer	Amy Wertheimer
Advertiser	FedEx, "Enchanted Forest"

A cheerful FedEx van rumbles through an animated forest populated by singing animals, pixies, and trees with wise old faces. But the cartoon trimmings vanish one by one as the narrator explains that while the story of a shipping giant that befriended a forest may sound like a fairy tale, FedEx really has invested in electric trucks, recycled shipping materials and low pollution planes. When reality has taken charge, only a lone cartoon frog remains in the van driver's cab. "Oops – forgot one."

Direction & Cinematography

Agency	BETC, Paris	**Sound Prod.**	Gum
Creative Director	Stéphane Xiberras	**Music**	Eric Cervera
Copywriter	Jean-Christophe Royer		Near Deaf Experience
Art Director	Eric Astorgue	**DOP**	Joost Van Gelder
Production	Soixante Quinze, Paris	**Editor**	Jono Griffiths
Director	Matthijs Van Heijningen	**Advertiser**	Canal+, "The Bear"
Producers	Yuki Suga		
	Isabelle Menard		
	David Green		

We're in the middle of a violent medieval battle: clashing swords, rearing horses, hurtling cannon balls, explosions. A heroine in armour slashes her way through the enemy hordes. And then: "Cut!" The hotshot director – who appears to be a bear – comes on set to make a few suggestions. "He's an amazing director," the actress tells us in an interview. Over the next few scenes we see the bear at work: passionate, egotistical, obsessed with ever bigger explosions.

He loves cinema so much that he even conducts the film's score. At the end, we find out why: he's a bearskin rug, and has spent much of his life in front of a TV watching Canal+. "I've seen so many great films over the years that I thought – why not me?"

Agencies	Fred & Farid,
	Paris & Shanghai
Creative Directors	Fred & Farid
Copywriters	Fred & Farid
Art Directors	Fred & Farid
Production	Gorgeous, London
Director	Peter Thwaites
Producers	Anna Hashmi
	Kate Talor
Advertiser	Martini Royale,
	"Luck is an Attitude"

This stylish split screen film shows two sides of our hero Yuri (cast by Martini fans via a Facebook competition) as he goes about his day. On one side of the screen we see a humble, somewhat diffident Yuri, while on the other we see an impulsive, romantic and self-confident character. They both make their way to a chic bar. But it's the shy Yuri who seizes the day, when he finds the courage to embrace his dream girl in the rain. All shot in elegantly retro black and white.

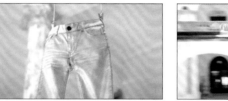 

Agency	BETC, Paris
Creative Directors	Rémi Babinet
	Florence Bellisson
Copywriter	Véronique de Surmont
Art Director	Marie-Eve Schoettl
Production	Caviar
Director	Angelin Preljocaj
Producer	Fabrice Brovelli
Advertiser	Air France, "L'Envol"

Beneath a vast blue sky in a desert landscape, two dancers perform a ballet on a surface that mirrors their movements. Their graceful dance captures the uplifting experience of an Air France flight, where "the sky is the best place on earth". The effect was achieved by placing a 400 square metre mirror on the desert floor in Morocco.

Agency	Selmore, Amsterdam
Copywriter	Niels Westra
Art Director	Jakko Achterberg
Production	Xsaga, Amsterdam
Directors	Clara Van Gool
	Nanine Linning
Producers	Patrick Roubroeks
	Hein Scheffer
	Marga Bierema
DOP	Nils Post
Editor	Kevin Whelan
Advertiser	De Bijenkorf Department
	Store, "Crazy Dance"

At sale time you sometimes have to fight for the most desirable items – a situation depicted here in the form of a perfectly choreographed dance. It features a woman struggling to take possession of a chic pair of white jeans – something she eventually achieves, attaining goddess-like status in the process.

Agencies	Marcel, Paris	**Agency**	Ogilvy France, Paris
	Publicis Conseil, Paris	**CCO**	Chris Garbutt
	Wam, Paris	**Creative Director**	Thierry Chiumino
Production	Quad Productions	**Copywriters & ADs**	Baptiste Clinet
Director	Bruno Aveillan		Nicolas Lautier
Producer	Martin Coulais		Florian Bodet
DOP	Patrick Duroux	**Production**	Soixante Quinze
Soundtrack	Pierre Adenot	**Director**	Johan Renck
Post Production	Digital District	**Producers**	Annabelle Fournier
Advertiser	Cartier,		Laure Bayle
	"Cartier Odyssey"	**Post Production**	Mikros Image
		DOP	Simon Chaudoir
		Advertiser	Perrier, "The Drop"

Some online films have the production values of Hollywood blockbusters. That's certainly the case with this three and a half minute epic directed by Bruno Aveillan. Showing Cartier's signature jewelled panther springing to life and travelling the world, it combines live action with digital post-production to create a blend of dream and reality.

The sun has become so hot that it is beginning to melt planet earth. A beautiful astronaut, who appears to share a wardrobe with Barbarella, blasts off with a bottle of Perrier to cool the sun down. Arriving at her destination, 149.6 million kilometres later, she feels a bit thirsty. Fortunately the last drop from her empty Perrier bottle is also sufficient to refresh the sun, much to the relief of all mankind. From the spacewoman's glass spaceship to the boiling sun itself, the film, under the assured direction of Johan Renck, is an alluring drop of sci-fi fantasy.

Life changing
SEE MORE AT LOTTERYGOODCAUSES.ORG.UK

Real holidays.

Switzerland.
get natural.

MySwitzerland.com

Agency	AMV BBDO, London	
Creative Directors	Mike Hannett	
	Dave Buchanan	
Copywriters & ADs	Alex Grieve	
	Adrian Rossi	
Production	Stink, London	
Director	John Hillcoat	
Producers	Olly Chapman	
	Malachy McAnenny	
Editor	Tim Lindsay	
Sound	Factory	
Sound Design	Anthony Moore	
Advertiser	The National Lottery	

The spot opens with the distressed face of an old man in extreme close-up. As the camera pans back, we see that he is strolling around a military encampment in the jungle. For the moment the soldiers are relaxed, chatting or resting. Suddenly the enemy arrives and a brutal battle begins: explosions, flying bullets, planes roaring overhead. The old man looks on. The battle scene fades and we see that he's standing in a graveyard. He's an army veteran making his peace with the past. A charity donation from National Lottery funds helped him return to the Far East.

Agency	Spilmann/Felser/
	Leo Burnett, Zurich
Creative Directors	Peter Brönnimann
	Diana Rossi
	Simon Staub
Copywriter	Fabian Windhager
Art Directors	Niels Schäfer
	Marco Donada
Production	Stories, Zurich
Director	Michael Fueter
Producers	Yves Bollag
	Suzana Kovacevic
Advertiser	Switzerland Tourism

The land famous for its timepieces abolishes time in this amusing tale, featuring the two Swiss mountaineers who are the faces of the country's tourism authority. Here they disable clocks, watches and even cuckoo clocks so visitors to Switzerland can truly relax. The film exudes gentle humour while discreetly showing us some of the country's tourist attractions.

308 Editing & Special Effects

Agency	RKCR/Y&R, London	The BBC's Natural History Unit is acclaimed
Creative Director	Mark Roalfe	worldwide. And Sir David Attenborough,
Copywriter	Ted Heath	who narrates many BBC wildlife films, is a
Art Director	Paul Angus	national treasure in the UK. To pay homage
Production	Red Bee Media,	to the work of the NHU, awe-inspiring shots
	London	of nature filmed by the BBC over the years
Directors	Ted Heath	are skilfully edited to reflect the lyrics of the
	Paul Angus	Louis Armstrong song "Wonderful World",
Producer	Kate Woodhouse	which Sir David recites in his distinctively
Editor	Thomas Ioannou	warm voice. It's a wonderful world – watch
Advertiser	BBC One,	it with the BBC.
	"Wonderful World"	

Agency	Publicis Conseil, Paris
CCO	Anne de Maupeou
Creative Director	Steve O'Leary
Copywriter	Antonin Jacquot
Art Director	Philippe d'Orgeville
Production	Sonny, London
	Première Heure
Director	Guy Manwaring
Producers	Constance Guillou
	Pierre Marcus
	Guillaume Delmas
	Timothe Rosenberg
Music Production	Sean Atherton
	Sian Rogers
Sound Design	Anthony Moore
	Jon Clarke
Final Mixing	Schmooze
Post Production	Antoine Daubert
Advertiser	Coke Zero,
	"Unlock the 007 in You"

Bond film sponsor Coke Zero turns Mr Ordinary into a hero when he spots the girl of his dreams in a café. Unfortunately, she's surrounded by villainous thugs. He begins humming the distinctive James Bond theme – aided by everyone around him, including his adversaries – as he braves the baddies and everyday obstacles to catch up with the girl and share a victorious Coke with her. There's a bit of Bond in all of us.

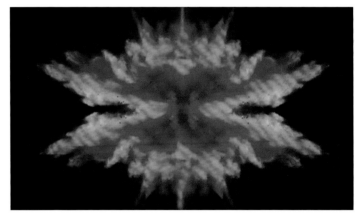

Agency	BETC, London
Creative Director	Neil Dawson
Copywriter	Clive Pickering
Art Director	Paul Copeland
Production	RSA London
Director	Jim Field Smith
Producers	Debbie Garvey
	Nikki Cramphorn
Advertiser	Cow & Gate,
	"Supergroup"

A group of toddlers let loose in a recording studio master the instruments to such an extent that they're able to play a rousing version of the 1980s pop song "Come On Eileen". As well as top notch editing, serious toddler wrangling was no doubt required in the making of this spot.

Agencies	Fred & Farid,
	Paris & Shanghai
Creative Directors	Fred & Farid
Copywriters	Fred & Farid
Art Directors	Julien-Pierre Mallet
	Volker Gehr
Production	RSA, London
Director	Mehdi Norowzian
Producers	Lisa Joseph
	Karim Naceur
Advertiser	Audi A1, "Millimeter"

We're not quite sure what's going on when we see a red light and hear the words: "This is one millimetre. One intensely bright red millimetre with monochromatic radiation." More bright lights, laboratories and technical terms follow, until we discover that we're being told about the effort put into just one millimetre of the new Audi A1 Sportback's rear light. Imagine the expertise poured into the entire vehicle.

310 **Editing & Special Effects**

Agency	DDB Brasil, Sao Paulo	Follow is a magazine that tracks the latest trends. This film captures the spirit of the publication through a series of statements along the lines of "brown is the new black". Each trend is accompanied by a witty stop-motion animation. For example, a heart shape printed by a vintage typewriter illustrates "Text message is the new love letter", while a crumpled tin can that magically springs back to perfection serves to inform us that "used is the new new".
Creative Directors	Sergio Valente Marco Versolato	
Copywriter	Caio Mattoso	
Art Director	Rodrigo Mendes	
Production	Ad Studio, Sao Paulo	
Directors	Jarbas Agnelli Doug Bello	
Producers	Rino Siveiro Gilberto Pires	
Advertiser	Follow Magazine, "Is the New"	

Agency	BBDO, New York	A satellite shot of Los Angeles. The camera dives down into the city, where a FedEx van pulls up. Pounding music creates a feeling of suspense. The van driver admits that a race against time to deliver vital Australian "bovine heart tissue" for a surgical operation "may seem like a trumped-up Hollywood premise", but he assures us that the story is quite real. As he does so, the film's action movie clichés – dramatic score, frenetic editing, 360° camera spin, car crashes – vanish one by one. But the driver allows the director to keep "the gratuitous supermodel cameo".
CCO	David Lubars	
Executive CDs	Greg Hahn Mike Smith	
Senior CDs	Tom Kraemer Nick Klinkert	
Creative Director	Chris Beresford-Hill	
Production	Saville Productions	
Director	Martin Campbell	
Producers	Rupert Maconick Diane Hill Amy Wertheimer	
Advertiser	FedEx, "Hollywood"	

UNHATE

UNITED COLORS
OF BENETTON.

Supports the Unhate Foundation
unhatefoundation.org

>> There is intelligence on earth.
The smart fortwo electric drive.

Agencies	Fabrica, Treviso
	72andSunny, Amsterdam
Creative Directors	Erik Ravelo
	Carlo Cavallone
	Paulo Martins
Production	Identity, New York
Director	Laurent Chanez
Producers	Joe Masi
	Claire Barnier
	Ellen Pot
	Sam Baerwald
Advertiser	Benetton, "Unhate"

Scenes of affection and violence tumble around one another. Sometimes it's difficult to tell them apart: is this crowd celebrating or protesting? Are those men hugging or grappling? But the images of suspicion and hate quickly lose out to depictions of love and passion. A veteran of controversial campaigns that go beyond the desire to sell, Benetton has a new message: "Unhate".

Agency	BBDO Proximity, Berlin
Copywriters	Jan Harbeck
	David Missing
Art Director	David Mously
Production	Cobblestone, Hamburg
Director	Robert Nylund
Producers	Silke Rochow
	Julia Diehl
Post Production	nhb Studio
DOP	Carl Sundberg
Editors	Alexander Kutka
	Thilo Both
Advertiser	Smart Fortwo ED

A man and a woman on a deserted dockside. In a dramatic farewell scene, the man tells his wife that he is leaving her forever. Then he reveals why: he rips off his face to reveal the slimy squid-like features of an alien, sent to earth to find evidence of intelligent life. On cue, his spaceship arrives overhead. But instead of beaming him up, it takes his car as evidence: the new Smart Fortwo Electric Drive. The alien awkwardly tries to put his mask back on. "Shall we take the bus?" he asks his horrified wife.

LET IT OUT.

LET IT OUT.

312 **Print Craft**

Agency	Wirz BBDO, Zurich
Creative Director	Philipp Skrabal
Art Director	Paul Labun
Illustrators	Isabelle Bühler
	Paul Labun
Graphic Design	Katja Schlosser
Advertiser	Caran d'Ache "Let it Out"

Agency	Jung von Matt, Hamburg	**Agency**	Leo Burnett, Mumbai
CCOs	Dörte Spengler-Ahrens	**Creative Directors**	K V Sridhar
	Jan Rexhausen		Nitesh Tiwari
Creative Director	Felix Fenz		Vikram Pandey
Copywriters	Andreas Hilbig	**Copywriter**	Vikram Pandey
	David Wegener	**Art Director**	Brijesh Parmar
Art Directors	Alexander Norvilas	**Photographer**	Amol Jadhav
	Michael Hess	**Advertiser**	Bajaj Exhaust Fans,
Photographer	Klaus Merz		"Get It Back" Campaign
Typographers	Kürten & Lechner		
Digital Artwork	Amina Warscheid		
	Marius Schwiegk		
Advertiser	Mercedes-Benz, "Look Twice"		

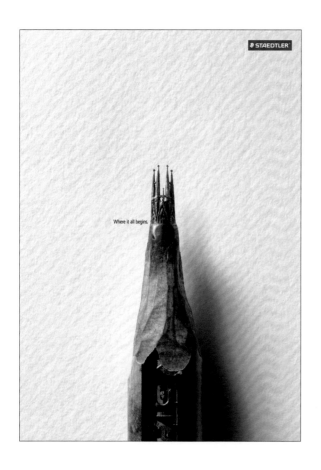

314 **Print Craft**

Agency	Leo Burnett, Hong Kong	Agency	DDB Group, Hong Kong
Creative Directors	Connie Lo	Creative Directors	Jeffry Gamble
	Adrian Lam		Ong Shi Ping
Copywriters	Fanny Lau		Paul Chan
	Wen Louie		Asawin Phanichwatana
Art Director	May Chan	Art Director	Ciff Luk
Photographer	Stephen Cheung	Illustrators	Surachai Puthikulangkura
Retouching	Henry Chan		Supachai U-Rairat
Consultant	Dalton M. Ghetti	Agency Producer	Annie Tong
Advertiser	Staedtler,	Advertiser	Westone, "Earphones"
	"The Pencil Church"		

Agency	CLM BBDO, Paris
Creative Directors	Gilles Fichteberg
	Jean-François Sacco
Art Director	Ronan Coursin
Photographer	Carlos Serrao
Retouching	Janvier
Art Buying	Sylvie Etchemaite
Planner	Laura Autier
Clients	Catherine Lescure
	Anne-Laure Meynial-Coumaros
	Hubert Blanquefort
	Virginie Maillebuau
Advertiser	EDF, "Olympic Heroes Campaign"

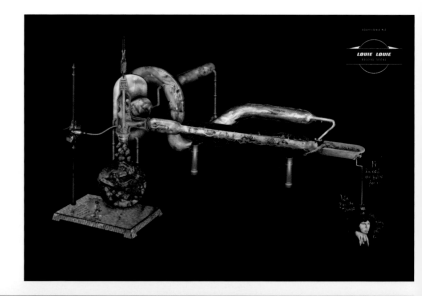

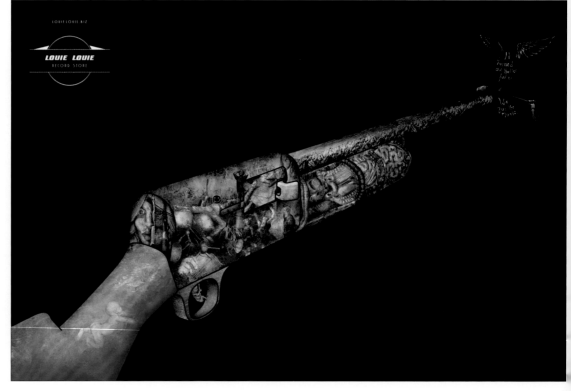

Agency	RKCR/Y&R, London
Creative Director	Mark Roalfe
Copywriter	Mike Boles
Art Director	Jerry Hollens
Photographer	Giles Revell
Typographer	Lee Aldridge
Advertiser	Department for Communities & Local Government-Fire Safety, "Fire Kills"

Agency	LAP Agencias de Comunicação, Lisbon
Executive CD	Erick Rosa
Creative Director	Luciana Cani
Copywriter	Pedro Ribeiro
Art Director	Fabio Cristo
Illustrators	Fabio Cristo
	Fabio Galindro
Typographer	Fabio Cristo
Account Team	Tiago Reis
	Beatriz Rebelo
Advertiser	Louie Louie, "We Got the Music"

SALE
HARVEY NICHOLS
STARTS 1ST JUNE

Agency	Y&R, Dubai
Creative Directors	Shahir Zag
	Kalpesh Patankar
Copywriter	Shahir Zag
Art Director	Kalpesh Patankar
Illustrator	Gitten Tom
Graphic Design	Shahir Zag
	Kalpesh Patankar
Producer	Amin Soltani
Account Team	Sarah Locke
	Pierre Farra
Client	Jean Atik
Advertiser	Land Rover, "Monologues"

Agency	Y&R, Dubai
Creative Directors	Shahir Zag
	Kalpesh Patankar
Copywriter	Shahir Zag
Art Director	Kalpesh Patankar
Photographer	The Remix Studio
Graphic Design	Kalpesh Patankar
Producer	Amin Soltani
Account Team	Zaakesh Mulla
	Line Hajjar
	Nazek Fawaz
Client	Madhu Chibber
Advertiser	Harvey Nichols, "Pelicans"

Advertising Photography

Agencies	Fred & Farid, Paris & Shanghai
Creative Directors	Fred & Farid
Copywriter	Feng Huang
Art Directors	Feng Huang Pierre Jouffray
Photographer	Rankin
Art Buying	Carmela Guiragossian
Advertiser	Weight Watchers, "Treat Yourself Better"

New York City, 1942

Agency	Marcel, Paris	Art Buying	Jean-Luc Chirio
Worldwide CD	Erik Vervroegen		Lauriane Dula
Creative Directors	Erik Vervroegen		Thomas Geffrier
	Eric Jannon	Planner	Rob Klingensmith
	Dimitri Guerassimov	Producer	Ruth Levy
Copywriter	Martin Rocaboy	Costume Design	Arianne Philips
Art Directors	Bastien Grisolet	Set Design	Rick Floyd
	Anaïs Boileau	Account Team	Alberto Scorticati
	Souen Le Van		Shannon Eddy
Photographer	Mark Seliger		Julie Amen
Digital Artwork	Asile	Client	Erika Ferszt
		Advertiser	Ray-Ban Legends, "75 Years of Legends"

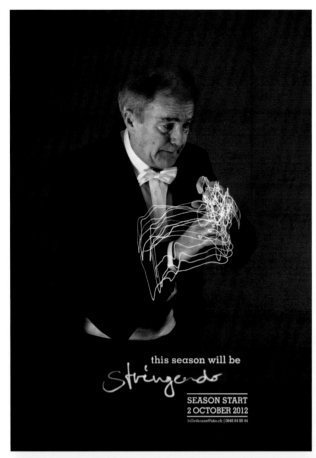

Agency	Havas Worldwide, Zurich
Creative Directors	Frank Bodin
	Axel Eckstein
Copywriter	Florian Birkner
Art Director	Inken Rohweder
Photographer	Peter Hebeisen
Graphic Design	Luca Schneider
Art Buying	Cara-Anne Specker
Composer	Simon Ianelli
Account Mgr.	Milena Elias
Advertiser	Zurich Chamber Orchestra,
	"Invisible Instruments"

Taps, showers and accessories. Beautifully handcrafted in Britain since 1820.

SAMUEL HEATH

samuel-heath.com
or call 0800 0191 282

Taps, showers and accessories. Beautifully handcrafted in Britain since 1820.

SAMUEL HEATH

samuel-heath.com
or call 0800 0191 282

CREDIT SUISSE

FASHION DESIGNER JEN KAO FOUND INSPIRATION BENEATH THE WAVES.

Credit Suisse has helped a new talent surface.

credit-suisse.com/clients

Agency	Cogent Elliott, Meriden	Agency	Havas Worldwide, London
Creative Director	Richard Payne	**Creative Director**	Gerry Moira
Copywriter	Nick Galanides	**Copywriter**	Tim Langford
Art Director	Richard Payne	**Art Director**	Dave Burn
Photographer	Manvir Rai	**Photographer**	Tim Walker
Digital Artwork	Vincent Jonecko	**Advertiser**	Credit Suisse, "Jen Kao"
Retouching	John Smith		
Advertiser	Samuel Heath, "The Graces"		

322 **Advertising Photography**

Agency	Scholz & Friends, Berlin
Creative Directors	Martin Pross
	Matthias Spaetgens
	Mirko Derpmann
	Christoph Blaschke
Copywriter	Mirko Derpmann
Art Directors	Christoph Keller
	Sebastian Frese
Graphic Design	Dustin Przibilla
Post Production	Fabian Behrendt
Account Mgr.	Sarah Westphal
Advertiser	City Cleaning Hamburg, "Trashcam Hamburg"

These images were taken by Hamburg's refuse collectors with their rubbish bins – converted into pinhole cameras thanks to a drilled hole and giant pieces of photographic paper. But the pictures are more than just a PR stunt to draw attention to the work of the city's bin men. They also stand alone as beautiful works of photographic art. And indeed they were exhibited at the Bucerius Art Forum, one of the most important museums for contemporary art in Germany.

Agency	Leo Burnett, Mumbai		Agency	Fallon, Minneapolis
Creative Directors	K V Sridhar		Creative Director	Leon Wilson
	Sujit Sawant		Art Director	Christy Peacock
Art Directors	Sujit Sawant		Photographer	Nadav Kander
	Mayuresh Natalkar		Advertiser	The Cosmopolitan
Photographers	Sujit Sawant			Hotel-Las Vegas
	M S Gopal			
Illustrator	Bhushan Patil			
Advertiser	Tide Detergent,			
	"Fisherman"			

324 **Advertising Photography**

Agency	The Martin Agency, Richmond
Creative Director	Alon Shoval
Copywriter	Neel Williams
Art Director	D'Arcy O'Neill
Photographer	Nadav Kander
Advertiser	Morgan Stanley, "What if"

Advertising Photography   **325**

Agency	Leo Burnett, London
Executive CD	Justin Tindall
Creative Team	Will Thacker
	Blake Waters
Photographer	Julia Fullerton-Batten
Head of Art	Lance Crozier
Art Buying	Simon Pedersen
Photo Rep.	Wyatt Clarke & Jones
Advertiser	Renaissance Photo Prize, "Everyone Has a Great Photograph in Them"

Agency	MK Norway, Oslo
Creative Director	Armando Zuniga
Copywriter	Jon Hjørnevik
Art Directors	Doffen Trellevik
	Ole Færøvik
	Armando Zuniga
Photographer	Adam Taylor
Graphic Design	Ole Færøvik
	Pedro Moreira
Acct. Director	Britt Hege Karlsen
Advertiser	Schweppes,
	"Your Taste"

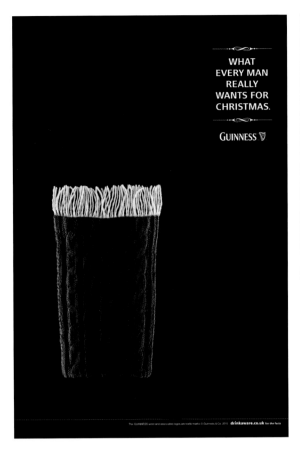

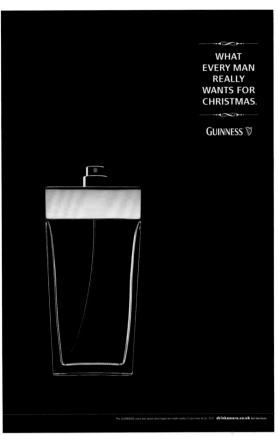

Agency	Abbott Mead Vickers BBDO, London	Agency	CHI & Partners, London
Creative Directors	Mike Hannett	Executive CD	Jonathan Burley
	Dave Buchanan	Copywriter	Daniel Fisher
Copywriter	Mike Sutherland	Art Director	Richard Brim
Art Director	Ant Nelson	Art Buying	Emma Modler
Photographer	Paul Zak	Planner	Ben Southgate
Typographer	Aaron Moss	Retouching	Rob Swainson
Retouching	Stefano Cherubini		Dave Turfitt
	Happy Finish	Account Team	Olivia Skone
Advertiser	Guinness, "Christmas		William Leabeater
	Poster Campaign"	Advertiser	The Sunday Times,
			"Rich List Campaign

Agency	adam&eveDDB, London	Planner	Tom Lloyd
Executive CD	Jeremy Craigen	Project Mgt.	Craig Neilson
Copywriter	Jonathan John		Jon Dewart
Art Director	David Mackersey	Media Agency	Mindshare
Illustrator	Garry Walton	Account Team	Anna Hopwood
Typographer	Garry Walton		Matthew Bundy
Digital Artwork	Trevor Slabber		Angharad Thomas
	Gutenberg Networks	Clients	Pankaj Sharma
Designer	Peter Mould		Nicola Waymark
Art Buying	Fiona Bailey		Joanne O'Riada
Retouching	Jamie May	Advertiser	Marmite Limited Edition Jubilee Jar, "Corgis"

The Queen of England is addressed as "Ma'am". Opinions about the monarchy in England are almost as divided as they are about the taste of Marmite spread. Nevertheless, to commemorate the Queen's diamond jubilee, Marmite launched a limited edition "Ma'amite" jar. Poster ads showcasing the jar featured Her Majesty's beloved corgis and a crown-shaped toast rack, as well as an appropriate variation on the Marmite slogan: "One either loves it or one hates it."

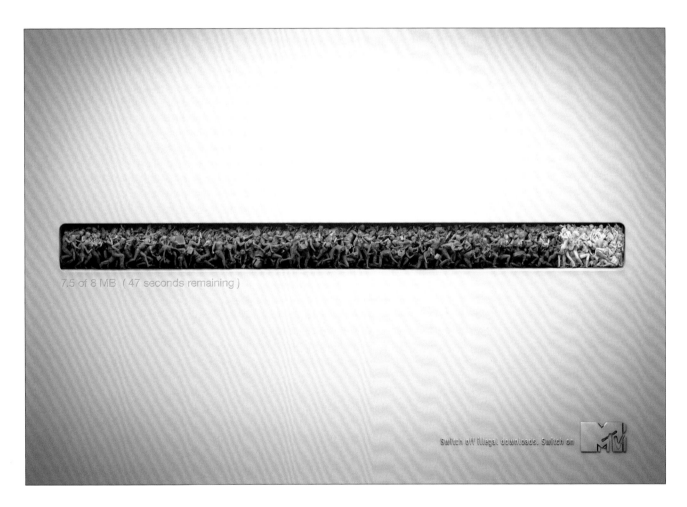

7.5 of 8 MB (47 seconds remaining)

Switch off illegal downloads. Switch on

Illustration   329

Agency	Ogilvy & Mather, Budapest
Creative Directors	Will Rust
	Ferenc Benesch
Copywriters	Karolina Galácz
	Balázs Vizi
Art Director	Zoltán Visy
Photographer	Thomas Mangold
Planner	Martin Alles
Acct. Director	Balázs Száday
Advertiser	Hot Wheels,
	"Toy Cars" Campaign

Agency	Ogilvy, Frankfurt
CCO	Stephan Vogel
Creative Directors	Matthias Storath
	Helmut Meyer
Copywriter	Haiko Hoernig
Art Director	Patrick Ackmann
Illustrators	Surachai Puthikulangkura
	Supachai U-Rairat
	Illusion, Bangkok
Art Buying	Valerie Opitz
Account Mgt.	Yves Rosengart
Client	Robin Karakash
Advertiser	MTV, "Downloadbar"

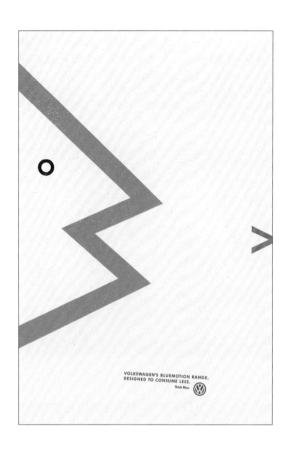

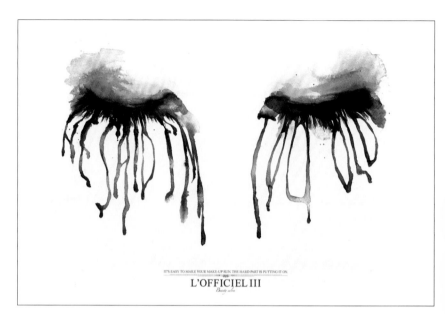

Agency	adam&eveDDB, London	**Agency**	Publicis Brasil, Sao Paulo
Creative Director	Jeremy Craigen	**Creative Directors**	Hugo Rodrigues
Copywriter	Jonathan John		Kevin Zung
Art Director	David Mackersey	**Copywriter**	Guilherme Nesti
Illustrator	Peter Mould	**Art Director**	Eduardo Pastor
Typographer	Peter Mould	**Illustrator**	Leo Dolfini
Designer	Peter Mould	**Producers**	Rita Vilarim
Project Managers	Tim Walther		Emerson Russo
	Craig Neilson	**Advertiser**	L'Officiel III Beauty Salon,
Advertiser	Volkswagen BlueMotion,		"Blurred Eyes"
	"Think Blue		
	Logo Campaign"		

THE MORE YOU TEXT, THE MORE YOU CAN PROTECT.
Text Coca-Cola package codes to donate. ArcticHome.com

THE MORE YOU TEXT, THE MORE YOU CAN PROTECT.
Text Coca-Cola package codes to donate. ArcticHome.com

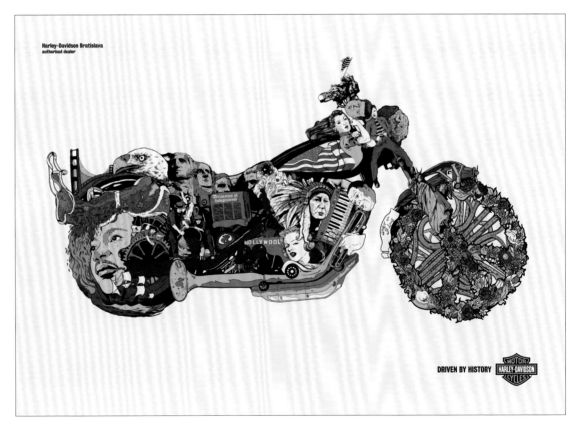

Harley-Davidson Bratislava
authorised dealer

DRIVEN BY HISTORY   HARLEY-DAVIDSON

Illustration   331

Agency	Leo Burnett, Chicago	Agency	Jandl, Bratislava
CCO	Susan Credle	Creative Directors	Pavel Fuksa
Executive CDs	Dave Loew		Eugen Suman
	Jon Wyville	Copywriters	Eugen Suman
Associate CDs	Chris von Ende		Samo Marec
	Mike Ward	Art Director	Lucia Cermakova
Copywriter	Mike Ward	Illustrator	Tim McDonagh
Art Director	Chris von Ende	Account Director	Rastislav Kuttner
Designer	Eing Omathikul	Advertiser	Harley Davidson,
Producer	Patrick Smith		"Driven by History"
Studio House	Visualwright		
Advertiser	Coca-Cola,		
	"Thumbprints"		

Agency	JWT, Shanghai	**Illustrators**	Surachai Puthikulangkura	**Agency**	Ogilvy & Mather, London
Creative Directors	Yang Yeo		Supachai U-Rairat	**Creative Director**	Gerry Human
	Elvis Chau	**Production**	Illusion, Bangkok	**Copywriter**	Laura Rogers
	Hattie Cheng	**Print Production**	Liza Law	**Art Director**	Trevallyn Hall
Copywriter	Chanfron Zhao		Joseph Yu	**Illustrator**	Keita Sagaki
Art Directors	Danny Li		Isaac Xu	**Typographer**	Trevallyn Hall
	Haoxi Lv		Chivel Miao	**Art Buying**	Brigitte Martin
Photographers	Surachai Puthikulangkura	**Client Service**	Carol Ma	**Account Director**	Stephen Hillcoat
	Kingkong	**Advertiser**	Maxam Toiletries,	**Advertiser**	Expedia City Breaks,
			"Civilization-Egypt"		"All You Can"

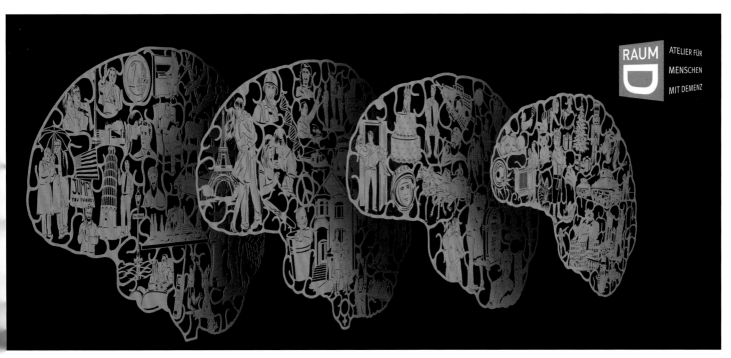

Illustration **333**

Agency	Abbott Mead Vickers BBDO, London	Agency	Ogilvy, Düsseldorf
		Executive CD	Thomas Schwarz
Creative Directors	Paul Brazier	Creative Director	Andreas Steinkemper
	Thiago De Moraes	Copywriters	Kajo Strauc
Copywriter	Paul Brazier		Jill Keehner
Art Director	Thiago De Moraes	Art Directors	Paul Kuna
Illustrator	Thiago De Moraes		Annika Fohler
Typographer	Thiago De Moraes		Rouven Maccario
Advertiser	Guinness,		Vitali Gahl
	"Rugby Poster Campaign"	Illustrator	Casper Franken
		Producer	Mario Kaltenbach
		Art Buying	Carol Redfield
		Advertiser	Raum D, "Vivid Memories"

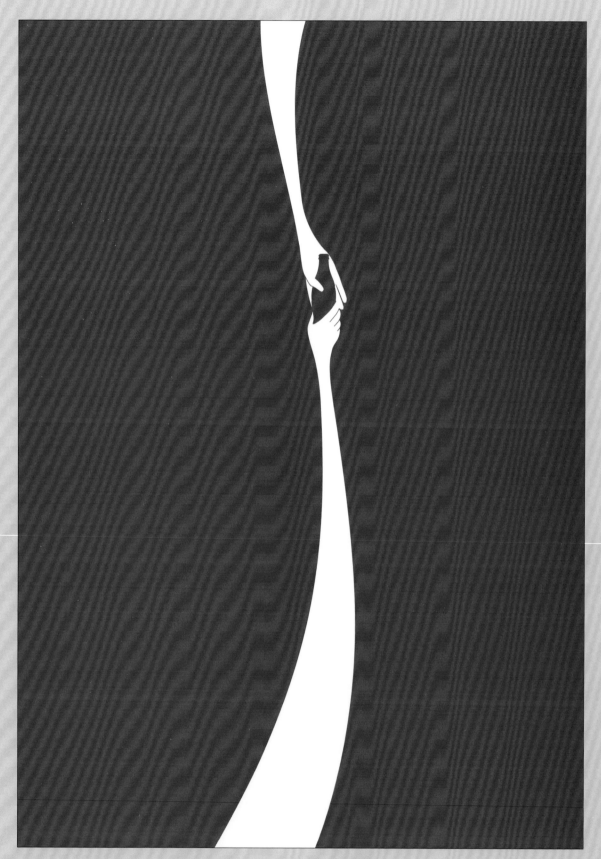

Agency	Ogilvy & Mather Advertising, Shanghai
Creative Directors	Graham Fink
	Francis Wee
Art Director	Jonathan Mak Long
Illustrators	Jonathan Mak Long
	Eno Jin
Planner	Mark Sinnock
Account Team	Martin Murphy
	Stephen Drummond
Advertiser	Coca-Cola, "Cokehands"

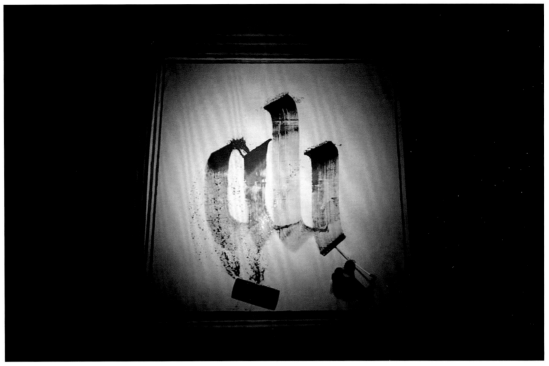

Agency	Ogilvy France, Paris	Muhammad Ali fought with words as much	**Agency**	Ogilvy Design, Lisbon

Agency Ogilvy France, Paris
CCO Chris Garbutt
Creative Director Kurt Novack
Copywriter Amandine Fabian
Art Director Adrien Havet
Production Steam Films
Producer Annette Hallum
Digital Producer Talla Seck
Project Mgrs. Adrien Leygues
Claude-Yves Duchatel
Director Stuart McIntyre
Advertiser Louis Vuitton, "Muhammed Ali"

Muhammad Ali fought with words as much as he did with his fists. To pay tribute to the boxing champ, Louis Vuitton invited rapper Yasiin Bey to reinterpret four of Muhammad Ali's poems in short films. During each performance calligrapher Neils "Shoe" Meulman transformed a word from each poem into a calligraphic artwork in the boxing ring. A virtual match between the written word and the spoken word.

Agency Ogilvy Design, Lisbon
Creative Director Rui Melo
Copywriter Miguel Castanheira
Art Directors Ricardo Capote
David Rafachinho
Illustrators Ricardo Capote
David Rafachinho
Producer Eduardo Vale
Advertiser Ogilvy Design, "Inspired by David"

When Ogilvy Design in Lisbon refurbished its reception area, it integrated the thoughts of adland legend David Ogilvy into the décor. A typographic image of Ogilvy's silhouette is made up of several of his most inspiring quotes. All the quotes were "handwritten" by designers, so it was possible to dedicate time and attention to each one. Now, when people visit the agency, it's not unusual to see them simply staring at the wall.

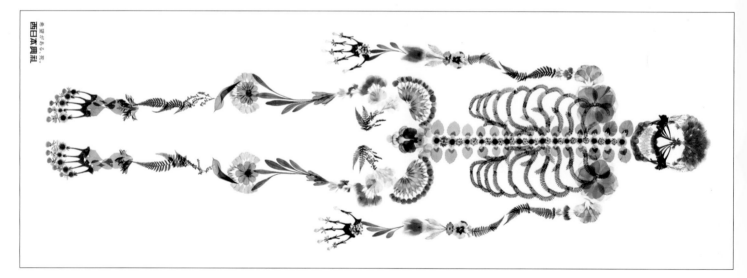

Agency	The Partners, London		**Agency**	I&S BBDO, Tokyo
Creative Directors	Greg Quinton		**Creative Director**	Mari Nishimura
	Nick Eagleton		**Copywriter**	Mari Nishimura
Senior Designer	Miranda Bolter		**Art Director**	Naomi Hou
Embroiderers	Jessica Aldred		**Designer**	Naomi Hou
	Genevieve Brading		**Advertiser**	Nishinihon Tenrei
	Kate Rolison			Funeral Parlor,
Account Manager	Suzanne Neal			"Life Is Endless"
Advertiser	Fine Cell Work,			
	"Sewn Guidelines"			

Fine Cell Work is a prison charity that teaches needlework skills to long-term inmates. With a small and over-stretched team, Fine Cell Work relies on volunteers for many of its tasks, including marketing. So it was hard for the charity to maintain consistency in its communications efforts. The agency was asked to create a set of guidelines that would act as a reference and a source of inspiration. A team of volunteers and prisoners created a set of guidelines like no other: a unique, one off piece of embroidery that hangs permanently on the wall of Fine Cell Work's office.

Funerals in Japan are traditionally black and white affairs. Breaking these codes is considered taboo. But the 2012 earthquake and tsunami had a traumatic effect on the country; issues of life and death, hope and despair became an all too real part of people's lives. In this new environment, the Nishinihon funeral parlour felt that funerals needed to play a new role; not only to reflect sorrow and tradition, but also to remember and celebrate the beauty of a lost person's life. So the agency created an unconventional poster; a life-sized image of what remains after death - a skeleton - made from pressed flowers.

Agency	Serviceplan, Munich
CCO	Alexander Schill
Executive CDs	Maik Kaehler
	Christoph Nann
Creative Producer	Florian Panier
Copywriters	Gesche Sander
	Michael Pilzweger
Art Directors	Manuel Wolff
	Fernando Santos
	Silvestrin
Graphic Design	Aletta Grolman
Advertiser	Serviceplan Recruitment, "1m² of Curiosity"

Serviceplan needs creatives who are searching for ideas everywhere and who are challenged by every blank sheet of paper. In order to find these rare individuals, the agency created 1m² do-it-yourself recruitment posters that don't reveal their content until people start rubbing them with crayons. Underneath each sheet of paper an embossed stencil gradually permitted its design and message to appear. Placed on the notice boards of design schools, the seven differently illustrated messages strongly appealed to the target group: creatives with imagination, patience and commitment.

SAVE THE ORANGUTAN

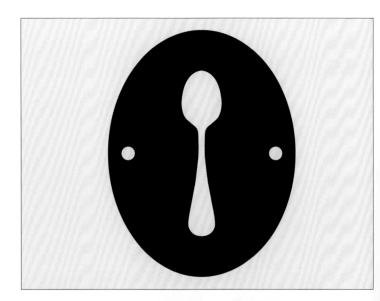

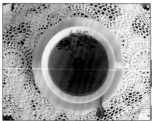

Agency	Futurniture, Stockholm	
Creative Director	Fredrik Nilsson	
Copywriter	Björn Wigenius	
Art Director	Kate Breineder	
Final Art	Andreas Slättner	
Acct. Executive	Jakob Lind	
Advertiser	Save the Orangutan, "The Monkey"	

Save The Orangutan are looking for people who would like to adopt an orangutan by making a donation. As the client had a small media budget it was important that the poster was "likeable", so the media would actually want to show it. The final appealing image consists of little more than a banana and two dots.

Agency	The Partners, London
Creative Director	Stuart Radford
Senior Designer	Leon Bahrani
Advertiser	Soho's Secret Tea Room

Soho's Secret Tea Room is a small, vintage-inspired tea room hidden in London's Soho. Customers have to phone in advance to book a table and ring the doorbell to be allowed inside. The logo had to communicate the truly secret nature of the venue. The design evokes the idea of peering through a keyhole into a secret room. And of course the keyhole itself is the shape of a tea spoon.

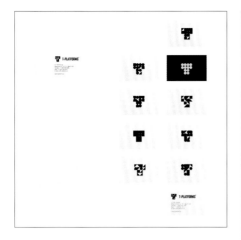

Agency	Tomatdesign, Moscow	T-Platforms produces supercomputers and high-end operating systems; for example the "Lomonosov" supercomputer can carry out 10 trillion operations per second. The company's new logo is based on the cluster systems (a group of loosely connected computers) that are the basis of any supercomputer. The logo contains four basic geometric figures in a free form, thus allowing for unlimited variations.
Creative Director	Andrey Tarakanov	
Art Director	Denis Bashev	
Advertiser	T-Platforms	

Agency	Bond, Helsinki	Attido is a service company that ensures the smooth operation of business information systems. The logo was designed to evoke the heraldic symbols found on knights' shields. And since the company's employees may feel like knights protecting their clients from system failures, they are depicted as tough guardians in the austere black-and-white photographs on the website.
Copywriter	Mikko Airas	
Photographers	Paavo Lehtonen Stefan Bremer	
Producer	Mirva Kaitila	
Strategy	Arttu Salovaara	
Graphic Design	Marko Salonen	
Advertiser	Attido IT Services	

Graphic Design

Agency	Juniper Park, Toronto	Story Planet is a space-themed learning centre in Toronto co-founded by author Dave Eggers. Its logo is as playful and imaginative as the activities the centre offers. These range from learning how to write stories to building plasticine monsters, writing poems to outer space and creating time capsules.
Executive CDs	Terry Drummond	
	Alan Madill	
	Barry Quinn	
Creative Director	Christina Gliha	
Designer	Louis Duarte	
Advertiser	Story Planet	

Agency	Kolle Rebbe, Hamburg	The challenge was to design almost every aspect of a new post-production company's identity, including the name, stationery and interior design. The solution was inspired by the company's credo: here the client's creative seed is sown, harvested and refined. So the surroundings at Harvest are handmade, earthy, authentic and yet stylish. Even the reception desk is a wood cabin.
Executive CD	Antje Hedde	
Copywriters	Sabine Kuckuck	
	Edgar Linscheid	
	Gereon Klug	
Art Directors	Antje Hedde	
	Christine Knies	
Photographers	Jonas von der Hude	
	Jan Burwick	
Graphic Design	Christine Knies	
	Katja Unterkofler	
	Reginald Wagner	
Advertiser	Harvest Digital Agriculture	

Agency	Scandinavian DesignLab, Copenhagen	Copenhagen Contemporary Art Centre is based in the former Nikolaj Church. The
Creative Director	Per Madsen	centre actively refers to this unusual location
Copywriter	Chresta Murmann	in its graphic identity and communications.
Designers	Per Madsen	Its slogans have a religious or provocative
	Robert Daniel Nagy	air, such as "Let there be art" or "I'm not
Project Manager	Christina Orth	a church". A stringent gold, yellow and
CEO	Anne-Mette Højland	black colour scheme ensures recognition
Advertiser	Nikolaj Kunsthal	and allows the communications material to stand out.

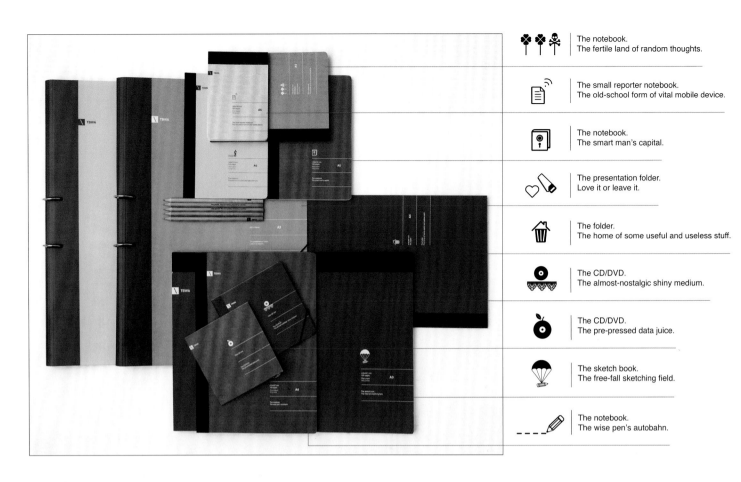

The notebook.
The fertile land of random thoughts.

The small reporter notebook.
The old-school form of vital mobile device.

The notebook.
The smart man's capital.

The presentation folder.
Love it or leave it.

The folder.
The home of some useful and useless stuff.

The CD/DVD.
The almost-nostalgic shiny medium.

The CD/DVD.
The pre-pressed data juice.

The sketch book.
The free-fall sketching field.

The notebook.
The wise pen's autobahn.

342   **Graphic Design**

Agency	TBWA\Istanbul
Creative Director	Ilkay Gurpinar
Copywriter	Ilkay Gurpinar
Art Director	Zeynep Orbay
Advertiser	TBWA, "The Stationary"

TBWA changed its corporate typeface to Helvetica globally, so the Istanbul agency needed to revamp its stationery items. In the Helvetica spirit it wanted them to look as Swiss as possible, so it incorporated precise info about the size, weight and material of each object. An icon and a slogan was created for each item to capture the meaning of the object in its users' lives: everything from cups and folders to CD cases. Other TBWA agencies soon started asking for samples.

Agency	Clark&Kent, New York
Creative Directors	Clark & Kent
Copywriter	Kent
Art Director	Clark
Advertiser	Clark&Kent, "Phone Booth Business Card"

The mysterious Clark & Kent claims to be the smallest ad agency in the world, with headquarters in a phone booth in New York. Naturally, the C&K business card is also a phone booth.

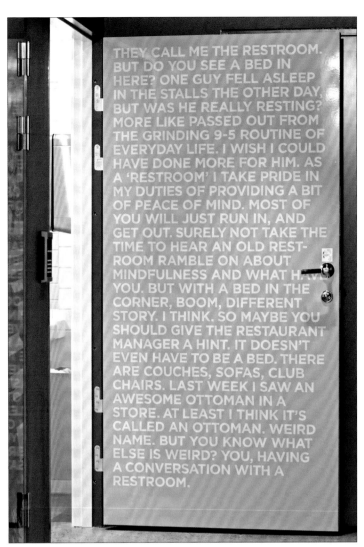

THEY CALL ME THE RESTROOM. BUT DO YOU SEE A BED IN HERE? ONE GUY FELL ASLEEP IN THE STALLS THE OTHER DAY, BUT WAS HE REALLY RESTING? MORE LIKE PASSED OUT FROM THE GRINDING 9-5 ROUTINE OF EVERYDAY LIFE. I WISH I COULD HAVE DONE MORE FOR HIM. AS A 'RESTROOM' I TAKE PRIDE IN MY DUTIES OF PROVIDING A BIT OF PEACE OF MIND. MOST OF YOU WILL JUST RUN IN, AND GET OUT. SURELY NOT TAKE THE TIME TO HEAR AN OLD RESTROOM RAMBLE ON ABOUT MINDFULNESS AND WHAT HAVE YOU. BUT WITH A BED IN THE CORNER, BOOM, DIFFERENT STORY. I THINK. SO MAYBE YOU SHOULD GIVE THE RESTAURANT MANAGER A HINT. IT DOESN'T EVEN HAVE TO BE A BED. THERE ARE COUCHES, SOFAS, CLUB CHAIRS. LAST WEEK I SAW AN AWESOME OTTOMAN IN A STORE. AT LEAST I THINK IT'S CALLED AN OTTOMAN. WEIRD NAME. BUT YOU KNOW WHAT ELSE IS WEIRD? YOU, HAVING A CONVERSATION WITH A RESTROOM.

Agency	JVD/Jacobson Vellinga Design, Stockholm	Yoi is a new fast food chain that opened its first location in Stockholm. It mixes the cuisines of Japan, Korea, Vietnam and Thailand into an Asian fusion with speedy service but "slow food" quality. The agency designed the entire concept, including brand name, graphics, interior design and communication. The concept is summed up by the main graphic device: a minimalist wok bowl logo next to a "stop burgers" sign. But the restaurant's mischievously alternative stance can be seen in everything from packaging to bathroom doors.
Creative Director	John Jacobson	
Copywriter	Olle Nordell	
	Nordell & Nordell, Stockholm	
Art Director	John Jacobson	
Photographers	John Jacobson	
	Olle Nordell	
	Åke E:son Lindman	
Web Production	Five Star Day, Malmö	
Account Mgr.	Johan Johansson	
	Xlent Strategy, Stockholm	
Advertiser	Yoi Asian Fast Food	

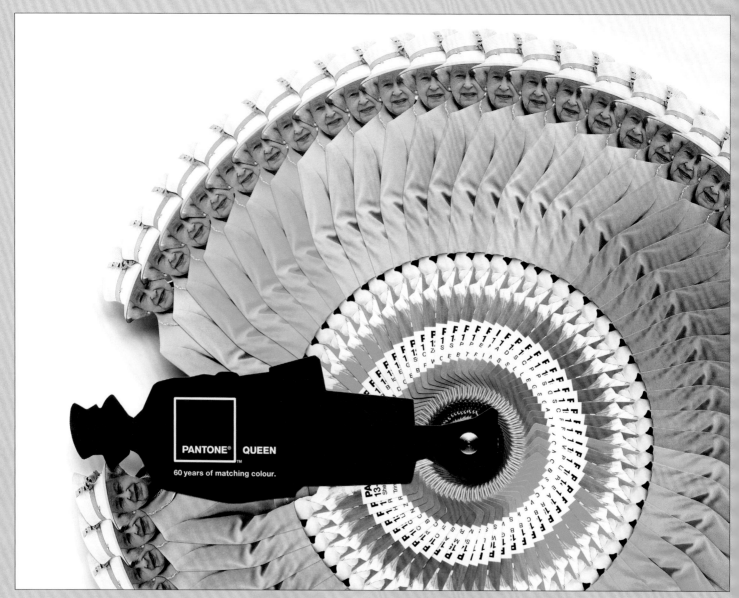

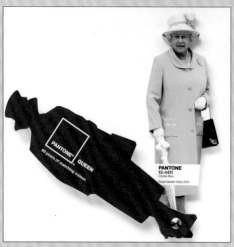

		Queen Elizabeth II is an icon of style. For
Agency	Leo Burnett, London	60 years she has colour matched her
Creative Director	Justin Tindall	outfits perfectly. Produced to celebrate
Copywriter	Blake Waters	her Diamond Jubilee, this Pantone colour
Art Director	Will Thacker	guide book teams Her Majesty's most
Producers	Janice Capewell	famous single colour ensembles with their
	Katie Lee	Pantone reference and the dates on which
Advertiser	Pantone,	she wore them. Buckingham Palace not
	"Pantone Queen"	only gave its permission – it loved the idea
		and made the Pantone Queen an official
		Diamond Jubilee souvenir.

Agency	Leo Burnett, Toronto	The Solstice Calendar offered solace to those yearning for light in the gloom of winter. As well as detailing the hours of light and darkness on any given day, each page became progressively lighter or darker according to the season. So the pages were pitch black at the beginning of the year but faded as spring and summer approached, before darkening again in winter.
CCO	Judy John	
Creative Director	Lisa Greenberg	
Copywriter	Morgan Kurchak	
Art Directors	Chris Duchaine	
	Scott Leder	
Producer	Kim Burchiel	
Designers	Scott Leder	
	Chris Duchaine	
	Trong Nguyen	
Advertiser	Leo Burnett,	
	"Solstice Calendar"	

Agency	Gürtlerbachmann, Hamburg	Flora Garten is one of Germany's most popular gardening magazines. To encourage readers to renew their subscriptions it created an unusual publication – a book about poisonous plants. "The Book of Poison" came in a skull slipcase and looked as if it was designed to warn children about toxic plants. But the avant-garde illustrations, wicked poems and twisted typography clearly appealed to adults too. The book was not available in stores: those who wanted it had to extend their subscriptions.
Creative Director	Reiner Fiedler	
Copywriter	Claudia Oltmann	
AD/Illustrator	Veronika Kieneke	
Production	Produktionsbüro Romey	
	von Malottky	
Project Mgr.	Katja Lesche	
Typography	Reiner Fiedler	
Final Art	Christiane Helm	
	Tobias Langkamp	
Imaging	Julian Hets	
Advertiser	Flora Garten,	
	"Book of Poison"	

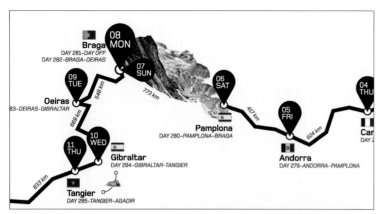

User's shooting skill becomes phenomenal

Agency	Y&R, Dubai
Creative Directors	Shahir Zag
	Kalpesh Patankar
Copywriters	Shahir Zag
	Guillaume Calmelet
Art Director	Kalpesh Patankar
Illustrator	Gitten Tom
Producer	Amin Soltani
Account Team	Sarah Locke
	Pierre Farra
	Jean Atik
Advertiser	Land Rover, "366 Days
	of Adventure"

Most people start the year intending to make the most of every day. Land Rover's 2012 calendar shows them how to do just that by inspiring them to hit the road. Leaving Dubai on January 1st, it traces a 136,709 km marathon across 95 countries on 7 continents over 366 days. With a new destination each day, it includes details like distances, ferry connections, places of interest and types of terrain. Recipients just need to supply their own visas, vaccinations and spirit of adventure. The calendar is a roadmap to the world, with every day bringing a new discovery.

Agency	I&S BBDO, Tokyo
Art Directors	Hiroyuki Nakazato
	Takahiro Sakai
Production	Tone Up, Tokyo
Producers	Tatsuya Watanabe
	Toru Hara
Planners	Peter Smyth
	Yosuke Yamauchi
Advertiser	KSC Corporation,
	"National Defense
	Calendar"

KSC is a Japanese toy gun manufacturer. Its calendar features one target every day so customers can hone their sharpshooting skills. To keep things interesting the pages grow smaller as the year wears on – and your shooting becomes more accurate.

Agency	Serviceplan, Munich		**Agency**	Kolle Rebbe, Hamburg

Agency — Serviceplan, Munich
CCO — Alexander Schill
Creative Directors — Christoph Everke
Cosimo Moeller
Alexander Nagel
Copywriter — Moritz Dornig
Art Director — Matthaeus Frost
Graphic Design — Mathias Noesel
Producer — Melanie Dienemann
Final Art — Alexandra Felbinger
Acct. Supervisor — Diana Guender
Advertiser — Verband Austria Solar,
"Solar Annual Report"

If you want to read this annual report from an association of solar energy providers, you'll have to expose its apparently blank pages to the light of the sun. Slowly, all the relevant facts and figures will emerge. But take the book out of the light and its pages fade.

Agency — Kolle Rebbe, Hamburg
Executive CDs — Sascha Hanke
Antje Hedde
Creative Director — Katrin Oeding
Copywriter — Gereon Klug
Art Director — Reginald Wagner
Photographers — Jan Burwick
Christoph Himmel
Production — Pasta Prima
Buchbinderei Zwang
Producer — Martin Lühe
Graphic Design — Christine Knies
Advertiser — Gerstenberg Publishing

Usually you're encouraged to eat everything in a cookbook apart from its pages. But in this case the pages were made of fresh pasta. Truly a book you could cook – and when you removed it from the oven it looked like the perfect lasagne. The book was devised by a small culinary and art publisher to send to its loyal customers and cook up a bit of publicity.

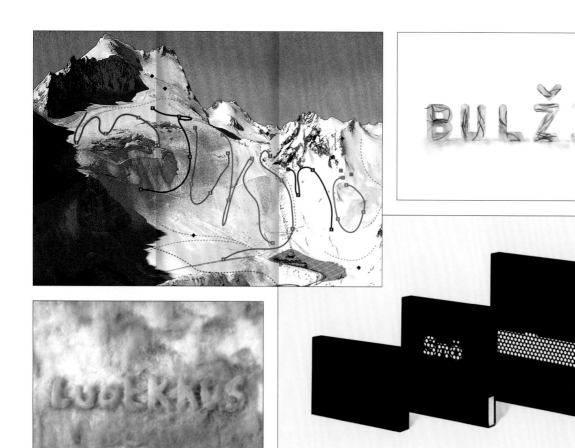

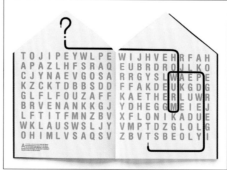

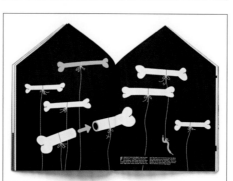

Agency	SapientNitro London	
European CCO	Malcolm Poynton	
Creative Directors	Ben Callis	
	Justin Barnes	
Copywriter	Claire Baker	
Art Director	Laura Fisher	
Producer	Dan Eagles	
Senior Designers	Adam Brewster	
	Marcos Quinn	
	Stephen Vaughan	
Planner	Andrew Gregoris	
Acct. Director	Kate Illott	
Advertiser	Volvo, "Snö"	

In Sweden people have such a close affinity with snow that their language has developed to describe its many forms and qualities. In fact, there are over 56 words for snow in Swedish. And they're all depicted in this publication, created as part of a campaign to increase dealer awareness and sales of the Volvo XC range. Because Volvo really knows snow.

Agency	Gürtlerbachmann, Hamburg
Copywriter	Claudia Oltmann
AD/Illustrator	Veronika Kieneke
Production	Produktionsbüro Romey von Malottky
Typography	Müllerditzen P.O.P. Werbeteam
Exec. Producer	Veronika Kieneke
Final Art	Tobias Langkamp
Imaging	Julian Hets
Acct. Executive	Anne Kukereit
Advertiser	Görtz Shoes

German footwear retailer Görtz has established a bird theme for the children's footwear section of its stores. Alongside colourful bird packaging, it has created a "Book of Birds": a big colourful book about our feathered friends, for kids to play with and marvel at.

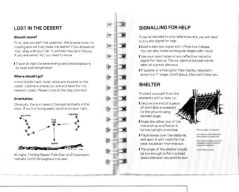

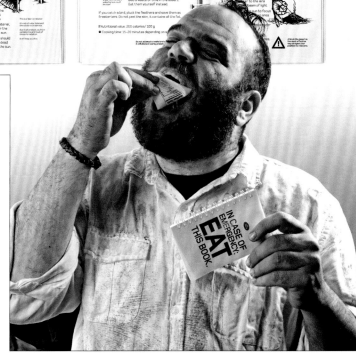

Agency	Y&R, Dubai
Creative Directors	Shahir Zag
	Joseph Bihag
Copywriters	Shahir Zag
	Guillaume Calmelet
	Khaled Said
Art Director	Joseph Bihag
Photographer	Mojtaba Komeili
Illustrators	Joseph Bihag
	Gitten Tom
Production Head	Amin Soltani
Advertiser	Land Rover, "Desert Survival Guide"

Driving a Land Rover can take you to challenging places, which is why it created this edible Desert Survival Guide. Learn how to avoid sandstorms, predators and sinkholes in the Arabian desert. Study the topography of the region. Find out which animals and plants might help you survive. And if you're really hungry, you can always eat the book. It's made out of edible ink and paper with a nutritional value close to that of a cheeseburger. Finally, you can use its reflective packaging to signal for help.

Agency	Serviceplan, Munich
CCO	Alexander Schill
Creative Directors	Christoph Everke
	Cosimo Moeller
	Alexander Nagel
Copywriters	Cosimo Moeller
	Katharina Keith
Art Director	Monika Steiner
Production	Buero Mirko Borsche, Munich
Acct. Supervisor	Anne Jordan
Advertiser	Intel Ultrabook

For the first time in its history Intel developed not just a processor, but a new generation of computers. The Ultrabook was fast, light and stylish. Now its young target audience had to be shown how cool it was. Giving away thousands of Ultrabooks was not practical – so how about actual books? The publication looked like an Ultrabook and its contents reflected the computer's character, covering topics like mobility, lifestyle, fashion and design. 20,000 of the books were distributed through design and fashion hotspots.

01 02 03 04 05 06 07 08 09 10 11 12 13 14 15 16 17 18 19 20 21 22 23 24 25 26 27 28 29
M G V S D L M M G V S D L M M G V S D L M M G V S D L M M

350 **Publication Design**

Agency	Leo Burnett, Milan	Every year printing firm Fontegrafica gives a creative talent carte blanche to design its calendar. This self-promotional item lets Fontegrafica's advanced printing techniques speak for themselves. In 2012 art director Azzurra Bacchetta of Leo Burnett Milan created this sabbatical calendar. Where in the world would you go if you had a year off (and presumably an unlimited budget)?
Executive CDs	Paolo Dematteis	
	Riccardo Robiglio	
Art Director	Azzurra Bacchetta	
Advertiser	Fontegrafica,	
	"Sabbatical Year"	

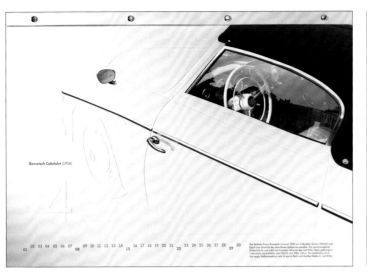

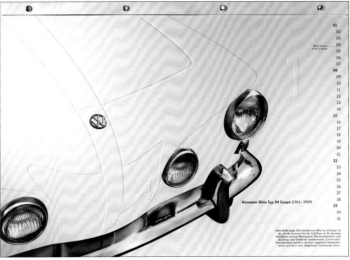

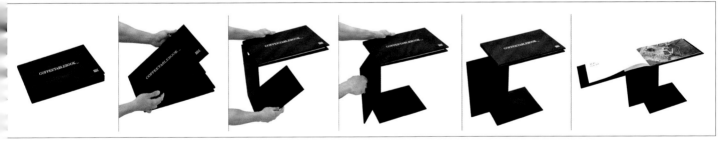

Agency	Grabarz & Partner, Hamburg	Volkswagen Classic is responsible for the maintenance and preservation of classic Volkswagen cars. This calendar shows why the cars are worth preserving, through sublime images of their distinctive lines and details. An embossing process means it's possible to run your fingers over each image, much as a classic car owner might caress the gleaming bodywork of their vehicle.
Creative Directors	Ralf Heuel	
	Ralf Nolting	
	Sven Rumpf	
Copywriters	Mareike Woischke	
	Jens Schlotiski	
Art Director	Roman-Geoffrey Lukowski	
Photographer	Emir Haveric	
Acct. Supervisor	Anna Christiane Roth	
Advertiser	Volkswagen Classic Calendar	

Agency	Serviceplan, Munich	A coffee table book that's also a coffee table. Created for Rolf Benz, a manufacturer of premium designer furniture made in Germany. From a distance, it looks like a coffee table, but on closer inspection it turns out to be a book containing the entire Rolf Benz coffee table collection, which was less well known than some of its other furniture. An ideal promotional tool for design fairs and at point of sale.
CCO	Alexander Schill	
Executive CD	Matthias Harbeck	
Creative Director	Oliver Palmer	
Copywriter	Frank Seiler	
Art Directors	Sandra Loibl	
	Franz Roeppischer	
Photographers	Lippert Studios	
	Bernd Opitz Photography	
Production	Foto Design Huber	
Graphic Design	Katharina Holzer	
Advertiser	Rolf Benz "Coffeetablebook"	

Agency	Family Business, Stockholm	**Account Team**	Anna Andrén Cecilia Steenberg Forsberg		
Creative Directors	John Lagerqvist Mårten Knutsson	**Clients**	Jonas Thålin Mattias Westphal		
Copywriter	Tove Norström		Jonas Thålin		
Art Director	Fredrik Lindquist		Louise Arén		
Photographer	Jens Mortensen		Anna Bergfeldt		
Final Art	Andy Chong Anna Jarl	**Advertiser**	Erik Näf Absolut Vodka, "Absolut Unique"		
Glass Works	Julia Schilleras Fredrik Källqvist Ardagh Group				

Vodka brand Absolut is famous for its distinctive bottle. It often comes up with attractive or amusing limited editions. But this time the challenge was even greater: to make four million unique bottles, so that each and every one was a limited edition. The production line was programmed to use every possible type of glass decoration technique in a random yet controlled way.

Coatings, patterns and painting methods were defined, but the final combination was left to the machines. Finally, each decorated bottle was numbered and the bottles were mixed up like cards being shuffled before the cases were sent out into the world.

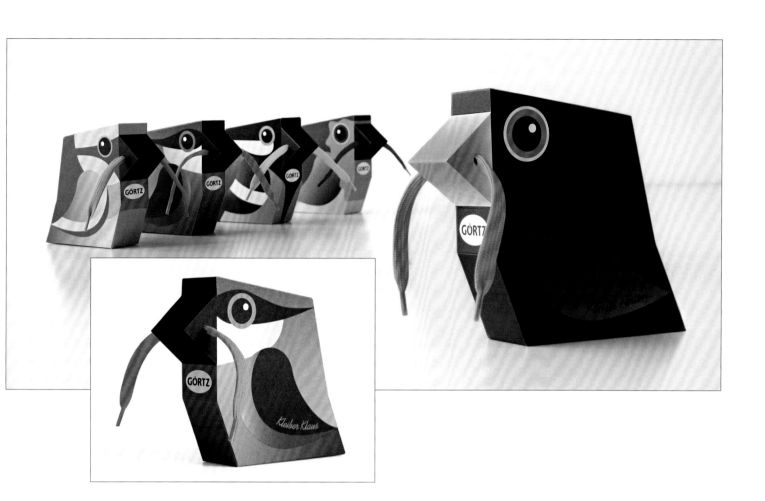

Agency	Gürtlerbachmann, Hamburg	
Copywriter	Claudia Oltmann	
AD/Illustrator	Veronika Kieneke	
Production	Produktionsbüro Romey von Malottky	
Typography	Müllerditzen P.O.P. Werbeteam	
Exec. Producer	Veronika Kieneke	
Imaging	Julian Hets	
Final Art	Tobias Langkamp	
Acct. Executive	Anne Kukereit	
Advertiser	Görtz Shoes	

German footwear retailer Görtz uses a bird theme to attract children and their parents to the kiddies' shoe section of its stores. Even the shoeboxes themselves are transformed into birds, with laces playing the role of worms caught in the creatures' beaks. Five lovingly designed birds encourage play and collection.

Agency	Gürtlerbachmann, Hamburg
Copywriter	Matthias Hardt
AD/Illustrator	Veronika Kieneke
Production	Produktionsbüro Romey von Malottky
Project Mgr.	Anna Lorenzen
Final Art	Tobias Langkamp
Imaging	Julian Hets
Advertiser	Closed Clothing, "The Four of Woolga"

The Four of Woolga are four family members – mum, dad, child and baby – featured on sock packaging from German clothing brand Closed. During a promotion, customers who spent more than 50 euros in the store received one of the packs for free. When they'd collected all four they found that the packs nestled inside one another in ascending order like Russian matryoshka dolls.

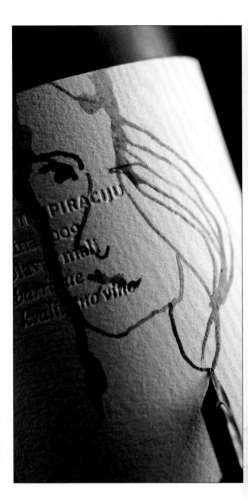

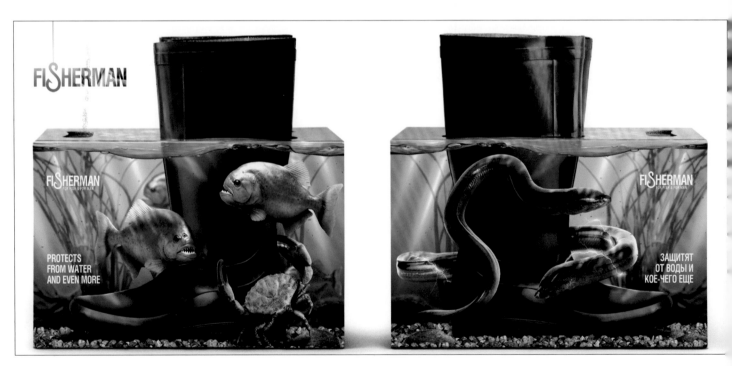

FISHERMAN

FISHERMAN

PROTECTS
FROM WATER
AND EVEN MORE

ЗАЩИТЯТ
ОТ ВОДЫ И
КОЕ-ЧЕГО ЕЩЕ

354   **Packaging Design**

Agencies	Brandoctor, Zagreb
	Bruketa&Žinić OM, Zagreb
Creative Directors	Davor Bruketa
	Nikola Žinić
Copywriters	Anja Bauer Minkara
	Maja Bencic
Art Directors	Davor Bruketa
	Nikola Žinić
Photographer	Domagoj Kunic
Designer	Sonja Surbatovic
Production Mgr.	Vesna Durasin
DTP	Radovan Radicevic
Advertiser	Stina Wine, "Inspiration"

Stina comes from the Adriatic island of Brač, which is known for its white limestone ("stina" actually means "stone"). The island and its paper-white stone have inspired sculptors, painters and novelists. And naturally, Stina wine inspires anyone who tastes it. So apart from the discreetly embossed lettering, its label is left blank to encourage creativity among its drinkers. Imagine turning a rogue trickle of red wine into a work of art.

Agency	Good Media, Almaty
Creative Director	Igor Mitin
Art Directors	Berik Yergaliyev
	Rustam Gareyev
Designers	Darina Baimukhanova
	Farhat Omirbaev
	Andrey Serduk
Account Team	Renat Abdrakhmanov
	Diana Saibekova
Advertiser	Fisherman Rubber Boots

Packaging with a difference for these rubber boots that are more than just waterproof. They also protect the wearer against environmental debris, biological threats, natural, chemical and electrical hazards. To communicate their protective features the boots appear to be standing in a tank of piranhas and other dangerous underwater creatures.

DELICIOUS HAND MADE PÂTÉ

TO DIE FOR

Made exclusively using freshest local ingredients, our free-range chicken livers and proper English butter create the most extraordinarily smooth pâté. Enhanced with a good splash of Cointreau or Armagnac, it's no wonder everyone wants in.

smashingpate.com

Agencies	Turner Duckworth, London & San Francisco
Creative Directors	David Turner
	Bruce Duckworth
Photographer	Craig Easton
Illustrator	Geoffrey Appleton
Design Director	Jamie McCathie
Designers	David Blakemore
	Jamie McCathie
Typographer	Nick Cooke
Artwork	James Norris
Retouching	Peter Ruane
Advertiser	Conté à Paris

Conté à Paris is a fine art brand that has specialised in pencils and pastels since 1795. The packaging shows scenes of Paris to inspire customers and underline the provenance of the brand. Each set is illustrated with an appropriate idea: for example, a set of black-only pastels features a black cat on a nocturnal Parisian cobbled street. A set of white pastels shows the famous white stone of the Sacré-Coeur basilica.

Agency	IAS b2b Marketing, Cheshire
Creative Director	Reuben Webb
AD/Illustrator	Stephen Lawlor
Photographer	Stephen Lawlor
Producer	Stephen Lawlor
Advertiser	Smashing Pâté

Smashing Pâté is so delicious that it's simply to die for, as the brand claims in its advertising. So it's packaged in a coffin. The concept is designed to stand out in the world of premium pâté, a category full of "finest farmhouse this" and "organically fed that".

MINTY MERMAID   BLACK SWAN   BORDEAUX BABY   WHITE SNAKE

CANDY CRUSH

356   **Packaging Design**

Agency	Mockup Advertising, Gothenburg	Hoses are hardly the sexiest objects on earth – or the prettiest things in the garden. But Garden Glory's designers changed all that by taking inspiration from iconic "it" bags produced by fashion houses like Chanel and Mulberry. They created high-quality hoses and wall mounts in eye-catching colours. The hoses were given names like Minty Mermaid, Candy Crush and Bordeaux Baby, turning hoses from pragmatic devices into luxury objects; "For glamorous people with dirty nails."	
Creative Director	Rosita Johnson		
Copywriter	Gabriella Zachrisson		
Art Director	Rosita Johnson		
Photographer	Jonathan Fernström		
Illustrator	Mikael Stenberg		
Acct. Manager	Erik Sanderoth		
Advertiser	Garden Glory Hoses, "For Glamorous People with Dirty Nails"		

Agency	Jung von Matt, Hamburg	Ricola is often the sweet of choice when your voice is a bit hoarse. Its blend of natural herbs eases sore throats and soothes vocal cords. Hence these wrappers, which turn the sweets into the heads of singers with constricted throats. Unwrap the sweet and the stars are free to warble once more.	
Creative Directors	Fabian Frese		
	Goetz Ulmer		
	Thimoteus Wagner		
	Martin Strutz		
Copywriter	Hannah Haeffner		
Art Director	Johannes Riffelmacher		
Photographers	Reinhard Hunger		
	Klaus Merz		
Illustrator	Julien Canavezes		
Designers	Lars Jakschik		
	Karina Riehle		
Advertiser	Ricola, "Unwrap"		

Shiraz
Rosé Wine · South African

Syrah
Vino Rosado · Argentina

Coteaux d'Aix en Provence
Appellation d'Origine Contrôlée

Bergerac
Appellation d'Origine Contrôlée

Côtes du Rhône
Appellation d'Origine Contrôlée

Montepulciano d'Abruzzo
Denominazione di origine controllata

Cabernet Sauvignon
Vino Tinto · Chile

Australian
White Wine · Chardonnay

Chardonnay
White Wine of California

Agency	Lavernia & Cienfuegos Diseño, Valencia	As part of its 365 range of affordable products, Belgian supermarket Delhaize offers a selection of wines from around the world. To capture the accessible qualities of the product, the labels feature the humble cork. But each cork is transformed into a funny character symbolising the wine's country of origin.
Creative Directors	Nacho Lavernia Alberto Cienfuegos	
Advertiser	Delhaize Private Label Wines, "Wines of the World"	

Agency	DDB & Tribal, Amsterdam
Copywriter	Stef Jongenelen
Art Director	Yona Hümmels
Production	Graveertechniek Nijdeken, Hengelo
Producer	Denise Wolterbeek
Advertiser	Amstel Beer, "Trophy Can"

Amsterdam's Amstel beer is the proud sponsor of the city's football club: Ajax. In 2012 Ajax won the Dutch National Championship, so Amstel gave fans the chance to raise their very own Championship Trophy. How? It turned the bottom of the Amstel can into the trophy itself, a silver platter. An image of the trophy was laser engraved on the bottom of 2,400 limited edition cans. The cans were available in four selected Amsterdam supermarkets the day after Ajax won the cup - and soon sold out. Examples were seen on eBay with prices up to 50 euros.

Agency	Tomatdesign, Moscow
Creative Director	Andrey Tarakanov
Art Directors	Andrey Tarakanov
	Denis Bashev
Advertiser	SPI Group, "JC Limited Edition Beer"

Leading drinks company SPI Group briefed the agency to design the label and packaging for a limited edition range of beer to be served during a private birthday party for a special guest, "famous French winemaker Jean Claude". It had to reflect two of the VIP guest's favourite things – richly flavoured dark beer, and sailing. The agency soon found a solution to the knotty problem.

Agency	Havas 360, Paris		This interactive bag for toy store Joupi
Executive CDs	Thomas Derouault		cleverly puts into action the retailer's brand
	Hugues Pinguet		promise: "Expert in children's smiles."
Creative Director	Thomas Derouault		Every bag depicts a child's face. When
Art Directors	Sabrina Leva		the bags are empty, the kids look sad. But
	Thomas de Belleville		when the bags are full and being carried
Advertising Mgr.	Marie-Claude Morat		out of the shop, the weight of the toy turns
Acct. Supervisor	Anne-Flore Seringe		a sad face into a smiling one.
PR	Delphine Le Floch		
CEOs	Vincent Mayet		
	Matthieu Habra		
Advertiser	Joupi Toy Store,		
	"Joupi Bag"		

Agency	New Moment		Supermarket shelves are full of pâté, so
	New Ideas Company		how to create a brand that stands out?
	Y&R, Belgrade		Adopt a cartoonish approach and a slightly
Creative Director	Dusan Drakalski		dark sense of humour. Each type of pate
Copywriters	Nikola Vojnov		features the relevant animal coming to a
	Ana Pop Stefanija		sticky and entirely unpremeditated end,
Art Director	Nikola Vojnov		underlining the claim that this particular
Illustrators	Jana Miseva		pâté is "naturally made".
	Hari Dudeski		
Advertiser	Pekabesko Pâté,		
	"Naturally Made Pâté"		

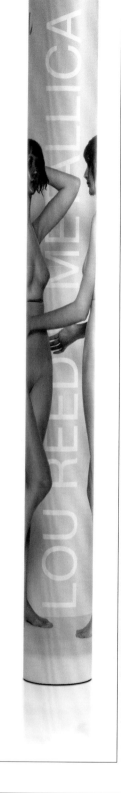

Agencies	Just Design, Cape Town
Copywriter	Ciara Louw
Illustrator	Studio Muti, Cape Town
Designer	Jay Badenhorst
Advertiser	Devil's Peak Beers

The Devil's Peak Brewing Company claims to produce brews unlike any other in South Africa. These designs reflect the intricacy of the different beer styles and the brewer's commitment to creating beers with unique character and depth. Craftsmanship and idiosyncratic style unite the four designs, which have the symmetry and mysticism of tarot cards.

Agency	Turner Duckworth Design, London & San Francisco
Creative Directors	David Turner
	Bruce Duckworth
	Sarah Moffat
Photographers	Stan Musilek
	Anton Corbijn
Designer	David Turner
Advertiser	Lou Reed & Metallica, "Lulu"

Lulu is a musical collaboration between Lou Reed and Metallica: an album based on Frank Wiedekind's Lulu plays from the early 1900s. Memorably portrayed by Louise Brooks in the 1929 film Pandora's Box, the seductive Lulu is pulled into a spiral of sex, deception and murder. The packaging design reflects the male characters' objectification of Lulu by melding the female form with the torso of a vintage mannequin found in the Museum der Dinge ("Museum of Things") in Berlin.

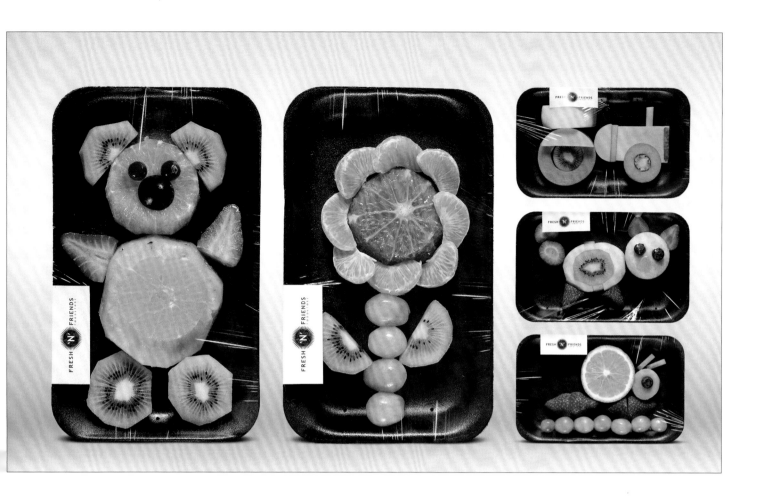

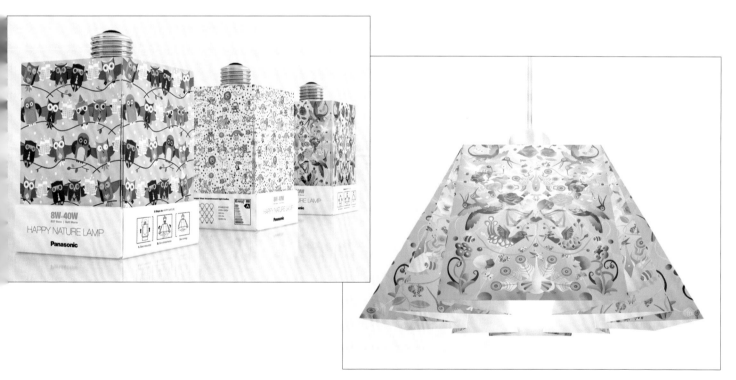

Agency	Scholz & Friends, Berlin	Fresh'N'Friends supermarket sells organic food for a healthy lifestyle. That's an easy message for adults to swallow, but how do you get children to eat fruit instead of sweets? This has become an important question in the face of rising rates of obesity. To convince children that fruit could be fun, "boring" fruits were rearranged into appealing shapes like a teddy bear, a kitten, a flower, a tractor…and other things kids love.	
Creative Directors	Martin Pross		
	Matthias Spaetgens		
	Wolf Schneider		
	Mathias Rebmann		
	Florian Schwalme		
Art Directors	Alexander Doepel		
	Sandra Krebs		
	Bjoern Kernspeckt		
	René Gebhardt		
	Loic Sattler		
	Jinhi Kim		
Advertiser	Fresh'N'Friends		

Agency	Scholz & Friends, Berlin	Panasonic makes energy saving light bulbs. Of course, so do lots of other people – and Panasonic wanted to stand out. To prove that its product was sustainable, it created an energy saving lamp. You don't throw away the packaging, you use it as a colourful lampshade. The natural designs enhance the message.	
Creative Directors	Martin Pross		
	Matthias Spaetgens		
	Michael Winterhagen		
	Nils Busche		
Copywriter	Michael Schoepf		
Art Director	Walter Ziegler		
Producer	Franziska Ibe		
Art Buying	Kirsten Rendtel		
Account Mgr.	Salvatore Amato		
Advertiser	Panasonic		
	Energy Saving Lamps,		
	"Happy Nature Lamp"		

362   **Packaging Design**

Agency	Scholz & Friends, Berlin	3M's ear plugs protect sensitive ears against	
Creative Directors	Martin Pross	extreme sounds. This was clearly demon-	
	Matthias Spaetgens	strated by packaging designed to look like	
	Robert Krause	the volume control on a hi-fi. When opening	
	Wolf Schneider	the pack, the user seems to be turning	
Copywriter	Nils Tscharnke	down the volume. The image appealed to	
Art Directors	Sebastian Frese	the target market of musicians and festi-	
	Ralf Schroeder	val-goers who love sound, but sometimes	
Producer	Benito Schumacher	need protection against excessive volume.	
Account Mgr.	Josef Hoehnow		
Advertiser	3M Solar Ear Plugs,		
	"The Volume-Down		
	Packaging"		

Agency	Kian Branding Agency,	In the future, cooking eggs will be as	
	Novosibirsk	easy as opening the package. The Gogol	
Creative Director	Kirill Konstantinov	Mogol project is a new way of packing,	
Art Director	Mary Sypko	storing and above all cooking eggs. Each	
Designer	Evgeny Morgalev	package is made from several layers of	
Advertiser	Gogol Mogol	recycled cardboard. Under the first layer	
	Design Project	is a special heating catalyst. Pulling a tab	
		starts a chemical reaction that begins to	
		cook the egg. Open the egg package a	
		couple of minutes later and – presto! – it's	
		time for breakfast.	

Agencies	Turner Duckworth,
	London & San Francisco
Creative Directors	David Turner
	Bruce Duckworth
Illustrators	John Geary
	Geoffrey Appleton
Design Director	Clem Halpin
Designers	Matt Lurcock
	Buzz Burman
	Brian Labus
Art Work	Adam Bentley
	James Norris
Advertiser	Toblerone

On one side of Toblerone's famous triangular packaging, the "N" is cropped to form a rooftop and chimney pot – where a silhouetted Santa and his reindeer get up to various adventures. The Matterhorn mountain logo makes the perfect backdrop, lending a sense of scale. On the other side, a "zoomed out" continuation of the story shows the consequences of Santa's mishaps.

Agencies	Fred & Farid,
	Paris & Shanghai
Creative Directors	Fred & Farid
Art Director	Amelie Pichon
Account Team	Hélène Camus
	Olivia Courbon
Clients	Hugues Pietrini
	Stanislas De Parcevaux
	Émilie De Fautereau
Advertiser	Schweppes Slim Cans

The challenge was to make Schweppes tonic relevant to night clubbers. The cans reflect the properties that make each flavour special, such as psychedelic citrus fruits or an exotic lemon. The "original" Indian Tonic features a leopard, while a black panther demonstrates the "dark side" of cola flavour. And because these are cans for night owls, they feature light-reflecting ink.

Food & Drink Interactive

Agency	Robert/Boisen & Like-Minded, Copenhagen	Producers	Christina Erritzoe Emilie Brandt
Creative Director	Michael Robert	Graphic Design	Peter Vojnovic
Art Directors	Mark Rif Torbensen		Morten Grundsøe
	René Sohn Kammersgaard	Programmers	Jorge Hernandez Ramiro Espada
	Anders Kure	Account Team	Søren Christensen
Director	Niels Nørløv		Mathias Birkvad
Production	Gobsmack		Martin Hörmann
	Productions, Molamil	Advertiser	Anthon Berg, "The Generous Store"

Generosity is a crucial part of Danish chocolate brand Anthon Berg's DNA. It wanted people to rediscover the brand and remind them how good it feels to be generous. Instead of advertising, it opened a unique pop-up chocolate shop. In fact, it was the world's first chocolate store where you didn't pay with cash or cards, but with good deeds.

Choose from a range of "fees": for example promise to make your loved one breakfas in bed; or to stop criticising their driving Make a pledge via Facebook so you'r obliged to stick to your promise. Then leav with your chocolates. The Pop-up stor was only open for a day but it had peopl queuing around the block to exchange ger erosity…for chocolates.

Agency	Lowe Brindfors, Stockholm
Creative Directors	Patrik Westerdahl
	Petter Lublin
Copywriter	Henrik Haeger
Production	Monterosa
	B-Reel
Web Design	Ellinor Bjarnolf
	Rasmus Sjöborg
Strategy Director	Oscar Erlandsson
Digital Producers	Lisa Flacké
	Sofia Jönsson
Tech. Producer	Tobias Löfgren
Sound	Plan8, Stockholm
Account Team	Tina Jarlerud
	Jessica Nordlund
	Emma Branting
Clients	Mick van Ettinger
	Sophie Galvani
	Alper Eroglu
	Camilla Scognamiglio
Advertiser	Magnum Ice Cream, "Pleasure Hunt Across Amsterdam"

Magnum wanted to reinforce its brand promise "For pleasure seekers" and introduce its new Infinity ice cream. So it created an artificial reality smartphone app that allowed people to play a "real life" version of Pac Man on the streets of Amsterdam. The game challenged them to collect points while outrunning the greedy mouths visible on their phones. It all worked with Google Maps and a bit of technical wizardry. Those who collected enough points could exchange them for a real Magnum Infinity.

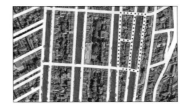

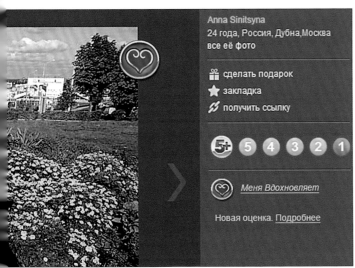

Agency	OMD OM Group, Moscow
Creative Directors	Dmitry Mordashov
	Alexander Balashov
	Ekaterina Pugina
Producers	OMD Digital
Graphic Design	Julia Tkacheva
MD	Dmitry Mordashov
Media Managers	Alexander Balashov
	Ekaterina Pugina
	Julia Tkacheva
Advertiser	Inspiration Chocolates, "You Inspire Me!"

Giving Inspiration chocolates is a gesture of love. The agency had noted that users of leading Russian social network Odnoklassniki often used the site to flirt, usually by "rating" photos of the person who'd caught their eye. Five is the highest rating, but the chocolate brand went a step further. It created an entirely new button reading "You Inspire Me". When recipients or other friends clicked on the button, it led to the Inspiration site, where giving chocolates was promoted as the perfect way of showing someone how you feel.

Agency	Great Works, Sthlm
Executive CD	Ted Persson
Creative Director	Kalle Söderquist
Lead Creative	Ingrid Sydow
Creative Concept	Johan Öhrn
	Jesper Klarin
Development	Isak Burström
Production	Teenage Engineering
	Kamisol
Director	Magnus Härdner
Producers	Anders Eklund
	Hakan Bilgin
Advertiser	Absolut Vodka

Over the years Absolut has worked with artists such as Andy Warhol and Damien Hirst. But this project featured a very special artist: you. Simply download the Absolut Blank app, a white Absolut bottle. Now fill it with inspiration by taking pictures and recording sounds with your phone. With a quick shake the app magically turns your inspirations into a multimedia artwork, which you can post to the Absolut Blank online gallery. The gallery also contains interviews with artists about how their creativity begins…with an absolute blank.

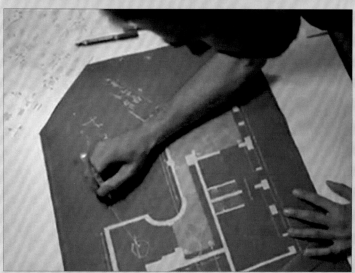

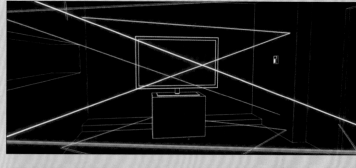

Agency	Åkestam Holst, Stockholm	**Graphic Design**	Oscar Gardö
Creative Director	Andreas Ullenius	**Digital Producer**	Johan Eklund
Copywriter	Joakim Labraaten	**Motion Designer**	Oskar Törnros
Art Director	Petra Albrektson	**Studio Assistant**	Kim Ihre
Photographer	Markus Kuhn	**Account Team**	Henrik Adenskog
Director	Nisse Axman		Anna Nolendorfs
Production	From Stockholm with Love Supermegacorp	**Advertiser**	Pause Home Entertainment, "The Heist"

Electronics retailer Pause wanted to show that it delivers the best home cinema experience. For one night, it turned the store into a scene from a heist movie – and invited the public to play burglar. An online trailer set the scene: a Pause staff member had been unfairly dismissed and wanted to wreak revenge by robbing the store. But he needed your help to avoid being linked to the crime. Lasers, motion detectors, strobe lights, alarms and smoke were installed.

Volunteers were invited to study the floor plan. Then they teamed up with a computer geek, who would hack the Pause website to get the door codes and take control of the security system. Meanwhile, the thief tried to lift an LED TV worth six grand. The closer they got without triggering the alarm, the bigger discounts they received on the store's home cinema products. At the end of the night, someone actually stole the TV.

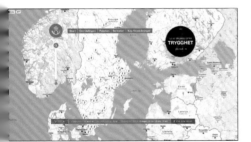  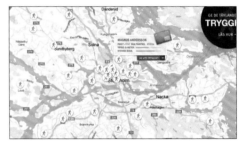

Agency	Åkestam Holst, Stockholm	**Web Designer**	Andreas Dagman	
Creative Director	Andreas Ullenius	**Motion Designer**	Nisse Axman	
Copywriter	Hanna Björk	**Digital Producer**	Johan Eklund	
Art Director	Lars Holthe	**Studio Assistant**	Kim Ihre	
Production	From Stockholm with Love	**Sound Design**	Plan8, Stockholm	
		Account Team	Göran Åkestam	
Producer	Leila El-Zein		Jacob Stjärne	
Graphic Design	Oscar Gardö		Daniel Sundin	
	Anna Forsberg		Maria Ljung	
Planner	Lars Friberg	**Advertiser**	The Swedish Post, "Sweden's Safest Hands"	

The Swedish Post wanted to remind customers that it always delivers parcels safely. So it launched a competition to find "Sweden's safest hands". It created a gaming app that turned anyone with an iPhone into a mail carrier on a virtual bicycle. At 6am, midday and 6pm every day, it released a virtual parcel filled with "secret stuff". Using the app, users had to cross the city and deliver their parcel safely. Sounds easy?

It wasn't – the game used the iPhone's technology to make keeping the bike balanced a tricky proposal. But you could drop by a post office to get extra "safety" points. You could also track rival mail carriers on a dedicated website. The first to deliver the parcel intact became "Sweden's safest hands" – and the contents of the virtual parcel was delivered to their home, by a real postman.

Agency	Crispin Porter + Bogusky, Gothenburg
CCO	Rob Reilly
Executive CD	Gustav Martner
Associate CD	Mattias Berg
Copywriter	Annica Brinck
Art Director	Dennis Rosenqvist
Interactive Head	Marcus Åslund
Exec. Producer	Marcus Scheffler
Digital Developers	Patrick Chan
	Bogdan Orlov
Advertiser	Scandinavian Airlines, "Point & Fly"

This cunning tablet ad for airline SAS took advantage of the device's built in compass and GPS. When the ad is activated, the compass points in the direction you're headed. Then it suggests potential destinations that lie in the same direction – but only if you fly from a nearby airport. It tells you the price of the flight, too. Naturally, if a destination captures your imagination, you can click there and then to book.

Agency	SMFB, Oslo
Copywriters	Hans Magne Ekre
	Alexander Gjersoe
Art Directors	Hans Magne Ekre
	Alexander Gjersoe
Designer	Nicklas Hellborg
Web Designer	Suzie Webb
Account Team	Kristian Kristiansen
	Jannicke Platou
Advertiser	Ikea Tidafors Sofa, "The Home Showroom"

When Norwegians are buying or selling a home, most of them do so through the same website, Finn, which utterly dominates the market. Ikea realised that people seeking homes may soon be looking for new furniture – a perfect opportunity to promote its new Tidafors sofa. So it contacted the people who were selling their homes through the site and got permission to place its sofa in their ads: "An idyllic country house with a very comfortable sofa." In return, the sellers got some help from Ikea in advertising their homes.

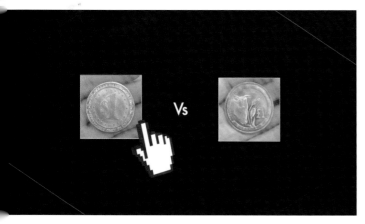

Consumer Services & Household Interactive   **369**

Agency	BBDO, Moscow	**Producers**	Valery Gorohov
Creative Directors	Luis Tauffer		Maria Yakushina
	Andres Vergara		Dmitriy Dobuzhinsky
Copywriter	Polina Zabrodskaya		Alexey Zinchenko
Art Directors	Luis Tauffer	**Digital Creative**	Ilya Andreyev
	Andres Vergara	**Digital Directors**	Ekaterina Smygina
	Lucas Zaiden		Evgeny Borisov
	Cloves Menezes	**Project Manager**	Igor Kholopov
Photographer	Artiom Gelvez	**Digital Manager**	Alena Aleksandrova
	Kostenko	**Music**	Goudron Music Factory
Production	Park Production	**Sound Studio**	CM Records
	INDEE Interactive	**Advertiser**	Intouch Car Insurance,
Production Mgr.	Andrey Grishin		"Car vs Piano"

In Russia, unexpected incidents are known as "falling pianos". Car insurance company Intouch interpreted this idea literally by training a webcam 24/7 on a grand piano suspended over a car by nine ropes. Over seven days, online participants were invited to flip a coin and bet twice a day on the probability of certain unlikely events occurring: for instance, temperatures in Moscow reaching 21° (they did). If one of the events occurred, one of the ropes would be cut.

On the site, a live Twitter feed was projected on the wall and a countdown heightened the suspense. Finally, on the sixth day, after one improbable event too many, the piano fell onto the car. This sent the message that, even if it can't protect cars from "falling pianos", at least Intouch can provide comprehensive insurance, covering owners for even the most unexpected events.

Agency	DDB DM9JaymeSyfu/Digit, Manila
Creative Directors	Merlee Jayme
	Eugene Demata
Copywriter	Aste Gutierrez
Art Directors	Biboy Royong
	Buboy Paguio
Production	Tower of Doom
Producer	Carlo Perlas
Programmer	Buboy Paguio
Account Director	Gabbie Santiago
Advertiser	Gabriela, "Bury the Past Project"

The Philippines has a problem with so-called "sex scandal videos": amateur sex tapes, often shot many years ago and posted online without the women's permission. There are one million of these videos online and 300,000 searches for them every month, with the result that many women are now living in shame in this predominantly Catholic society. Women's rights organisation Gabriela wanted to help them start afresh. The "Bury the Past" campaign aimed to make sex scandal videos far less easy to dig up.

The solution was simple: through a PR, online and print campaign, people were persuaded to add the word "Scandal" to their name on Facebook. With the aid of further search engine optimisation the growth of the "Scandal" community meant that real scandal videos were buried as many as 30 pages deep in search results. In addition, each person who changed their name on Facebook was effectively promoting the campaign.

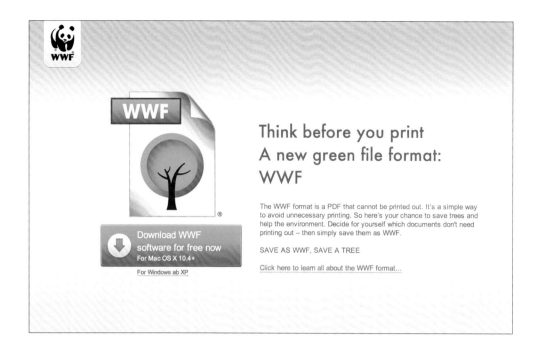

Think before you print
A new green file format:
WWF

The WWF format is a PDF that cannot be printed out. It's a simple way
to avoid unnecessary printing. So here's your chance to save trees and
help the environment. Decide for yourself which documents don't need
printing out – then simply save them as WWF.

SAVE AS WWF, SAVE A TREE

Click here to learn all about the WWF format...

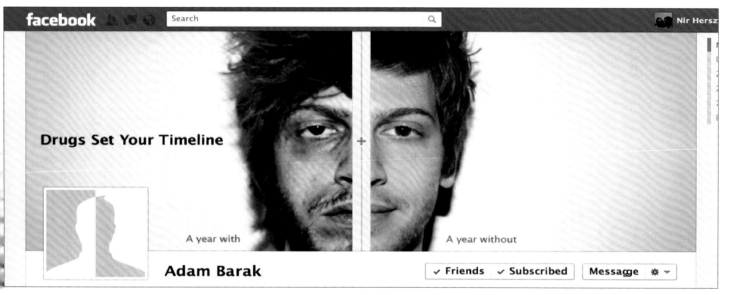

Agency	Jung von Matt, Hamburg	WWF (the Worldwide Fund For Nature) was concerned that too many trees were being cut down to produce paper. So it wanted to discourage people from printing out PDF documents unnecessarily. To raise awareness of the issue and literally stop wasteful printing, it developed a new, green file format: "Save as WWF." A format that can't be printed out. A simple idea that saves trees. At the time of writing, 53,000 companies, organizations and individuals worldwide have already downloaded the WWF software.
Creative Directors	Dörte Spengler-Ahrens	
	Jan Rexhausen	
Copywriters	Michael Kittel	
	Henning	
	Müller-Dannhausen	
Art Director	Alexander Norvilas	
Producer	Florian Panier	
Programmers	Knud Alex Müller	
	Florian Paul	
	Lana Nugent	
Project Mgr.	Michael Behrens	
Advertiser	WWF, "Save as WWF"	

Agency	McCann Digital, Tel Aviv	The Israel Anti-Drug Authority (IADA) identified a rise in drug users aged 18-to-24. As 94% of young Israelis use social networks, this was the ideal place to reach them. But how? Then Facebook introduced Timeline, a new way of telling your life story in chronological order, like an autobiography. So a character named Adam Barak suddenly appeared on Facebook. Unusually, his Timeline was split in two: one side showed a year without drugs, the other a parallel year as a user. The target audience saw what their lives might look like if they abused drugs.
Creative Director	Nir Refuah	
Copywriter	Daniel Barak	
Art Director	Nir Hersztadt	
Photographer	Guli Cohen	
Producer	Inbal Fanan	
Advertiser	Israel Anti-Drug Authority, "Drugs Set Your Timeline"	

The Ad Makeover

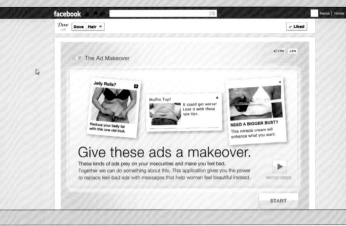

Give these ads a makeover.

These kinds of ads prey on your insecurities and make you feel bad. Together we can do something about this. This application gives you the power to replace feel-bad ads with messages that help women feel beautiful instead.

WATCH VIDEO

START

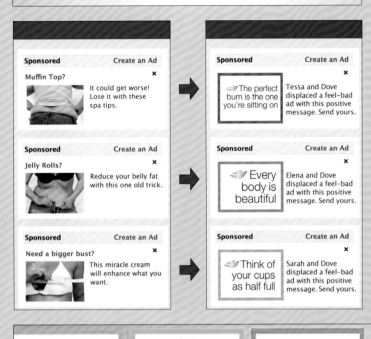

Sponsored	Create an Ad
Muffin Top? ✕	It could get worse! Lose it with these spa tips.

Sponsored	Create an Ad
Jelly Rolls? ✕	Reduce your belly fat with this one old trick.

Sponsored	Create an Ad
Need a bigger bust? ✕	This miracle cream will enhance what you want.

Sponsored	Create an Ad
✕	The perfect bum is the one you're sitting on — Tessa and Dove displaced a feel-bad ad with this positive message. Send yours.

Sponsored	Create an Ad
✕	Every body is beautiful — Elena and Dove displaced a feel-bad ad with this positive message. Send yours.

Sponsored	Create an Ad
✕	Think of your cups as half full — Sarah and Dove displaced a feel-bad ad with this positive message. Send yours.

Claudia White was tagged in Chloe Taylor's photo.

The queen of the party

Like · Comment · 9 hours ago

Elizabeth Andrews likes this.

Write a com...

Sponsored — See All

Beauty is an all-ages show — Sharly & Dove replaced a feel-bad ad with this positive message. Send yours.

The perfect bum is the one you're sitting on

When it comes to your body, love the one you're with

Your birthday suit suits you

The perfect bum is the one you're sitting on

Hello beautiful

Your birthday suit suits you

Think of your cups as half full

Every body is beautiful

Beauty is an all-ages show

Think of your cups as half full

Be your beautiful self

Every body is beautiful

Hora de curtir algo mais no Facebook: você mesma

Beleza não tem idade

Oi linda!

Hora de curtir algo mais no Facebook: você mesma

Seja bonita como você mesma

Beleza não tem idade

O bumbum perfeito é aquele em que você está sentada

Suas medidas estão sempre na medida

Suas medidas estão sempre na medida

Você já nasceu com o look que melhor combina com você

O bumbum perfeito é aquele em que você está sentada

Você já nasceu com o look que melhor combina com você

Health, Beauty & Fashion Interactive

Agency	Ogilvy & Mather London
Creative Directors	Gerry Human Ivan Pols
Copywriters	Margo Young Laura Rogers
Art Director	Trevallyn Hall
Production	The Mill London
Producer	Fiona Renfrew
Creative Tech.	Craig Blagg
Digital Producer	Sasha Dunn
Content Architect	Anthony Butterfield
Developer	Martin Robertson
Designer	Simone Zahradka
Digital Strategy	Giles Rhys-Jones
Advertiser	Dove, "The Dove Ad Makeover"

Dove is committed to raising the self-esteem of real women. Now the battle has moved to social networks. The information available from women's social media activity was being used to serve them negative banner advertising: everything from weight loss ads to cosmetic surgery and dating sites: "27 and still single?" The solution: the ad makeover application. This was initially promoted through conventional PR and advertising.

Then the fun began. The app user selects a positive message, then chooses a keyword typically purchased by advertisers: "love, careers, travel" and so on. The ad uses Facebook's "ad auction" service to bid double the usual amount for those keywords, magically overriding the negative messages with positive ones. In short, the app puts women in control of the advertising they see. Together, they replaced more than 171 million negative banners.

Agency	DDB Brasil, Sao Paulo
Creative Directors	Sergio Valente
	Marco Versolato
	Moacyr Netto
	Ricardo Tronquini
	Cristian Mazzeo
Copywriters	Marcelo Pascoa
	Vinicius Malinoski
	Helio Marques
Art Directors	Marcelo Bruzzesi
	Estela Padilha
	Caio Cardoso
Advertiser	C&A, "Look Block"

Girls, don't you just hate it when someone at a party is wearing the same outfit as you? If only there was a way of preventing that from happening! Fashion retailer C&A did just that. Introducing the Look Block. Accessing the online store through Facebook, shoppers could buy a look from the new collection and "block" it so none of their friends could buy the same outfit. For every piece of clothing they bought, a post was published on their friends' walls, in which they bragged about their exclusive purchase.

Agency	DDB Brasil, Sao Paulo
Creative Directors	Sergio Valente
	Marco Versolato
	Ricardo Tronquini
	Cristian Mazzeo
Copywriters	Helio Marques
	Flavio Reghini
Art Directors	Caio Cardoso
	Marcelo Bruzzesi
	Rodrigo Ghiorzi
Production	Cricket Design
Graphic Design	Marco Loschiavo
Advertiser	C&A, "Fashion Like"

Shopping alone for clothes presents a problem – how can you get a second opinion about an outfit you're thinking of buying? C&A solved this problem by putting its collection on Facebook and encouraging users to "like" the various pieces. Meanwhile, the "fashion likes" for each outfit were totted up in real time on electronic hangars in the stores. So hesitant shoppers could identify the most popular pieces, right there at the point of sale.

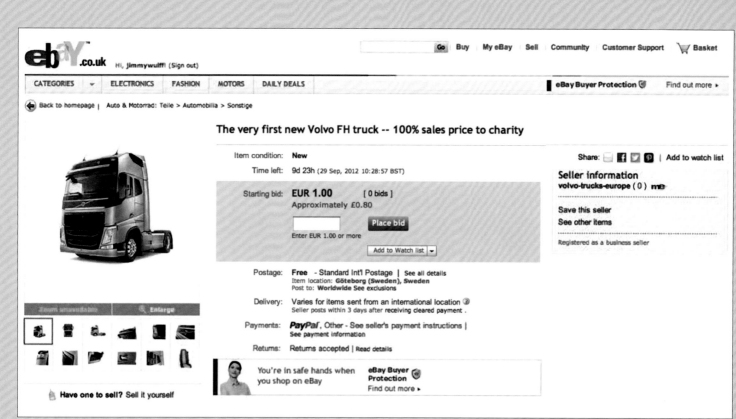

eBaY.co.uk Hi, jimmywulffl (Sign out)

[Go] Buy | My eBay | Sell | Community | Customer Support | Basket

CATEGORIES ▾ | ELECTRONICS | FASHION | MOTORS | DAILY DEALS

eBay Buyer Protection | Find out more ▸

◂ Back to homepage | Auto & Motorrad: Teile > Automobilia > Sonstige

The very first new Volvo FH truck -- 100% sales price to charity

Item condition: **New**

Time left: 9d 23h (29 Sep, 2012 10:28:57 BST)

Starting bid: **EUR 1.00** [0 bids]
Approximately £0.80

[Place bid]
Enter EUR 1.00 or more

[Add to Watch list ▾]

Postage: **Free** - Standard Int'l Postage | See all details
Item location: **Göteborg (Sweden), Sweden**
Post to: **Worldwide** See exclusions

Delivery: Varies for items sent from an international location ⓘ
Seller posts within 3 days after receiving cleared payment.

Payments: **PayPal**, Other - See seller's payment instructions |
See payment information

Returns: Returns accepted | Read details

You're in safe hands when you shop on eBay
eBay Buyer Protection
Find out more ▸

Share: 📧 f 🐦 p | Add to watch list

Seller information
volvo-trucks-europe (0) me

Save this seller
See other items

Registered as a business seller

🛍 **Have one to sell?** Sell it yourself

The very first new Volvo FH truck -- 100% sales price to charity

Item condition: **New**

Time left: 9d 23h (29 Sep, 2012 10:28:57 BST)

Starting bid: **EUR 1.00** [0 bids]
Approximately £0.80

[Place bid]
Enter EUR 1.00 or more

[Add to Watch list ▾]

Postage: **Free** - Standard Int'l Postage | See all details
Item location: **Göteborg (Sweden), Sweden**
Post to: **Worldwide** See exclusions

Delivery: Varies for items sent from an international location ⓘ
Seller posts within 3 days after receiving cleared payment.

2. HANDLING QUALITIES

This vehicle has Individual Front Suspension (IFS) and rack and pinion steering, two world-first features on the new Volvo FH that improve comfort and safety. Please note: this feature is not available on the right hand drive version.

A completely new chassis including redesigned rear suspension and more powerful damper springs improve yaw damping by 100 percent. Other handling features of this 4X2 tractor truck include Electronic Stability Control (ESP) and Anti-lock Braking System (ABS).

For a demonstration of the precise handling of this vehicle, watch slackliner Faith Dickey as she walks the line between two Volvo FH trucks speeding down a highway in Croatia.

A quick glance is all it should take to know what you need to know. That's the idea behind the new, clear instrument panel. The right buttons and controls are at your fingertips. And the buttons you use most often are easy to move closest to hand.

D. Steering wheel controls
A switch on the steering wheel lets you manage the driver's instrument group and the secondary display. The buttons themselves are more ergonomic -- among other things a thumb wheel helps to control instruments and scroll through menus

BID ON THE VERY FIRST NEW VOLVO FH

Starting bid: 1 euro (No reserve)

GO TO AUCTION ▸

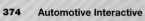

Agency	Forsman & Bodenfors, Gothenburg	**Content Architect**	Johan Wingård
Copywriters	Martin Ringqvist	**Editorial Writer**	Simon Coe
	Björn Engström	**Designer**	Jerry Wass
Art Directors	Sophia Lindholm	**Account Team**	Cilla Glenberg
	Anders Eklind		Britta Malmberg
Producers	Peter Gaudiano		Jenny Edwardsson
	Alexander Blidner	**Advertiser**	Volvo FH Truck, "Launch Site on eBay"

Truck drivers are tough to reach through conventional media. However, they often trawl eBay for spare parts. This gave Volvo an idea for the launch of its new FH Truck. It auctioned a truck on eBay, at a starting price of one euro. The auction was promoted via a multimedia campaign that included an online trailer, a Volvo webzine that acted as a brochure for the truck and PR activity. The buzz was huge and the truck sold for way over its market value within ten days.

"The design is a celebration of truck drivers"

Agency	Forsman & Bodenfors, Gothenburg
Copywriters	Martin Ringqvist
	Björn Engström
Art Directors	Sophia Lindholm
	Anders Eklind
	Staffan Lamm
Producers	Alexander Blidner
	Lina Strandäng
	Peter Gaudiano
	Stefan Thompson
Designer	Jerry Wass
Advertiser	Volvo FH Truck

As part of the launch of the new Volvo FH Truck, a suspenseful online film showcased the truck's rock-steady handling. A high-wire walker crossed a line stretched between two trucks as they raced side-by-side towards a tunnel. But the Ballerina Stunt it was only a teaser to create interest in the new truck. After a live broadcast from six European cities, a digital magazine with several films and interactive modules was released on all platforms, including eBay. It was the first time anyone used eBay as a complete launch site.

Agency	BBDO Proximity, Berlin
Creative MDs	David Mously
	Jan Harbeck
Creative Directors	Ton Hollander
	Rens Ringena
Copywriters	Lukas Liske
	Fredric Antonsson
Art Directors	Daniel Schweinzer
	Sebastian Forsman
	Thomas Tulinius
Production	Gahrens & Battermann
	Pflanz Werbemittelprod'n
Advertiser	Smart Fortwo ED, "Eball"

The Smart Fortwo Electric Drive is an economic little car with surprisingly powerful acceleration. At a unique test drive event at the Frankfurt Motor Show, the cars became rackets in a new take on the classic video game Pong. But instead of using a joystick, players must hit the virtual "ball" by driving their cars back and forth. Each driver experienced the car's impressive performance – and had a lot of fun too.

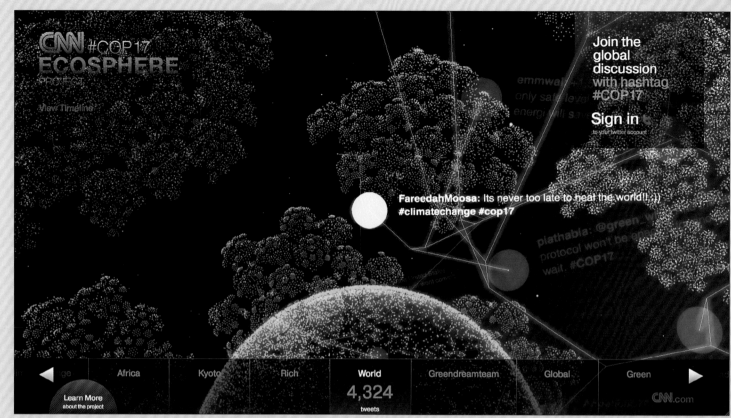

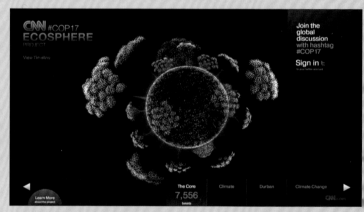

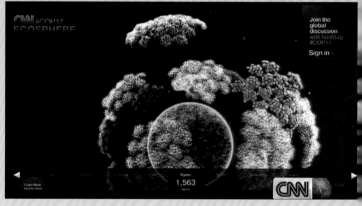

Agency	Heimat, Berlin	**Programmers**	Victor Firsanov	The UN invited delegates to discuss climate change at the COP17 Conference in Durban, South Africa. CNN wanted to get people talking about the issue of climate change and promote its coverage of the event. The result was the Ecosphere: a "living" digital ecosystem that thrived on tweets tagged with #COP17. Every tweet stimulated growth in one of the numerous branches growing out of the Ecosphere, represent-ing topics like Sustainability or Carbon.
Creative Directors	Myles Lord		Ralph de Haan	
	Martien Delfgaauw	**Tech. Direction**	Dan Lewis	
	Luc Schurgers		Victor Firsanov	
Copywriter	Ramin Schmiedekampf		Luc Schurgers	
Art Director	Frank Hose	**Digital Production**	James Britton	
Production	Stink Digital		Marc Pytlik	
Director	Minivegas		Nils Schwemer	
Producer	Jessica Valin		Jess Fletcher	
Graphic Design	Jue Alt		Ellen Utrecht	
	Jared Leistner	**Client**	Jörg Buddenberg	
	Alexander Suchy	**Advertiser**	CNN International,	
Screen Design	Alexander Brimijoin		"The CNN Ecosphere"	

The size, colour and growth rate of the digital forest gave users a real-time view of how the international conversation was evolving. In the run-up to the conference the project was promoted on CNN, which encouraged social network users to "plant a thought and watch it grow". Other media picked up on the idea. At the conference itself, a digital installation displayed the Ecosphere and put delegates in touch with the global debate on climate change.

UNIVERSAL ORCHESTRA   TELEPORTER   SKETCHBOTS   DATA TRACER   LAB TAG EXPLORER

Agency	They, Amsterdam
Production	Moblio.nl
Advertiser	They-Christmas Gift App, "Avoid the Shopping Crowds"

Meet the world's first anti-social media application. The mobile app was first developed as an agency Christmas gift. It helps people monitor crowds at leading local shopping centres in order to have a more relaxing Christmas break. It scans social media check-ins and provides users with an update of the busiest places in the city. In this way, it enables you do the exact opposite of what social media sites are intended for: not connect with people, but avoid them.

Agency	Google Creative Lab, London
Creative Team	Google Creative Lab
Production	Bibliothèque, London
	B-Reel, London
	Fraser Randall, London
	Tellart, Providence
	Universal Design Studio, London
	Weir + Wong, London
Digital Designer	Karsten Schmidt
Advertiser	Google Chrome, "Chrome Web Lab"

Google Chrome is Google's super-fast web browser. Google wanted to make the invisible magic of the web more tangible. So it set up five real-life experiments at the Science Museum in London and allowed users to interact with them online. For example, the universal orchestra shows how the web helps people collaborate by encouraging you to make music with other users. And the "sketchbots" draw your portrait in real time, showing how the web can connect to physical objects. Web Lab was a first-of-its-kind global museum experience.

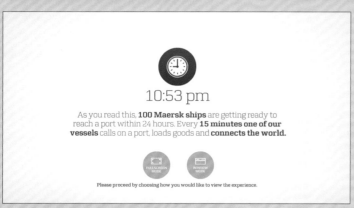

10:53 pm

As you read this, **100 Maersk ships** are getting ready to reach a port within 24 hours. Every **15 minutes one of our vessels** calls on a port, loads goods and **connects the world.**

Please proceed by choosing how you would like to view the experience.

Maersk Deliverer
Semi-submersible drilling rig

Drilling for
hidden treasure

3,000 meters

10,000 meters

Oil can no longer be retrieved in open pools. Today's reservoirs are mainly found in **inaccessible offshore places** that require **highly specialized drilling rigs.**

Our state-of-the-art drilling rigs operate in some of the most challenging environments on the planet. Drilling rigs, some of the most complicated man-made structures ever built, have even been compared to space crafts.

Harsh conditions require different types of efficient, high-performance equipment.

The depths of many oil reserves present some of the greatest challenges. Most drilling rigs, except

semi-submersibles, cannot operate in deep water, or water more than 175 meters deep. When the full pontoons of drilling rigs are submerged, they are less sensitive to wave action than drill ships.

5,544,139

Good exports: 95,770,803,525

Service exports: 60,404,954,157

Income payments: 21,446,335,493

8°C Wind 15 mph NW

PLAY FILM

We move
mountains

The computer **you're using**, the food you eat, what you wear, and even your chair, most of it comes from remote manufacturers. **Every day Maersk moves mountains of goods around the world.**

Agency	LBi, Copenhagen	Shipping giant Maersk was perceived as old fashioned and had trouble attracting graduates. Recently it has adopted a new strategy of transparency. One of the results of this was wearemaersk.com: a digital storytelling platform. Enter the site and a short film introduces the idea: pick any point on the globe and Maersk won't be far away. Click on the map and open one of ten films describing Maersk's activities around the world. IP detection allows the site to back up the films by delivering graphics, animations and images of potential interest to the user.
Creative Director	Rasmus Frandsen	
Copywriters	Pia Leichter	
	Susanne Sayers	
Art Director	Toke Kristensen	
Cr. Technologists	Dennis Green-Lieber	
	Mads Viktor Hartvig Hansen	
	Rasmus Elken	
Developers	Rasmus Bangsted Pedersen	
	Klaus Mandal Hansen	
Account Mgr.	Mikkel Havmand	
Client	Lars Ørum Andersen	
Advertiser	A.P Møller Maersk Shipping	

mittens!

BERÖRA
vottekit

IKEA-katalogen er klar for iPad.
Er vottene dine?

IKEA

Agency	SMFB, Oslo
Copywriters	Hans Magne Ekre
	Alexander Gjersoe
Art Directors	Hans Magne Ekre
	Alexander Gjersoe
Designer	Nicklas Hellborg
Account Team	Kristian Kristiansen
	Hanne Grobstock
	Tonje Skjetne Bjornerem
Advertiser	Ikea iPad Catalogue,
	"Ikea Beröra"

Norwegians love the great outdoors, even if it's cold and snowy. Problem: gloved fingers don't work on touchscreen mobile devices. Ikea used this insight as a way of launching its new iPad catalogue through an inexpensive banner ad. It created a new product called Beröra ("to touch"): a sewing kit with a special conductive thread to sew into your favourite gloves or mittens. Then they'd work on a touchscreen. Users ordered the kit by clicking on the banner and received it in the post. Then they could browse the new Ikea catalogue – even in freezing temperatures.

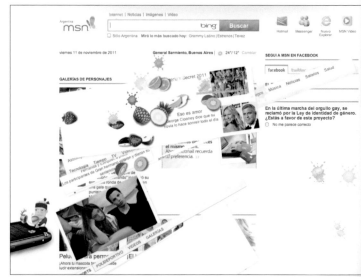
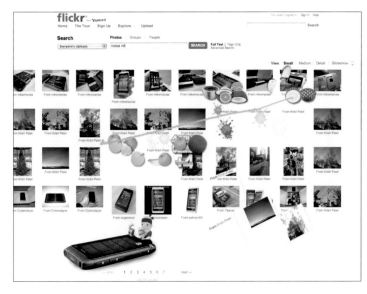
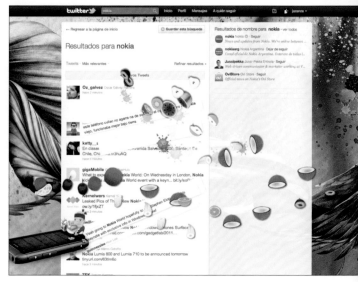

Agency	Wunderman, Buenos Aires
Creative Directors	José Azanza Arias
	Alfonso Cornejo Lavín
Copywriter	Julia Stoger
Art Director	Nicolas Bugari
Interactive Mgr.	Verónica Schvimer
Project Manager	Dalila Di Menna
Account Team	Emiliano Galvan
	Yolanda Vazquez
	Gonzalez
Advertiser	Nokia N8, "Gaming"

The objective was to communicate that popular games Angry Birds and Fruit Ninja could be downloaded to the new Nokia N8 phone for free. The strategy was to combine the two games into a free installation that allowed the birds and the ninjas to "destroy" websites on your phone. Just install the app from the interactive banner or the Nokia N8 website. Then you're ready to attack web pages and Facebook profiles with exploding birds and aggressive fruits. And share your tales of destruction with friends.

PARKING DOUCHE

Agency	Look At Media, Moscow
Creative Directors	Katya Bazilevskaya
	Grisha Sorokin
Art Director	Vladimir Shreyder
Creative Strategy	Alexey Artyukhov
Production	Look At Media
Project Manager	Alya Gabdurakhmanova
Technical Director	Alexander Rybyakov
App Developer	Alexander Simonov
Flash Developer	Alexander Redinger
Advertiser	The-Village.ru
	Online City Guide,
	"Parking Douche"

Selfish "douche" parking is a problem in Russian cities. There aren't enough spaces, so drivers park anywhere and anyhow. Moscow online city newspaper The Village decided make such behaviour socially unacceptable. It created a free app enabling people to take pictures of badly parked cars and save the registration and other details. Using IP addresses, this data was streamed live as pop-up ads to people in locations near the parking outrage.

The pop-ups annoyed you right in the middle of other online activity. Hovering over the ads let you see the car that was irritating everyone in a street nearby. Users had to share the picture of the "parking douche" in social media before the pop-up would close. Lots of people saw neighbours, colleagues, serial douches – even themselves. The douches were named and shamed; and less selfish drivers got their revenge.

Agency	Duval Guillaume Modem, Antwerp		
Creative Directors	Geoffrey Hantson Katrien Bottez		
Copywriter	Dieter De Ridder		
Art Director	Ad Van Ongeval		
Director	Koen Mortier		
Production	Czar, Brussels		
Producer	Marc Van Buggenhout		
Advertiser	TNT, "Push to Add Drama"		

American TV channel TNT was launching in Belgium. The channel's promise is "We know drama". So the agency placed a big red button in the middle of a town square. Above it, the words "Push to add drama." When an unwitting passer-by did so, they unleashed a pre-planned sequence of dramatic events, including a full-blown shootout, all of which referred to series on TNT.

At the end of the experience, a banner unfurled on a nearby building reading: "Your daily dose of drama, from 10/04 on Telenet: TNT." In just one week on YouTube, a film of the stunt attracted millions of views and hundreds of thousands of likes. According to the agency, it also became the second most shared commercial...ever.

Online Films 383

Agency	Abbott Mead Vickers BBDO, London
Creative Directors	Mike Hannett
	Dave Buchanan
Copywriter	Mike Sutherland
Art Director	Ant Nelson
Production	Thomas Thomas
Director	Kevin Thomas
Producers	Paul Goodwin
	Louise Richardson
	Trent Simpson
Editor	Scott Crane
Advertiser	Guinness, "Sheepdog"

St. Patrick's Day is the perfect excuse to get together with your mates for a pint of Guinness. But blokes are terrible at organising group outings. According to this viral video, help is at hand. It shows a sheepdog "rounding up" a group of mates and herding them away from the usual distractions – sport on the TV, an Indian restaurant, disco-dancing girls, angry texts from wives – to get them safely into the pub. Round up your mates for a Guinness this St Patrick's Day.

Integrated Campaigns

Agency	DDB, Stockholm	**Graphic Design**	Patrik Pagréus	
Creative Directors	Magnus Jakobsson	**Business Director**	Johan Dannemann	
	Fredrik Simonsson	**Planners**	Adam Sandahl	
Copywriters	Jeffrey Salomonsson		Cornelia Wangel	
	Martin Lundgren	**Digital Design**	Robin Karlsson	
Art Directors	Lisa Granberg	**Developer**	Sebastian Ross	
	Daniel Mencàk	**Account Team**	Sandra Kaludjercic	
Web Production	B-Reel		Bergman	
Event Production	Atomgruppen		Tina Munck	
Producer	Elisabet Halming	**Advertiser**	Swedish Armed Forces, "Who Cares?"	

The Swedish Armed Forces need young men and women who are willing to sacrifice their own comfort in order to help others. To see how many people would do this for real, a person was locked up in an enclosed box in the middle of Stockholm. He agreed to remain there until someone else willingly replaced him. But the next person would also have to wait until they were relieved. The event was promoted on TV, in press ads and on live banners.

It could also be followed on a live billboard placed near the installation, but the only way to help was to act - by physically entering the box yourself. So who cared? Over a total of 89 hours, 74 people entered the box to free the person inside. Some even travelled across the country just to replace the "imprisoned" person. As for the army, by the end of the campaign it had received 9,930 applications – more than twice the target.

UNHATE

UNITED COLORS
OF BENETTON.

Supports the Unhate Foundation
unhatefoundation.org

President of the US   President of Venezuela

UNHATE

UNITED COLORS
OF BENETTON.

Supports the Unhate Foundation
unhatefoundation.org

Prime Minister of Is...   President of the Palestinian National Authority

UNHATE

MADE OF 15,000 BULLET CASINGS FROM GLOBAL WAR ZONES

UNHATE

UNITED COLORS
OF BENETTON.

Agencies	Fabrica, Treviso
	72andSunny, Amsterdam
Creative Directors	Erik Ravelo
	Carlo Cavallone
	Paulo Martins
	Robert Nakata
Production	Identity, New York
Director	Laurent Chanez
Producers	Maria Perez
	Ellen Pot
Advertiser	Benetton,
	"Unhate" Campaign

Benetton returned to the cause-related campaigns of its past with a new message of tolerance: Unhate. A film depicted the world's delicate balance of love and hate, tilting the scales towards love. A controversial poster campaign showed naturally opposed leaders embracing. Giant versions of the ads appeared in cities around the world for one day only, generating media buzz. As the Vatican denounced the fake image of the Pope embracing Sheikh Ahmed Mohamed El-Tayeb, a leading Imam, a global debate about tolerance began.

Benetton launched the Unhate Foundation, which supports educational and community projects around the world. In Tripoli, it erected a dove sculpture made of 15,000 bullet casings. Benetton's Unhate website was viewed by thousands; Benetton became a top trending topic on Twitter and its Facebook fans doubled to one million in two weeks. Unhate was not just a campaign, it was a true conversation starter.

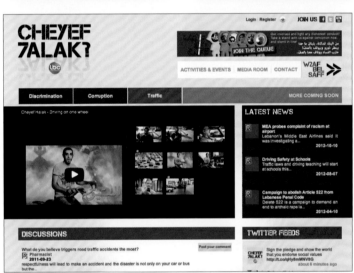

386   **Integrated Campaigns**

Agency	Impact BBDO, Beirut	**Producers**	Omar Frangieh
Creative Director	Walid Kanaan		Rawad Keyrouz
Copywriters	Miriam Jbeili	**Head of Design**	Davar Azarbeygui
	Chris Jabre	**Content Mgr.**	Omar Sadek
	Marie-Noelle	**Digital Acct. Mgr.**	Jocelyne Twak
	de Chaderevian	**Acct. Executive**	Nayla Kheyreddine
Art Director	Nay Abou Chahla	**Advertiser**	LBCI TV,
Production	Sunny Side Up		"Cheyef Halak"

In Lebanon the sarcastic expression "cheyef halak" means, roughly speaking, "So are you proud of yourself?" Leading Lebanese TV station LBCI used the phrase to draw attention to the issue of reckless and illegal behaviour on the roads. Four darkly amusing TV commercials featuring road rebels launched the campaign and its website. An app was created allowing Lebanese citizens to capture uncivilised road use on their phones and upload the images to an online "wall of shame".

The results could be shared across soci[a] networks. The movement was continue[d] through blogs, seminars and the tradition[al] al media. "Cheyef halak" tickets were eve[n] handed out to bad drivers. In a count[ry] where there are no traffic cameras [or] radars, the citizens are now keeping an ey[e] on reckless road users.

facebook Search

Carla

⌨ Works

📅 Born o

💬 Write

Write so

NO RIGHTS NO WOMEN

DID YOU KNOW THAT IN LEBANON THERE IS NO LAW THAT PROTECTS WOMEN FROM DOMESTIC VIOLENCE?

DID YOU KNOW THAT IN LEBANON THERE IS NO LAW THAT PROTECTS WOMEN FROM SEXUAL HARASSMENT IN HER WORK ENVIRONMENT?

DID YOU KNOW THAT YOUR NON-LEBANESE HUSBAND AND CHILDREN CANNOT INHERIT FR OM YOU?

DID YOU KNOW THAT AS A LEBANESE WOMAN YOU CANNOT PASS DOWN YOUR NATIONALITY TO YOUR KIDS?

DID YOU KNOW THAT THERE IS NO LAW TO PROTECT WOMEN FROM MARITAL RAPE? ♥ ♥ ♥

DID YOU KNOW THAT YOUR RAPIST CAN GET AWAY WITH HIS CRIME IF HE MARRIES YOU?

Integrated Campaigns 387

Agency	Leo Burnett, Beirut
CCO/ECD	Bechara Mouzannar
Creative Director	Areej Mahmoud
Copywriters	Rana Khoury
	Diala Haidar
Art Directors	Roula Asmar
	Lea Salibi
	Natasha Maasri
Deputy MD	Nada Abi Saleh
PR Executive	Hala Akiki
Advertiser	No Rights - No Women

Under Lebanese law, men and women are not equal. Women have no custody rights over their children and there is no law protecting them against domestic violence. So a local women's rights movement asked the question: rather than remaining half citizens, why don't women just become men? Their rallying cry: "No rights – no women." On Facebook, thousands of Lebanese women added moustaches to their profile pictures and changed their gender. They posted statements about the discriminatory laws and invited others to join the debate.

Posters were placed around town asking women to dress as men on March 8th, International Women's day. Many complied – and that that night, hundreds demonstrated near the parliament building. The event generated international exposure in magazines, newspapers, radio broadcasts and blogs. Five months later, the government scrapped a law mitigating the sentence of those who claim they killed or injured wives or daughters to protect the family "honour."

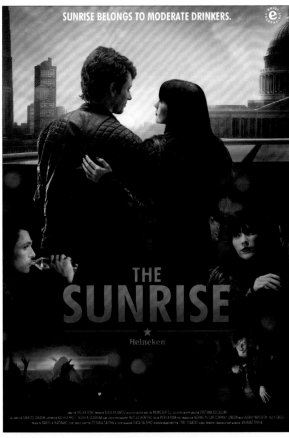

388   **Integrated Campaigns**

Agency	Publicis, Milan	Director	Fredrik Bond	
Creative Directors	Bruno Bertelli	Producer	Mariella Maiorano	
	Cristiana Boccassini	Post Production	Moving Picture	
Copywriters	Rachele Proli		Company, London	
	Michela Talamona	Planning Director	Alastair Maclean	
	Michele Picci	Digital Agency	AKQA, London	
	Francesca Bonomi	Digital CD	Kevin Russell	
Art Directors	Fabrizio Tamagni	Account Team	Stefania Savona	
	Marco Viganò		Giada Salerno	
	Valeria Vanzulli		Bela Ziemann	
	Costanza Rossi	Client	Anuraag Trikha	
Production	Sonny London	Advertiser	Heineken,	
			"Reach the Sunrise"	

Heineken wanted to convince young adults that moderate drinking is the key to a great night out. Its message: "When you know your limits, there are no limits." The starting point was a film featuring a cool guy who drinks moderately at a club and ends up walking into the sunrise with gorgeous DJ Audrey Napoleon. The film was projected in front of a million people in Times Square on New Year's Eve. Napoleon herself composed and performed the film's soundtrack, "My Sunrise".

Posters and beer coasters in bars and clubs helped to spread the message – Heineken even made its own branded water to help clubbers get through the night. For those who made it to dawn, Heineken sofas were placed in the world's best sunrise spots, where users could tweet their location to a sunrise Facebook map. The uploaded photos were used to create a new music video for "My Sunrise", which was seen in nightspots around the world. The result: thousands of people got home sober at sunrise – and maybe not alone.

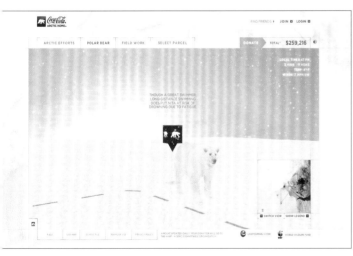

Agencies	Leo Burnett, Chicago	Production	HSI, New York
	Arc Worldwide, Chicago	Director	Ryan Ebner
Global CCO	Mark Tutssel	Producers	Jeff Zimmerman
CCO	Susan Credle		Patrick Smith
Executive CD	Dave Loew	Production Head	Chris Rossiter
	Jon Wyville	Content Architect	Vincent Geraghty
Creative Directors	Leyla Dailey		Rob Tripas
	Matt Denten	Digital Strategy	Joe Kehoe
Associate CDs	Melanie Larsen	Senior Analyst	Jessica Muniz
	Chris von Ende	Web Production	Acne, LA
	Mike Ward	Design Agency	Turner Duckworth
Copywriter	Mike Ward	Advertiser	Coca-Cola,
Art Director	Chris von Ende		"Arctic Home"

The polar bear is the star of Coca-Cola's Christmas advertising. Coke is also behind Arctic Home, a partnership with the WWF which aims to preserve the polar bears' habitat. But this has to compete for attention with a number of other worthy causes during the festive season. As a symbol of the brand's commitment to the effort, it took a dramatic step – and turned the iconic red Coca-Cola can white, for the first time in history. 1.4 billion white cans created instant global awareness. Packaging and point-of-sale encouraged people to donate via text and visit ArcticHome.com. A three-dimensional flash site and iPad app brought the Arctic to consumers, allowing them to track actual polar bears in real time weather conditions. The idea was amplified in television and cinema, while outdoor and online ads also called for donations. Branded Facebook and Twitter platforms brought the campaign into the heart of social networks. It all added up to the largest integrated marketing platform in the history of Coca-Cola – and the first part of a three-year initiative.

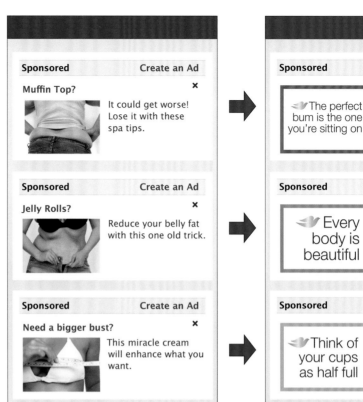

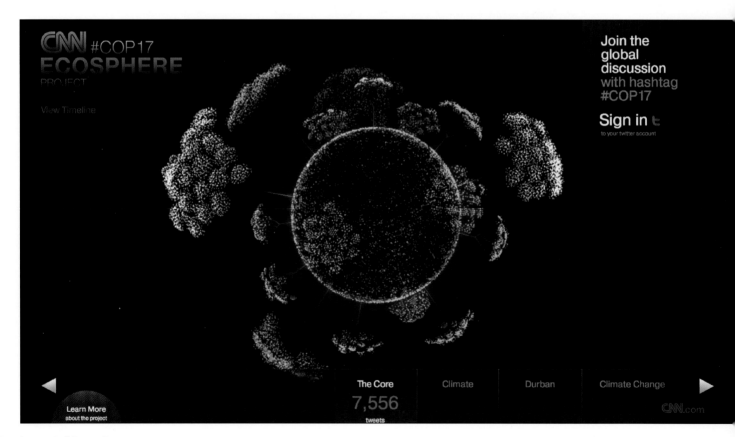

Agency	Ogilvy & Mather, London
Creative Directors	Gerry Human
	Ivan Pols
Copywriter	Margo Young
Art Director	Trevallyn Hall
Production	The Mill, London
Producer	Fiona Renfrew
Cr. Technologist	Craig Blagg
Digital Producer	Sasha Dunn
Content Architect	Anthony Butterfield
Developer	Martin Robertson
Designer	Simone Zahradka
Advertiser	Dove, "Ad Makeover"

Dove's mission is to help women feel beautiful, but only 4% of women describe themselves this way. The solution was an app that empowered women to replace negative banner advertising on Facebook with positive messages promoting healthy self-esteem – and over 171 million banners were displaced this way. But although the campaign had a social core, it was a fully integrated operation that encompassed PR, traditional advertising and online, as well as expanding into international news media via coverage on sites such as the Huffington Post and Mashable.

Agency	Heimat, Berlin
Creative Directors	Myles Lord
	Martien Delfgaauw
	Luc Schurgers
Copywriter	Ramin Schmiedekampf
Art Director	Frank Hose
Film Director	Minivegas
Production	Stink Digital
Agency Producer	Jessica Valin
Graphic Design	Jue Alt
	Jared Leistner
	Alexander Suchy
Advertiser	CNN, "The Ecosphere"

CNN wanted to get people talking about the climate change and promote its coverage of the COP17 conference in Durban. In the run-up to the conference, it unveiled its idea: an evolving digital ecosystem created by tweets. CNN asked users to "plant an idea and watch it grow". Every #COP17 tweet would boost the growth of colourful shoots, each representing a climate change issue. The idea captured the imagination of rival media and by the time the conference began, a digital installation showed a flourishing and ever-expanding Ecosphere.

The world's safest Volvo

AIRING CUPBOARD AND BUNK BED. STANDARD IN THE NEW VOLVO.

World premiere for the new Volvo FH truck. **VOLVO**

JCDecaux

Brunnsparken

THE NEW VOLVO HAS ROOM FOR A PUSHCHAIR AND 40 TONS OF TIMBER.

World premiere for the new Volvo FH truck. **VOLVO**

THE NEW VOLVO HAS ROOM FOR THE KING. AND HIS HORSE.

World premiere for the new Volvo FH truck. **VOLVO**

Agency	Forsman & Bodenfors, Gothenburg	**Content Architect**	Johan Wingård	
Copywriters	Martin Ringqvist	**Designer**	Jerry Wass	
	Björn Engström	**Editorial Writers**	Per Torberger	
Art Directors	Sophia Lindholm		Simon Coe	
	Anders Eklind	**Account Team**	Olle Victorin	
	Staffan Lamm		Cilla Glenberg	
Producers	Alexander Blidner		Jenny Edwardsson	
	Lina Strandäng		Britta Mlamberg	
	Peter Gaudiano		Alison Arnold	
		Advertiser	Volvo FH Truck	
			Launch Campaign	

Volvo pulled out all the stops to launch its new FH Truck. At the heart of the campaign was a digital idea – a truck was auctioned on eBay with the starting price of one euro. But many other media supported the launch, from the spectacular viral film "The Ballerina Stunt" to posters that teased the truck as an extremely spacious family car. An industry launch event was broadcast live on the web from six countries around Europe. Directly afterwards, Volvo launched a digital magazine that used films and interactive modules to show the truck from every angle.

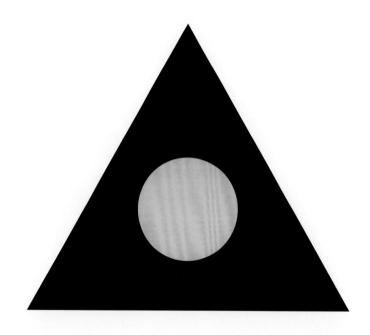

Network of the Year at Epica 2012